...ILOSOPHY AND ...

Richard Rorty was educated at the University of Chicago and Yale. He has been Stuart Professor of Philosophy at Princeton University and Emeritus Professor of Humanities at the University of Virginia; he is presently Professor of Comparative Literature at Stanford University. He is the author of *Philosophy and the Mirror of Nature, Contingency, Irony and Solidarity* and *Achieving Our Country: Leftist Thoughts in Twentieth-Century America.*

RICHARD RORTY

Philosophy and Social Hope

PENGUIN BOOKS

[Eng]land
[New] York 10014, USA
Penguin Books Australia Ltd, Ringwood, Victoria, Australia
Penguin Books Canada Ltd, 10 Alcorn Avenue, Toronto, Ontario, Canada M4V 3B2
Penguin Books (NZ) Ltd, Private Bag 102902, NSMC, Auckland, New Zealand

Penguin Books Ltd, Registered Offices: Harmondsworth, Middlesex, England

First published in Penguin Books 1999
10 9 8 7 6 5 4 3 2

Set in 10/12.5 pt Monotype Baskerville
Typeset by Rowland Phototypesetting Ltd,
Bury St Edmunds, Suffolk
Printed in England by Clays Ltd, St Ives plc

To the University of Virginia

Contents

IV Politics

V Contemporary America

Acknowledgements

The pieces in this book were originally published in the following places (copyright Richard Rorty unless otherwise marked):

Introduction: 'Relativism: Finding and Making': *Debating the State of Philosophy: Habermas, Rorty and Kolokowski*, Jozef Nizńik and John T. Sanders, eds. (Praeger, 1996). Copyright © Institute of Philosophy and Sociology of the Polish Academy of Science, 1996. Reprinted by permission.

1. 'Trotsky and the Wild Orchids': *Wild Orchids and Trotsky: Messages from American Universities*, Mark Edmundson, ed. (New York: Viking, 1993). Copyright © Viking, 1993. Reprinted by permission.

2. 'Truth without Correspondence to Reality': First appearance in English; a German translation appeared in my *Hoffnung statt Erkentniss* (Vienna: Passagen Verlag, 1994); a French translation appeared in my *L'espoir au lieu de savoir* (Paris: Albin Michel, 1995).

3. 'A World without Substances or Essences': First appearance in English; a German translation appeared in my *Hoffnung statt Erkentniss* (Vienna: Passagen Verlag, 1994); a French translation appeared in my *L'espoir au lieu de savoir* (Paris: Albin Michel, 1995).

4. 'Ethics without Principles': First appearance in English; a German translation appeared in my *Hoffnung statt Erkentniss* (Vienna: Passagen Verlag, 1994); a French translation appeared in my *L'espoir au lieu de savoir* (Paris: Albin Michel, 1995).

5. 'The Banality of Pragmatism and the Poetry of Justice': *Pragmatism in Law and Society*, Michael Brint and William Weaver, eds. (Boulder, Colorado: Westview Press, 1991), pp. 89–97. First published in *Southern California Law Review*. Copyright © Southern California Law Review, 1990. Reprinted by permission.

6. 'Pragmatism and Law: A Response to David Luban': *Cardozo Law Review*, vol. XXVIII, no. 1. Copyright © 1996, Yeshiva University. Reprinted by permission.

7. 'Education as Socialization and as Individualization': originally published as 'Education without Dogma', *Dissent* (Spring 1989), pp. 198–204. Copyright © Dissent, 1989. Reprinted by permission.

8. 'The Humanistic Intellectual: Eleven Theses': *ACLS Occasional Papers* (November 1989), no. 10, pp. 9–12. Reprinted by permission.

9. 'The Pragmatist's Progress: Umberto Eco on Interpretation': *Interpretation and Overinterpretation*, Stefan Collini, ed. (Cambridge: Cambridge University Press, 1992), pp. 89–108. Copyright © Cambridge University Press, 1992. Reprinted by permission.

10. 'Religious Faith, Intellectual Responsibility and Romance': *The Cambridge Companion to William James*, Ruth Anna Putnam, ed. (Cambridge: Cambridge University Press, 1997), pp. 84–102. Copyright © Cambridge University Press, 1997. Reprinted by permission.

11. 'Religion as Conversation-stopper': *Common Knowledge* (Spring 1994), vol. III, no. 1, pp. 1–6. Copyright © Common Knowledge, 1994. Reprinted by permission.

12. 'Thomas Kuhn, Rocks and the Laws of Physics': *Common Knowledge* (Spring 1997), vol. VI, no. 1. Copyright © Common Knowledge, 1997. Reprinted by permission.

13. 'On Heidegger's Nazism': Originally published as 'Another Possible World' in the *London Review of Books* (8 February 1990), p. 21. Copyright © London Review of Books, 1990. Reprinted by permission.

14. 'Failed Prophecies, Glorious Hopes': First appeared as 'Endlich sieht man Freudenthal' in *Frankfurter Allgemeine Zeitung*, 20 February 1998. Copyright © FAZ, 1998. Reprinted by permission.

15. 'A Spectre is Haunting the Intellectuals: Derrida on Marx': *European Journal of Philosophy* (December 1995), vol. III, no. 3, pp. 289–98. Copyright © European Journal of Philosophy, 1995. Reprinted by permission.

16. 'Love and Money': *Common Knowledge* (Spring 1992), vol. I, no. 1, pp. 12–16. Copyright © Common Knowledge, 1992. Reprinted by permission.

17. 'Globalization, the Politics of Identity and Social Hope': originally published as 'Global Utopias, History and Philosophy' in *Cultural Pluralism, Identity and Globalization*, Luiz Soares, ed. (Rio de Janiero: UNESCO/ISSC/EDUCAM, 1996), pp. 457–69.

18. 'Looking Backwards from the Year 2096': originally published as 'Fraternity Reigns' in *The New Times Magazine*, 28 September 1996, pp. 155–8.

19. 'The Unpatriotic Academy': *The New York Times*, 13 February 1994, section 4, p. 15 (op-ed page). Copyright © *The New York Times*, 1994. Reprinted by permission.

20. 'Back to Class Politics': *Dissent* (Winter 1997), pp. 31–4. Copyright © Dissent, 1997. Reprinted by permission.

Preface

Most of what I have written in the last decade consists of attempts to tie in my social hopes – hopes for a global, cosmopolitan, democratic, egalitarian, classless, casteless society – with my antagonism towards Platonism. These attempts have been encouraged by the thought that the same hopes, and the same antagonism, lay behind many of the writings of my principal philosophical hero, John Dewey.

'Platonism' in the sense in which I use the term does not denote the (very complex, shifting, dubiously consistent) thoughts of the genius who wrote the *Dialogues*. Instead, it refers to a set of philosophical distinctions (appearance–reality, matter–mind, made–found, sensible–intellectual, etc.): what Dewey called 'a brood and nest of dualisms'. These dualisms dominate the history of Western philosophy, and can be traced back to one or another passage in Plato's writings. Dewey thought, as I do, that the vocabulary which centres around these traditional distinctions has become an obstacle to our social hopes.

Much of the material in this volume repeats theses and arguments previously put forward in the three volumes of *Philosophical Papers* which I have published with Cambridge University Press.[1] Those volumes consisted of papers written for philosophical journals, or for conferences attended mostly by philosophy professors. In this volume, I am reprinting pieces of two other sorts: first, lectures intended for a so-called 'general audience' (that is, students and teachers in colleges and universities, as opposed to gatherings of specialists in philosophy); second, occasional contributions to newspapers and magazines, mostly on political or semi-political topics. Most of these essays contain fewer footnotes than do those included in *Philosophical Papers*. I hope that this new collection may interest an audience wider than the one to which those volumes were directed.

Section I of this volume is a bit of autobiography, explaining how, early on, I found myself moving away from Plato in the direction of Dewey. Section II consists of three lectures given in Vienna and Paris in 1993 under the heading 'Hope in Place of Knowledge', originally published in French and German.[2] I thought about expanding and revising them, but have finally decided to publish them in English pretty much as given. They offer a fairly simple, albeit sketchy, outline of my own version of pragmatism. This version makes no pretence of being faithful to the thoughts of either James or Dewey (much less Peirce, whom I barely mention). Rather, it offers my own, sometimes idiosyncratic, restatements of Jamesian and Deweyan themes.

My choice of themes, and my ways of rephrasing them, result from my conviction that James's and Dewey's main accomplishments were negative, in that they explain how to slough off a lot of intellectual baggage which we inherited from the Platonic tradition. Each of the three essays, therefore, has a title of the form '— without —', where the first blank is filled by something we want to keep and the second something which James and Dewey enabled us, if not exactly to throw away, at least to understand in a radically un-Platonic way.

The title 'Hope in Place of Knowledge' is a way of suggesting that Plato and Aristotle were wrong in thinking that humankind's most distinctive and praiseworthy capacity is to know things as they really are – to penetrate behind appearance to reality. That claim saddles us with the unfortunate appearance–reality distinction and with metaphysics: a distinction, and a discipline, which pragmatism shows us how to do without. I want to demote the quest for knowledge from the status of end-in-itself to that of one more means towards greater human happiness.

My candidate for the most distinctive and praiseworthy human capacity is our ability to trust and to cooperate with other people, and in particular to work together so as to improve the future. Under favourable circumstances, our use of this capacity culminates in utopian political projects such as Plato's ideal state, Christian attempts to realize the kingdom of God here on earth, and Marx's vision of the victory of the proletariat. These projects aim at improving our institutions in such a way that our descendants will be still better able to trust and cooperate, and will be more decent people than we ourselves have managed to be. In our century, the most plausible project of this sort has been the one to which Dewey devoted his political efforts: the creation of a social democracy; that is, a classless, casteless, egalitarian society. I interpret James and Dewey as giving us advice on how, by getting rid of the old dualisms, we can make this project as central to our intellectual lives as it is to our political lives.

In section III, I embark on some little expeditions out from philosophy into various neighbouring areas of culture: jurisprudence, literary criticism, religion, science and, in a little paper written just for kicks, Heidegger – not exactly an area of culture but now the name given, as Auden said of Freud, to a whole climate of opinion. In these pieces, which were inspired by one or another current controversy, I try to show how these areas look when seen through pragmatist eyes.

Section IV is also made up mostly of pieces which take sides in some current debate, but here the debates are explicitly about politics. The four pieces in this section discuss our chances of achieving a democratic utopia. For various reasons which these pieces spell out, I think these chances are pretty dim. But I do not think that is a reason to change our political goal. There is no more worthy project at hand; we have nothing better to do with our lives.

In the concluding section V, I have included pretty much everything I published about the present sociopolitical situation in the United States prior to my *Achieving Our Country* (Harvard University Press, 1998). These pieces are run-ups to that book. By including them I hope to supplement the more general reflections on contemporary politics which make up section IV with discussion of some concrete problems.

Because I keep finding myself referred to as a 'postmodernist relativist', I have begun this volume with an essay called 'Relativism: Finding and Making' and ended it with an Afterword called 'Pragmatism, Pluralism and Postmodernism' (the only previously unpublished piece in the book).

I think that 'relativism' and 'postmodernism' are words which never had any clear sense, and that both should be dropped from our philosophical vocabulary. A philosophical view which was propounded in detail before the First World War is not happily described as 'postmodern', even though there is considerable overlap between that view and those held by such post-Nietzschean European thinkers as Heidegger and Derrida. 'Relativism' is as misleading a description of the views of these latter figures as it is of those of James or Dewey. Serious discussion of any of these four philosophers is only possible if one does not assume that lack of an appearance–reality distinction entails that every action or belief is as good as every other.

I hope that the papers in this volume may help convince people that relativism is a bugbear, and that the real question about the utility of the old Platonic dualisms is whether or not their deployment weakens our sense of human solidarity. I read Dewey as saying that discarding these dualisms will help bring us together, by enabling us to realize that trust, social cooperation and social hope are where our humanity begins and ends.

I am grateful to Stefan McGrath for the suggestion that I collect some of my recent non-technical pieces for this volume, and to Sally Holloway for careful copy-editing and many helpful suggestions.

I have dedicated this collection to the institution at which its contents were written: the University of Virginia, of which I was Emeritus Professor of the Humanities. By offering me a non-departmental university professorship – a sort of freelance arrangement unique, I believe, to US universities – Mr Jefferson's university made it possible for me to teach and write about anything I pleased, when and as I pleased. I am most grateful both to the university itself, and to the colleagues and students who made my 15 years in Charlottesville so happy and so productive.

* * * *

NOTES

1 My *Objectivity, Relativism and Truth: Philosophical Papers* and *Essays on Heidegger and Others: Philosophical Papers 2* were both published by Cambridge University Press in 1991. *Truth and Progress: Philosophical Papers 3* was published in 1998.
2 *Hoffnung statt Erkentniss* (Vienna: Passagen Verlag, 1994); *L'espoir au lieu de savoir* (Paris: Albin Michel, 1995).

Introduction:
Relativism: Finding and Making

(1996)

The epithet 'relativist' is applied to philosophers who agree with Nietzsche that ' "Truth" is the will to be master of the multiplicity of sensations'. It is also applied to those who agree with William James that 'the "true" is simply the expedient in the way of believing' and to those who agree with Thomas Kuhn that science should not be thought of as moving towards an accurate representation of the way the world is in itself. More generally, philosophers are called 'relativists' when they do not accept the Greek distinction between the way things are in themselves and the relations which they have to other things, and in particular to human needs and interests.

Philosophers who, like myself, eschew this distinction must abandon the traditional philosophical project of finding something stable which will serve as a criterion for judging the transitory products of our transitory needs and interests. This means, for example, that we cannot employ the Kantian distinction between morality and prudence. We have to give up on the idea that there are unconditional, transcultural moral obligations, obligations rooted in an unchanging, ahistorical human nature. This attempt to put aside both Plato and Kant is the bond which links the post-Nietzschean tradition in European philosophy with the pragmatic tradition in American philosophy.

The philosopher whom I most admire, and of whom I should most like to think of myself as a disciple, is John Dewey. Dewey was one of the founders of American pragmatism. He was a thinker who spent 60 years trying to get us out from under the thrall of Plato and Kant. Dewey was often denounced as a relativist, and so am I. But of course we pragmatists never call *ourselves* relativists. Usually, we define ourselves in negative terms. We call ourselves 'anti-Platonists' or 'antimeta-physicians' or 'antifoundationalists'. Equally, our opponents almost never call themselves 'Platonists' or 'metaphysicians' or 'foundationalists'. They usually call themselves defenders of common sense, or of reason.

Predictably, each side in this quarrel tries to define the terms of the quarrel in a way favourable to itself. Nobody wants to be called a Platonist, just as nobody wants to be called a relativist or an irrationalist. We so-called 'relativists' refuse, predictably, to admit that we are enemies of reason and common sense. We say that we are only criticizing some antiquated, specifically philosophical, dogmas. But, of course, what we call dogmas are exactly what our opponents call common sense. Adherence to these dogmas is what they call being rational. So discussion between us and our opponents tends to get bogged down in, for example, the question of whether the slogan 'truth is correspondence to the intrinsic nature of reality' expresses common sense, or is just a bit of outdated Platonist jargon.

In other words, one of the things we disagree about is whether this slogan embodies an obvious truth which philosophy must respect and protect, or instead simply puts forward one philosophical view among others. Our opponents say that the correspondence theory of truth is so obvious, so self-evident, that it is merely perverse to question it. We say that this theory is barely intelligible, and of no particular importance – that it is not so much a theory as a slogan which we have been mindlessly chanting for centuries. We pragmatists think that we might stop chanting it without any harmful consequences.

One way to describe this impasse is to say that we so-called 'relativists' claim that many of the things which common sense thinks are found or discovered are really made or invented. Scientific and moral truths, for example, are described by our opponents as 'objective', meaning that they are in some sense out there waiting to be recognized by us human beings. So when our Platonist or Kantian opponents are tired of calling us 'relativists' they call us 'subjectivists' or 'social constructionists'. In their picture of the situation, we are claiming to have discovered that something which was supposed to come from outside us really comes from inside us. They think of us as saying that what was previously thought to be objective has turned out to be merely subjective.

But we anti-Platonists must not accept this way of formulating the issue. For if we do, we shall be in serious trouble. If we take the distinction between making and finding at face value, our opponents will be able to ask us an awkward question, viz., Have we *discovered* the surprising fact that what was thought to be objective is actually subjective, or have we *invented* it? If we claim to have discovered it, if we say that it is an objective fact that truth is subjective, we are in danger of contradicting ourselves. If we say that we invented it, we seem to be being merely whimsical. Why should anybody take our invention seriously? If truths are merely convenient fictions, what about the truth of the claim that that is what they are? Is that too a convenient fiction? Convenient for what? For whom?

I think it is important that we who are accused of relativism stop using the distinctions between finding and making, discovery and invention, objective and subjective. We should not let ourselves be described as subjectivists, and perhaps calling ourselves 'social constructionists' is too misleading. For we cannot formulate our point in terms of a distinction between what is outside us and what is inside us. We must repudiate the vocabulary our opponents use, and not let them impose it upon us. To say that we must repudiate this vocabulary is to say, once again, that we must avoid Platonism and metaphysics, in that wide sense of metaphysics in which Heidegger said that metaphysics *is* Platonism. (Whitehead was making the same point when he said that all of Western philosophy is a series of footnotes to Plato. Whitehead's point was that we do not call an inquiry 'philosophical' unless it revolves around some of the distinctions which Plato drew.)

The distinction between the found and the made is a version of that between the absolute and the relative, between something which is what it is apart from its relations to other things, and something whose nature depends upon those relations. In the course of the centuries, this distinction has become central to what Derrida calls 'the metaphysics of presence' – the search for a 'full presence beyond the reach of play', an absolute beyond the reach of relationality. So if we wish to abandon that metaphysics we must stop distinguishing between the absolute and the relative. We anti-Platonists cannot permit ourselves to be called 'relativists', since that description begs the central question. That central question is about the utility of the vocabulary which we inherited from Plato and Aristotle.

Our opponents like to suggest that to abandon that vocabulary is to abandon rationality – that to be rational consists precisely in respecting the distinctions between the absolute and the relative, the found and the made, object and subject, nature and convention, reality and appearance. We pragmatists reply that if that were what rationality was, then no doubt we are, indeed, irrationalists. But of course we go on to add that being an irrationalist in *that* sense is not to be incapable of argument. We irrationalists do not foam at the mouth and behave like animals. We simply refuse to talk in a certain way, the Platonic way. The views we hope to persuade people to accept cannot be stated in Platonic terminology. So our efforts at persuasion must take the form of gradual inculcation of new ways of speaking, rather than of straightforward argument within old ways of speaking.

To sum up what I have said so far: We pragmatists shrug off charges that we are 'relativists' or 'irrationalists' by saying that these charges presuppose precisely the distinctions we reject. If we have to describe ourselves, perhaps it would be best for us to call ourselves anti-dualists. This does not, of course, mean that we are against what Derrida calls 'binary oppositions': dividing the world up into the good Xs and the bad non-Xs will always be an indispensable tool of inquiry. But we are against a certain *specific* set of distinctions, the Platonic distinctions. We have to admit that these distinctions have become part of Western common sense, but we do not regard this as a sufficient argument for retaining them.

So far I have been speaking of 'we so-called relativists' and of 'we anti-Platonists'. But now I need to become more specific and name names. As I said at the outset, the group of philosophers I have in mind includes a tradition of post-Nietzschean European philosophy and also a tradition of post-Darwinian American philosophy, the tradition of pragmatism. The great names of the first tradition include Heidegger, Sartre, Gadamer, Derrida and Foucault. The great names of the second tradition include James, Dewey, Kuhn, Quine, Putnam and Davidson. All of these philosophers have been fiercely attacked as relativists.

Both traditions have attempted to cast doubt on the Kantian and Hegelian distinction between subject and object, on the Cartesian distinctions which Kant and Hegel used to formulate their problematic, and on the Greek distinctions which provided the framework for Descartes' own thought. The most important thing that links the great names of each tradition to one other, and thus links the two traditions together, is suspicion of the same set of Greek distinctions, the distinctions which make it possible, natural, and almost inevitable to ask, 'Found or made?', 'Absolute or relative?', 'Real or apparent?'

Before saying more about what binds these two traditions together, however, I should say a little about what separates them. Although the European tradition owes a lot to Darwin by way of Nietzsche and Marx, European philosophers have typically distinguished quite sharply between what empirical scientists do and what philosophers do. Philosophers in this tradition often sneer at 'naturalism' and 'empiricism' and 'reductionism'. They sometimes condemn recent Anglophone philosophy without a hearing, because they assume it to be infected by these diseases.

The American pragmatist tradition, by contrast, has made a point of breaking down the distinctions between philosophy, science and politics. Its representatives often describe themselves as 'naturalists', though they deny that they are reductionists or empiricists. Their objection to both traditional British empiricism and the scientistic reductionism characteristic of the Vienna Circle is precisely that neither is sufficiently naturalistic. In my perhaps chauvinistic view, we Americans have been more consistent than the Europeans. For American philosophers have realized that the idea of a distinctive, autonomous, cultural activity called 'philosophy' becomes dubious when the vocabulary which has dominated that activity is called into question. When Platonic dualisms go, the distinction between philosophy and the rest of culture is in danger.

Another way of exhibiting the difference between the two traditions is to say that the Europeans have typically put forward a distinctive, new, post-Nietzschean 'method' for philosophers to employ. Thus in early Heidegger and early Sartre we find talk of 'phenomenological ontology', in late Heidegger of something mysterious and wonderful called 'Thinking', in Gadamer of 'hermeneutics', in Foucault of 'the archaeology of knowledge' and of 'genealogy'. Only Derrida seems free from this temptation; his term 'grammatology' was evanescent whimsy, rather than a serious attempt to proclaim the discovery of a new philosophical method or strategy.

By contrast, the Americans have not been much given to such proclamations. Dewey, it is true, talked a lot about bringing 'scientific method' into philosophy, but he never was able to explain what this method was, nor what it was supposed to add to the virtues of curiosity, open-mindedness and conversability. James sometimes spoke of 'the pragmatic method', but this meant little more than the insistence on pressing the anti-Platonist question, 'Does our purported theoretical difference make any difference to practice?' That insistence was not so much the employment of a method as the assumption of a sceptical attitude towards traditional philosophical problems and vocabularies. Quine, Putnam and Davidson are all labelled 'analytic philosophers', but none of the three thinks of himself as practising a method called 'conceptual analysis', nor any other method. The so-called 'postpositiv-istic' version of analytic philosophy which these three philosophers have helped to create is notably free of methodolatry.

The various contemporary contributors to the pragmatist tradition are not much inclined to insist on either the distinctive nature of philosophy or the pre-eminent place of philosophy within culture as a whole. None of them believes that philosophers think, or should think, in ways dramatically different from the ways in which physicists and politicians think. They would all agree with Thomas Kuhn that science, like politics, is problem-solving. So they would be content to describe themselves as solving philosophical problems. But the main problem which they want to solve is the origin of the problems which the philosophical problem has bequeathed to us: why, they ask, are the standard, textbook problems of philosophy both so intriguing and barren? Why are philosophers, now as in Cicero's day, still arguing inconclusively, tramping round and round the same dialectical circles, never convincing each other but still able to attract students?

This question, the question of the nature of the problems which the Greeks, Descartes, Kant and Hegel have bequeathed to us, leads us back around to the distinction between finding and making. The philosophical tradition has insisted that these problems are *found*, in the sense that they are inevitably encountered by any reflective mind.

The pragmatist tradition has insisted that they are *made* – are artificial rather than natural – and can be *un*made by using a different vocabulary than that which the philosophical tradition has used. But such distinctions between the found and the made, the natural and the artificial are, as I have already said, not distinctions with which pragmatists can be comfortable. So it would be better for pragmatists to say simply that the vocabulary in which the traditional problems of Western philosophy were formulated were useful at one time, but are no longer useful. Putting the matter that way would obviate the appearance of saying that whereas the tradition dealt with what was not really there, we pragmatists are dealing with what *is* really there.

Of course we pragmatists cannot say *that*. For we have no use for the reality–appearance distinction, any more than for the distinction between the found and the made. We hope to replace the reality–appearance distinction with the distinction between the more useful and the less useful. So we say that the vocabulary of Greek metaphysics and Christian theology – the vocabulary used in what Heidegger has called 'the onto-theological tradition' – was a useful one for our ancestors' purposes, but that *we* have different purposes, which will be better served by employing a different vocabulary. Our ancestors climbed up a ladder which we are now in a position to throw away. We can throw it away not because we have reached a final resting place, but because we have different problems to solve than those which perplexed our ancestors.

So far I have been sketching the pragmatists' attitude towards their opponents, and the difficulties they encounter in avoiding the use of terms whose use would beg the question at issue between them and their opponents. Now I should like to describe in somewhat more detail how human inquiry looks from a pragmatist point of view – how it looks once one stops describing it as an attempt to correspond to the intrinsic nature of reality, and starts describing it as an attempt to serve transitory purposes and solve transitory problems.

Pragmatists hope to break with the picture which, in Wittgenstein's words, 'holds us captive' – the Cartesian–Lockean picture of a mind seeking to get in touch with a reality outside itself. So they start with a Darwinian account of human beings as animals doing their best to cope with the environment – doing their best to develop tools which will enable them to enjoy more pleasure and less pain. Words are among the tools which these clever animals have developed.

There is no way in which tools can take one out of touch with reality. No matter whether the tool is a hammer or a gun or a belief or a statement, tool-using is part of the interaction of the organism with its environment. To see the employment of words as the use of tools to deal with the environment, rather than as an attempt to represent the intrinsic nature of that environment, is to repudiate the question of whether human minds are in touch with reality – the question asked by the epistemological sceptic. No organism, human or non-human, is ever more or less in touch with reality than any other organism. The very idea of 'being out of touch with reality' presupposes the un-Darwinian, Cartesian picture of a mind which somehow swings free of the causal forces exerted on the body. The Cartesian mind is an entity whose relations with the rest of the universe are representational rather than causal. So to rid our thinking of the vestiges of Cartesianism, to become fully Darwinian in our thinking, we need to stop thinking of words as representations and to start thinking of them as nodes in the causal network which binds the organism together with its environment.

Seeing language and inquiry in this biologistic way, a way made familiar in recent years by the work of Humberto Maturana and others, permits us to discard the picture of the human mind as an interior space within which the human person is located. As the American philosopher of mind Daniel Dennett has argued, it is only this picture of a Cartesian Theatre which makes one think that there is a big philosophical or scientific problem about the nature of the origin of consciousness. We should substitute a picture of an adult human organism as one whose behaviour is so complex that it can be predicted only by attributing intentional states – beliefs and desires – to the organism. On this account, beliefs and desires are not prelinguistic modes of consciousness, which may or may not be expressible in language. Nor are they names of immaterial events. Rather, they are what in philosophical jargon are called 'sentential attitudes' – that is to say, dispositions on the part of organisms, or of computers, to assert or deny certain sentences. To attribute beliefs and desires to non-users of language (such as dogs, infants and thermostats) is, for us pragmatists, to speak metaphorically.

Pragmatists complement this biologistic approach with Charles Sanders Peirce's definition of a belief as a habit of action. On this definition, to ascribe a belief to someone is simply to say that he or she will tend to behave as I behave when I am willing affirm the truth of a certain sentence. We ascribe beliefs to things which use, or can be imagined to use, sentences, but not to rocks and plants. This is not because the former have a special organ or capacity – consciousness – which the latter lack, but simply because the habits of action of rocks and plants are sufficiently familiar and simple that their behaviour can be predicted without ascribing sentential attitudes to them.

On this view, when we utter such sentences as 'I am hungry' we are not making external what was previously internal, but are simply helping those around to us to predict our future actions. Such sentences are not used to report events going on within the Cartesian Theatre which is a person's consciousness. They are simply tools for coordinating our behaviour with those of others. This is not to say that one can 'reduce' mental states such as beliefs and desires to physiological or behavioural states. It is merely to say that there is no point in asking whether a belief represents reality, either mental reality or physical reality, accurately. That is, for pragmatists, not only a bad question, but the root of much wasted philosophical energy.

The right question to ask is, 'For what purposes would it be useful to hold that belief?' This is like the question, 'For what purposes would it be useful to load this program into my computer?' On the Putnamesque view I am suggesting, a person's body is analogous to the computer's hardware, and his or her beliefs and desires are analogous to the software. Nobody knows or cares whether a given piece of computer software represents reality accurately. What we care about is whether it is the software which will most efficiently accomplish a certain task. Analogously, pragmatists think that the question to ask about our beliefs is not whether they are about reality or merely about appearance, but simply whether they are the best habits of action for gratifying our desires.

On this view, to say that a belief is, as far as we know, true, is to say that no alternative belief is, as far as we know, a better habit of acting. When we say that our ancestors believed, falsely, that the sun went around the earth, and that we believe, truly, that the earth goes round the sun, we are saying that we have a better tool than our ancestors did. Our ancestors might rejoin that their tool enabled them to believe in the literal truth of the Christian Scriptures, whereas ours does not. Our reply has to be, I think, that the benefits of modern astronomy and of space travel outweigh the advantages of Christian fundamentalism. The argument between us and our medieval ancestors should not be about which of us has got the universe right. It should be about the point of holding views about the motion of heavenly bodies, the ends to be achieved by the use of certain tools. Confirming the truth of Scripture is one such aim, space travel is another.

Another way of making this last point is to say that we pragmatists cannot make sense of the idea that we should pursue truth for its own sake. We cannot regard truth as a goal of inquiry. The purpose of inquiry is to achieve agreement among human beings about what to do, to bring about consensus on the ends to be achieved and the means to be used to achieve those ends. Inquiry that does not achieve coordination of behaviour is not inquiry but simply wordplay. To argue for a certain theory about the microstructure of material bodies, or about the proper balance of powers between branches of government, is to argue about what we should do: how we should use the tools at our disposal in order to make technological, or political, progress. So, for pragmatists there is no sharp break between natural science and social science, nor between social science and politics, nor between politics, philosophy and literature. All areas of culture are parts of the same endeavour to make life better. There is no deep split between theory and practice, because on a pragmatist view all so-called 'theory' which is not wordplay is always already practice.

To treat beliefs not as representations but as habits of action, and words not as representations but as tools, is to make it pointless to ask, 'Am I discovering or inventing, making or finding?' There is no point in dividing up the organisms' interaction with the environment in this way. Consider an example. We normally say that a bank account is a social construction rather than an object in the natural world, whereas a giraffe is an object in the natural world rather than a social construction. Bank accounts are made, giraffes are found. Now the truth in this view is simply that if there had been no human beings there would still have been giraffes, whereas there would have been no bank accounts. But this causal independence of giraffes from humans does not mean that giraffes are what they are apart from human needs and interests.

On the contrary, we describe giraffes in the way we do, *as* giraffes, because of our needs and interests. We speak a language which includes the word 'giraffe' because it suits our purposes to do so. The same goes for words like 'organ', 'cell', 'atom', and so on – the names of the parts out of which giraffes are made, so to speak. All the descriptions we give of things are descriptions suited to our purposes. No sense can be made, we pragmatists argue, of the claim that some of these descriptions pick out 'natural kinds' – that they cut nature at the joints. The line between a giraffe and the surrounding air is clear enough if you are a human being interested in hunting for meat. If you are a language-using ant or amoeba, or a space voyager observing us from far above, that line is not so clear, and it is not clear that you would need or have a word for 'giraffe' in your language. More generally, it is not clear that any of the millions of ways of describing the piece of space time occupied by what we call a giraffe is any closer to the way things are in themselves than any of the others. Just as it seems pointless to ask whether a giraffe is really a collection of atoms, or really a collection of actual and possible sensations in human sense organs, or really something else, so the question, 'Are we describing it as it really is?' seems one we never need to ask. All we need to know is whether some competing description might be more useful for some of our purposes.

The relativity of descriptions to purposes is the pragmatist's principal argument for his antirepresentational view of knowledge – the view that inquiry aims at utility for us rather than an accurate account of how things are in themselves. Because every belief we have must be formulated in some language or other, and because languages are not attempts to copy what is out there, but rather tools for dealing with what is out there, there is no way to divide off 'the contribution to our knowledge made by the object' from 'the contribution to our knowledge made by our subjectivity'. Both the words we use and our willingness to affirm certain sentences using those words and not others are the products of fantastically complex causal connections between human organisms and the rest of the universe. There is no way to divide up this web of causal connections so as to compare the relative amount of subjectivity and of objectivity in a given belief. There is no way, as Wittgenstein has said, to come between language and its object, to divide the giraffe in itself from our ways of talking about giraffes. As Hilary Putnam, the leading contemporary pragmatist, has put it: 'elements of what we call "language" or "mind" penetrate so deeply into reality that the very project of representing ourselves as being "mappers" of something "language-independent" is fatally compromised from the start'.

The Platonist dream of perfect knowledge is the dream of stripping ourselves clean of everything that comes from inside us and opening ourselves without reservation to what is outside us. But this distinction between inside and outside, as I have said earlier, is one which cannot be made once we adopt a biologistic view. If the Platonist is going to insist on that distinction, he has got to have an epistemology which does not link up in any interesting way with other disciplines. He will end up with an account of knowledge which turns its back on the rest of science. This amounts to making knowledge into something supernatural, a kind of miracle.

The suggestion that everything we say and do and believe is a matter of fulfilling human needs and interests might seem simply a way of formulating the secularism of the Enlightenment – a way of saying that human beings are on their own, and have no supernatural light to guide them to the Truth. But of course the Enlightenment replaced the idea of such supernatural guidance with the idea of a quasi-divine faculty called 'reason'. It is this idea which American pragmatists and post-Nietzschean European philosophers are attacking. What seems most shocking about their criticisms of this idea is not their description of natural science as an attempt to manage reality rather than to represent it. Rather, it is their description of moral choice as always a matter of compromise between competing goods, rather than as a choice between the absolutely right and the absolutely wrong.

Controversies between foundationalists and antifoundationalists on the theory of knowledge look like the sort of merely scholastic quarrels which can safely be left to the philosophy professors. But quarrels about the character of moral choice look more important. We stake our sense of who we are on the outcome of such choices. So we do not like to be told that our choices are between alternative goods rather than between good and evil. When philosophy professors start saying that there is nothing either absolutely wrong or absolutely right, the topic of relativism begins to get interesting. The debates between the pragmatists and their opponents, or the Nietzscheans and theirs, begin to look too important to be left to philosophy professors. Everybody wants to get in on the act.

This is why philosophers like myself find ourselves denounced in magazines and newspapers which one might have thought oblivious of our existence. These denunciations claim that unless the youth is raised to believe in moral absolutes, and in objective truth, civilization is doomed. Unless the younger generation has the same attachment to firm moral principles as we have, these magazine and newspaper articles say, the struggle for human freedom and human decency will be over. When we philosophy teachers read this sort of article, we find ourselves being told that we have enormous power over the future of mankind. For all it will take to overturn centuries of moral progress, these articles suggest, is a generation which accepts the doctrines of moral relativism, accepts the views common to Nietzsche and Dewey.

Dewey and Nietzsche of course disagreed about a lot of things. Nietzsche thought of the happy, prosperous masses who would inhabit Dewey's social democratic utopia as 'the last men', worthless creatures incapable of greatness. Nietzsche was as instinctively antidemocratic in his politics as Dewey was instinctively democratic. But the two men agree not only on the nature of knowledge but on the nature of moral choice. Dewey said that every evil is a rejected good. William James said that every human need has a prima facie right to be gratified, and the only reason for refusing to gratify it is that it conflicts with another human need. Nietzsche would have entirely agreed. He would have phrased this point in terms of competition between bearers of the will to power, whereas James and Dewey would have found the term 'power', with its sadistic overtones, a bit misleading. But these three philosophers made identical criticisms of Enlightenment, and specifically Kantian, attempts to view moral principles as the product of a special faculty called 'reason'. They all thought that such attempts were disingenuous attempts to keep something like God alive in the midst of a secular culture.

Critics of moral relativism think that unless there is something absolute, something which shares God's implacable refusal to yield to human weakness, we have no reason to go on resisting evil. If evil is merely a lesser good, if all moral choice is a compromise between conflicting goods, then, they say, there is no point in moral struggle. The lives of those who have died resisting injustice become pointless. But to us pragmatists moral struggle is continuous with the struggle for existence, and no sharp break divides the unjust from the imprudent, the evil from the inexpedient. What matters for pragmatists is devising ways of diminishing human suffering and increasing human equality, increasing the ability of all human children to start life with an equal chance of happiness. This goal is not written in the stars, and is no more an expression of what Kant called 'pure practical reason' than it is of the Will of God. It is a goal worth dying for, but it does not require backup from supernatural forces.

The pragmatist view of what opponents of pragmatism call 'firm moral principles' is that such principles are abbreviations of past practices – way of summing up the habits of the ancestors we most admire. For example, Mill's greater-happiness principle and Kant's categorical imperative are ways of reminding ourselves of certain social customs – those of certain parts of the Christian West, the culture which has been, at least in words if not in deeds, more egalitarian than any other. The Christian doctrine that all members of the species are brothers and sisters is the religious way of saying what Mill and Kant said in non-religious terms: that considerations of family membership, sex, race, religious creed and the like should not prevent us from trying to do unto others as we would have them do to us –

should not prevent us from thinking of them as people like ourselves, deserving the respect which we ourselves hope to enjoy.

But there are other firm moral principles than those which epitomize egalitarianism. One such principle is that dishonour brought to a woman of one's family must be paid for with blood. Another is that it would be better to have no son than to have one who is homosexual. Those of us who would like to put a stop to the blood feuds and the gaybashing produced by these firm moral principles call such principles 'prejudices' rather than 'insights'. It would be nice if philosophers could give us assurance that the principles which we approve of, like Mill's and Kant's, are 'rational' in a way that the principles of the blood-revengers and the gaybashers are not. But to say that they are more rational is just another way of saying that they are more universalistic – that they treat the differences between women of one's own family and other women, and the difference between gays and straights, as relatively insignificant. But it is not clear that failure to mention particular groups of people is a mark of rationality.

To see this last point, consider the principle 'Thou shalt not kill'. This is admirably universal, but is it more or less rational than the principle 'Do not kill unless one is a soldier defending his or her country, or is preventing a murder, or is a state executioner, or a merciful practitioner of euthanasia'? I have no idea whether it is more or less rational, and so do not find the term 'rational' useful in this area. If I am told that a controversial action which I have taken has to be defended by being subsumed under a universal, rational principle, I may be able to dream up such a principle to fit the occasion, but sometimes I may only be able to say, 'Well, it seemed like the best thing to do at the time, all things considered.' It is not clear that the latter defence is less rational than some universal-sounding principle which I have dreamed up *ad hoc* to justify my action. It is not clear that all the moral dilemmas to do with population control, the rationing of health care, and the like – should wait upon the formulation of principles for their solution.

As we pragmatists see it, the idea that there must be such a legitimating principle lurking behind every right action amounts to the idea that there is something like a universal, super-national court of law before which we stand. We know that the best societies are those which are governed by laws rather than by the whim of tyrants or mobs. Without the rule of law, we say, human life is turned over to emotion and to violence. This makes us think that there must be a sort of invisible tribunal of reason administering laws which we all, somewhere deep down inside, recognize as binding upon us. Something like this was Kant's understanding of moral obligation. But, once again, the Kantian picture of what human beings are like cannot be reconciled with history or with biology. Both teach us that the development of societies ruled by laws rather than men was a slow, late, fragile, contingent, evolutionary achievement.

Dewey thought that Hegel was right, against Kant, when he insisted that universal moral principles were useful only insofar as they were the outgrowth of the historical development of a particular society – a society whose institutions gave content to the otherwise empty shell of the principle. Recently Michael Walzer, a political philosopher best known for his earlier work *Spheres of Justice*, has come to Hegel's and Dewey's defence. In his more recent book *Thick and Thin*, Walzer argues that we should not think of the customs and institutions of particular societies as accidental accretions around a common core of universal moral rationality, the transcultural moral law. Rather, we should think of the thick set of customs and institutions as prior, and as what commands moral allegiance. The thin morality which can be abstracted out of the various thick moralities is not made up of the commandments of a universally shared human faculty called 'reason'. Such thin resemblances between these thick moralities as may exist are contingent, as contingent as the resemblances between the adaptive organs of diverse biological species.

Someone who adopts the anti-Kantian stance common to Hegel, Dewey and Walzer and is asked to defend the thick morality of the society with which she identifies herself will not be able to do so by talking about the rationality of her moral views. Rather, she will have to talk about the various concrete advantages of her society's practices over those of other societies. Discussion of the relative advantages of different thick moralities will, obviously, be as inconclusive as discussion of the relative superiority of a beloved book or person over another person's beloved book or person.

The idea of a universally shared source of truth called 'reason' or 'human nature' is, for us pragmatists, just the idea that such discussion *ought* to be capable of being made conclusive. We see this idea as a misleading way of expressing the hope, which we share, that the human race as a whole should gradually come together in a global community, a community which incorporates most of the thick morality of the European industrialized democracies. It is misleading because it suggests that the aspiration to such a community is somehow built into every member of the biological species. This seems to us pragmatists like the suggestion that the aspiration to be an anaconda is somehow built into all reptiles, or that the aspiration to be an anthropoid is somehow built into all mammals. This is why we pragmatists see the charge of relativism as simply the charge that we see luck where our critics insist on seeing destiny. We think that the utopian world community envisaged by the Charter of the United Nations and the Helsinki Declaration of Human Rights is no more the *destiny* of humanity than is an atomic holocaust or the replacement of democratic governments by feuding warlords. If either of the latter is what the future holds, our species will have been unlucky, but it will not have been irrational. It will not have failed to live up to its moral obligations. It will simply have missed a chance to be happy.

I do not know how to argue the question of whether it is better to see human beings in this biologistic way or to see them in a way more like Plato's or Kant's. So I do not know how to give anything like a conclusive argument for the view which my critics call 'relativism' and which I prefer to call 'antifoundationalism' or 'antidualism'. It is certainly not enough for my side to appeal to Darwin and ask our opponents how they can avoid an appeal to the supernatural. That way of stating the issue begs many questions. It is certainly not enough for my opponents to say that a biologistic view strips human beings of their dignity and their self-respect. That too begs most of the questions at issue. I suspect that all that either side can do is to restate its case over and over again, in context after context. The controversy between those who see both our species and our society as a lucky accident, and those who find an immanent teleology in both, is too radical to permit of being judged from some neutral standpoint.

I

Autobiographical

1. Trotsky and the Wild Orchids

(1992)

If there is anything to the idea that the best intellectual position is one which is attacked with equal vigour from the political right and the political left, then I am in good shape. I am often cited by conservative culture warriors as one of the relativistic, irrationalist, deconstructing, sneering, smirking intellectuals whose writings are weakening the moral fibre of the young. Neal Kozody, writing in the monthly bulletin of the Committee for the Free World, an organization known for its vigilance against symptoms of moral weakness, denounces my 'cynical and nihilistic view' and says 'it is not enough for him [Rorty] that American students should be merely mindless; he would have them positively mobilized for mindlessness'. Richard Neuhaus, a theologian who doubts that atheists can be good American citizens, says that the 'ironist vocabulary' I advocate 'can neither provide a public language for the citizens of a democracy, nor contend intellectually against the enemies of democracy, nor transmit the reasons for democracy to the next generation'. My criticisms of Allan Bloom's *The Closing of the American Mind* led Harvey Mansfield – recently appointed by President Bush to the National Council for the Humanities – to say that I have 'given up on America' and that I 'manage to diminish even Dewey'. (Mansfield recently described Dewey as a 'medium-sized malefactor'.) His colleague on the council, my fellow philosopher John Searle, thinks that standards can only be restored to American higher education if people abandon the views on truth, knowledge and objectivity that I do my best to inculcate.

Yet Sheldon Wolin, speaking from the left, sees a lot of similarity between me and Allan Bloom: both of us, he says, are intellectual snobs who care only about the leisured, cultured élite to which we belong. Neither of us has anything to say to blacks, or to other groups who have been shunted aside by American society. Wolin's view is echoed by Terry Eagleton, Britain's leading Marxist thinker. Eagleton says that 'in [Rorty's] ideal society the intellectuals will be "ironists", practising a suitably cavalier, laid-back attitude to their own belief, while the masses, for whom such self-ironizing might prove too subversive a weapon, will continue to salute the flag and take life seriously'. *Der Spiegel* said that I 'attempt to make the yuppie regression look good'. Jonathan Culler, one of Derrida's chief disciples and expositors, says that my version of pragmatism 'seems altogether appropriate to the age of Reagan'. Richard Bernstein says that my views are 'little more than an ideological *apologia* for an old-fashioned version of Cold War liberalism dressed up in fashionable "post-modern" discourse'. The left's favourite word for me is 'complacent', just as the right's is 'irresponsible'.

The left's hostility is partially explained by the fact that most people who admire Nietzsche, Heidegger and Derrida as much as I do – most of the people who either classify themselves as 'postmodernist' or (like me) find themselves thus classified willynilly – participate in what Jonathan Yardley has called the 'America Sucks Sweepstakes'. Participants in this event compete to find better, bitterer ways of describing the United States. They see our country as embodying everything that is wrong with the rich post-Enlightenment West. They see ours as what Foucault called a 'disciplinary society', dominated by an odious ethos of 'liberal individualism', an ethos which produces racism, sexism, consumerism and Republican presidents. By contrast, I see America pretty much as Whitman and Dewey did, as opening a prospect on illimitable democratic vistas. I think that our country – despite its past and present atrocities and vices, and despite its continuing eagerness to elect fools and knaves to high office – is a good example of the best kind of society so far invented.

The right's hostility is largely explained by the fact that rightist thinkers don't think that it is enough just to *prefer* democratic societies. One also has to believe that they are Objectively Good, that the institutions of such societies are grounded in Rational First Principles. Especially if one teaches philosophy, as I do, one is expected to tell the young that their society is not just one of the better ones so far contrived, but one which embodies Truth and Reason. Refusal to say this sort of thing counts as the 'treason of the clerks' – as an abdication of professional and moral responsibility. My own philosophical views – views I share with Nietzsche and Dewey – forbid me to say this kind of thing. I do not have much use for notions like 'objective value' and 'objective truth'. I think that the so-called postmodernists are right in most of their criticisms of traditional philosophical talk about 'reason'. So my philosophical views offend the right as much as my political preferences offend the left.

I am sometimes told, by critics from both ends of the political spectrum, that my views are so weird as to be merely frivolous. They suspect that I will say anything to get a gasp, that I am just amusing myself by contradicting everybody else. This hurts. So I have tried, in what follows, to say something about how I got into my present position – how I got into philosophy, and then found myself unable to use philosophy for the purpose I had originally had in mind. Perhaps this bit of autobiography will make clear that, even if my views about the relation of philosophy and politics are odd, they were not adopted for frivolous reasons.

When I was 12, the most salient books on my parents' shelves were two red-bound volumes, *The Case of Leon Trotsky* and *Not Guilty*. These made up the report of the Dewey Commission of Inquiry into the Moscow Trials. I never read them with the wide-eyed fascination I brought to books like Krafft-Ebing's *Psychopathia Sexualis*, but I thought of them in the way in which other children thought of their family's Bible: they were books that radiated redemptive truth and moral splendour. If I were a really *good* boy, I would say to myself, I should have read not only the Dewey Commission reports, but also Trotsky's *History of the Russian Revolution*, a book I started many times but never managed to finish. For in the 1940s, the Russian Revolution and its betrayal by Stalin were, for me, what the Incarnation and its betrayal by the Catholics had been to precocious little Lutherans 400 years before.

My father had almost, but not quite, accompanied John Dewey to

Mexico as PR man for the Commission of Inquiry which Dewey chaired. Having broken with the American Communist Party in 1932, my parents had been classified by the *Daily Worker* as 'Trotskyites', and they more or less accepted the description. When Trotsky was assassinated in 1940, one of his secretaries, John Frank, hoped that the GPU would not think to look for him in the remote little village on the Delaware river where we were living. Using a pseudonym, he was our guest in Flatbrookville for some months. I was warned not to disclose his real identity, though it is doubtful that my schoolmates at Walpack Elementary would have been interested in my indiscretions.

I grew up knowing that all decent people were, if not Trotskyites, at least socialists. I also knew that Stalin had ordered not only Trotsky's assassination but also Kirov's, Ehrlich's, Alter's and Carlo Tresca's. (Tresca, gunned down on the streets of New York, had been a family friend.) I knew that poor people would always be oppressed until capitalism was overcome. Working as an unpaid office boy during my twelfth winter, I carried drafts of press releases from the Workers' Defense League office off Gramercy Park (where my parents worked) to Norman Thomas's (the Socialist Party's candidate for president) house around the corner, and also to A. Philip Randolph's office at the Brotherhood of Pullman Car Porters on 125th Street. On the subway, I would read the documents I was carrying. They told me a lot about what factory owners did to union organizers, plantation owners to sharecroppers, and the white locomotive engineers' union to the coloured firemen (whose jobs white men wanted, now that diesel engines were replacing coal-fired steam engines). So, at 12, I knew that the point of being human was to spend one's life fighting social injustice.

But I also had private, weird, snobbish, incommunicable interests. In earlier years these had been in Tibet. I had sent the newly enthroned Dalai Lama a present, accompanied by warm congratulations to a fellow eight-year-old who had made good. A few years later, when my parents began dividing their time between the Chelsea Hotel and the mountains of north-west New Jersey, these interests switched to orchids. Some 40 species of wild orchids occur in those mountains, and I eventually found 17 of them. Wild orchids are uncommon, and rather hard to spot. I prided myself enormously on being the only person around who knew where they grew, their Latin names and their blooming times. When in New York, I would go to the 42nd Street public library to reread a nineteenth-century volume on the botany of the orchids of the eastern US.

I was not quite sure why those orchids were so important, but I was convinced that they were. I was sure that our noble, pure, chaste, North American wild orchids were morally superior to the showy, hybridized, tropical orchids displayed in florists' shops. I was also convinced that there was a deep significance in the fact that the orchids are the latest and most complex plants to have been developed in the course of evolution. Looking back, I suspect that there was a lot of sublimated sexuality involved (orchids being a notoriously sexy sort of flower), and that my desire to learn all there was to know about orchids was linked to my desire to understand all the hard words in Krafft-Ebing.

I was uneasily aware, however, that there was something a bit dubious about this esotericism – this interest in socially useless flowers. I had read (in the vast amount of spare time given to a clever, snotty, nerdy only child) bits of *Marius the Epicurean* and also bits of Marxist criticisms of Pater's aestheticism. I was afraid that Trotsky (whose *Literature and Revolution* I had nibbled at) would not have approved of my interest in orchids.

At fifteen I escaped from the bullies who regularly beat me up on the playground of my high school (bullies who, I assumed, would somehow wither away once capitalism had been overcome) by going off to the so-called Hutchins College of the University of Chicago. (This was the institution immortalized by A. J. Liebling as 'the biggest collection of juvenile neurotics since the Children's Crusade'.) Insofar as I had any project in mind, it was to reconcile Trotsky and the orchids. I wanted to find some intellectual or aesthetic framework which would let me – in a thrilling phrase which I came across in Yeats – 'hold reality and justice in a single vision'. By *reality* I meant, more or less, the Wordsworthian moments in which, in the woods around Flatbrookville (and especially in the presence of certain coralroot orchids, and of the smaller yellow lady slipper), I had felt touched by something numinous, something of ineffable importance. By *justice* I meant what Norman Thomas and Trotsky both stood for, the liberation of the weak from the strong. I wanted a way to be both an intellectual and spiritual snob and a friend of humanity – a nerdy recluse and a fighter for justice. I was very confused, but reasonably sure that at Chicago I would find out how grown-ups managed to work the trick I had in mind.

When I got to Chicago (in 1946), I found that Hutchins, together with his friends Mortimer Adler and Richard McKeon (the villain of Pirsig's *Zen and the Art of Motorcycle Maintenance*), had enveloped much of the University of Chicago in a neo-Aristotelian mystique. The most frequent target of their sneers was John Dewey's pragmatism. That pragmatism was the philosophy of my parents' friend Sidney Hook, as well as the unofficial philosophy of most of the other New York intellectuals who had given up on dialectical materialism. But according to Hutchins and Adler, pragmatism was vulgar, 'relativistic', and self-refuting. As they pointed out over and over again, Dewey had no absolutes. To say, as Dewey did, that 'growth itself is the only moral end', left one without a criterion for growth, and thus with no way to refute Hitler's suggestion that Germany had 'grown' under his rule. To say that truth is what works is to reduce the quest for truth to the quest for power. Only an appeal to something eternal, absolute, and good – like the God of St Thomas, or the 'nature of human beings' described by Aristotle – would permit one to answer the Nazis, to justify one's choice of social democracy over fascism.

This quest for stable absolutes was common to the neo-Thomists and to Leo Strauss, the teacher who attracted the best of the Chicago students (including my classmate Allan Bloom). The Chicago faculty was dotted with awesomely learned refugees from Hitler, of whom Strauss was the most revered. All of them seemed to agree that something deeper and weightier than Dewey was needed if one was to explain why it would be better to be dead than to be a Nazi. This sounded pretty good to my 15-year-old ears. For moral and philosophical absolutes sounded a bit like my beloved orchids – numinous, hard to find, known only to a chosen few. Further, since Dewey was a hero to all the people among whom I had grown up, scorning

Dewey was a convenient form of adolescent revolt. The only question was whether this scorn should take a religious or a philosophical form, and how it might be combined with striving for social justice.

Like many of my classmates at Chicago, I knew lots of T. S. Eliot by heart. I was attracted by Eliot's suggestions that only committed Christians (and perhaps only Anglo-Catholics) could overcome their unhealthy preoccupation with their private obsessions, and so serve their fellow humans with proper humility. But a prideful inability to believe what I was saying when I recited the General Confession gradually led me to give up on my awkward attempts to get religion. So I fell back on absolutist philosophy.

I read through Plato during my fifteenth summer, and convinced myself that Socrates was right – virtue *was* knowledge. That claim was music to my ears, for I had doubts about my own moral character and a suspicion that my only gifts were intellectual ones. Besides, Socrates *had* to be right, for only then could one hold reality and justice in a single vision. Only if he were right could one hope to be both as good as the best Christians (such as Alyosha in *The Brothers Karamazov*, whom I could not – and still cannot – decide whether to envy or despise) and as learned and clever as Strauss and his students. So I decided to major in philosophy. I figured that if I became a philosopher I might get to the top of Plato's 'divided line' – the place 'beyond hypotheses' where the full sunshine of Truth irradiates the purified soul of the wise and good: an Elysian field dotted with immaterial orchids. It seemed obvious to me that getting to such a place was what everybody with any brains really wanted. It also seemed clear that Platonism had all the advantages of religion, without requiring the humility which Christianity demanded, and of which I was apparently incapable.

For all these reasons, I wanted very much to be some kind of Platonist, and from 15 to 20 I did my best. But it didn't pan out. I could never figure out whether the Platonic philosopher was aiming at the ability to offer irrefutable argument – argument which rendered him able to convince anyone he encountered of what he believed (the sort of thing Ivan Karamazov was good at) – or instead was aiming at a sort of incommunicable, private bliss (the sort of thing his brother Alyosha seemed to possess). The first goal is to achieve argumentative power over others – e.g., to become able to convince bullies that they should not beat one up, or to convince rich capitalists that they must cede their power to a cooperative, egalitarian commonwealth. The second goal is to enter a state in which all your own doubts are stilled, but in which you no longer wish to argue. Both goals seemed desirable, but I could not see how they could be fitted together.

At the same time as I was worrying about this tension within Platonism – and within any form of what Dewey had called 'the quest for certainty' – I was also worrying about the familiar problem of how one could possibly get a noncircular justification of any debatable stand on any important issue. The more philosophers I read, the clearer it seemed that each of them could carry their views back to first principles which were incompatible with the first principles of their opponents, and that none of them ever got to that fabled place 'beyond hypotheses'. There seemed to be nothing like a neutral standpoint from which these alternative first principles could be evaluated. But if there were no such standpoint, then the whole idea of 'rational certainty', and the whole Socratic-Platonic idea of replacing passion by reason, seemed not to make much sense.

Eventually I got over the worry about circular argumentation by deciding that the test of philosophical truth was overall coherence, rather than deducibility from unquestioned first principles. But this didn't help much. For coherence is a matter of avoiding contradictions, and St Thomas's advice, 'When you meet a contradiction, make a distinction,' makes that pretty easy. As far as I could see, philosophical talent was largely a matter of proliferating as many distinctions as were needed to wriggle out of a dialectical corner. More generally, it was a matter, when trapped in such a corner, of redescribing the nearby intellectual terrain in such a way that the terms used by one's opponent would seem irrelevant, or question-begging, or jejune. I turned out to have a flair for such redescription. But I became less and less certain that developing this skill was going to make me either wise or virtuous.

Since that initial disillusion (which climaxed about the time I left

Chicago to get a Ph.D. in philosophy at Yale), I have spent 40 years looking for a coherent and convincing way of formulating my worries about what, if anything, philosophy is good for. My starting point was the discovery of Hegel's *Phenomenology of Spirit*, a book which I read as saying: granted that philosophy is just a matter of out-redescribing the last philosopher, the cunning of reason can make use even of this sort of competition. It can use it to weave the conceptual fabric of a freer, better, more just society. If philosophy can be, at best, only what Hegel called 'its time held in thought', still, that might be enough. For by thus holding one's time, one might do what Marx wanted done – change the world. So even if there were no such thing as 'understanding the world' in the Platonic sense – an understanding from a position outside of time and history – perhaps there was still a social use for my talents, and for the study of philosophy.

For quite a while after I read Hegel, I thought that the two greatest achievements of the species to which I belonged were *The Phenomenology of Spirit* and *Remembrance of Things Past* (the book which took the place of the wild orchids once I left Flatbrookville for Chicago). Proust's ability to weave intellectual and social snobbery together with the hawthorns around Combray, his grandmother's selfless love, Odette's orchidaceous embraces of Swann and Jupien's of Charlus, and with everything else he encountered – to give each of these its due without feeling the need to bundle them together with the help of a religious faith or a philosophical theory – seemed to me as astonishing as Hegel's ability to throw himself successively into empiricism, Greek tragedy, Stoicism, Christianity and Newtonian physics, and to emerge from each, ready and eager for something completely different. It was the cheerful commitment to irreducible temporality which Hegel and Proust shared – the specifically anti-Platonic element in their work – that seemed so wonderful. They both seemed able to weave everything they encountered into a narrative without asking that that narrative have a moral, and without asking how that narrative would appear under the aspect of eternity.

About 20 years or so after I decided that the young Hegel's willingness to stop trying for eternity, and just be the child of his time, was the appropriate response to disillusionment with Plato, I found myself being led back to Dewey. Dewey now seemed to me a philosopher who had learned all that Hegel had to teach about how to eschew certainty and eternity, while immunizing himself against pantheism by taking Darwin seriously. This rediscovery of Dewey coincided with my first encounter with Derrida (which I owe to Jonathan Arac, my colleague at Princeton). Derrida led me back to Heidegger, and I was struck by the resemblances between Dewey's, Wittgenstein's and Heidegger's criticisms of Cartesianism. Suddenly things began to come together. I thought I saw a way to blend a criticism of the Cartesian tradition with the quasi-Hegelian historicism of Michel Foucault, Ian Hacking and Alasdair MacIntyre. I thought that I could fit all these into a quasi-Heideggerian story about the tensions within Platonism.

The result of this small epiphany was a book called *Philosophy and the Mirror of Nature*. Though disliked by most of my fellow philosophy professors, this book had enough success among nonphilosophers to give me a self-confidence I had previously lacked. But *Philosophy and the Mirror of Nature* did not do much for my adolescent ambitions. The topics it treated – the mind–body problem, controversies in the philosophy of language about truth and meaning, Kuhnian philosophy of science – were pretty remote from both Trotsky and the orchids. I had gotten back on good terms with Dewey; I had articulated my historicist anti-Platonism; I had finally figured out what I thought about the direction and value of current movements in analytic philosophy; I had sorted out most of the philosophers whom I had read. But I had not spoken to any of the questions which got me started reading philosophers in the first place. I was no closer to the single vision which, 30 years back, I had gone to college to get.

As I tried to figure out what had gone wrong, I gradually decided that the whole idea of holding reality and justice in a single vision had been a mistake – that a pursuit of such a vision had been precisely what led Plato astray. More specifically, I decided that only religion – only a nonargumentative faith in a surrogate parent who, unlike any real parent, embodied love, power and justice in equal measure – could do the trick Plato wanted done. Since I couldn't imagine becoming religious, and indeed had gotten more and more raucously secularist, I decided that the hope of getting a single vision by becoming a philosopher had been a self-deceptive atheist's way out. So I decided to write a book about what intellectual life might be like if one could manage to give up the Platonic attempt to hold reality and justice in a single vision.

That book – *Contingency, Irony and Solidarity* – argues that there is no need to weave one's personal equivalent of Trotsky and one's personal equivalent of my wild orchids together. Rather, one should try to abjure the temptation to tie in one's moral responsibilities to other people with one's relation to whatever idiosyncratic things or persons one loves with all one's heart and soul and mind (or, if you like, the things or persons one is obsessed with). The two will, for some people, coincide – as they do in those lucky Christians for whom the love of God and of other human beings are inseparable, or revolutionaries who are moved by nothing save the thought of social justice. But they need not coincide, and one should not try too hard to make them do so. So, for example, Jean-Paul Sartre seemed to me right when he denounced Kant's self-deceptive quest for certainty, but wrong when he denounced Proust as a useless bourgeois wimp, a man whose life and writings were equally irrelevant to the only thing that really mattered, the struggle to overthrow capitalism.

Proust's life and work were, in fact, irrelevant to that struggle. But that is a silly reason to despise Proust. It is as wrong-headed as Savonarola's contempt for the works of art he called 'vanities'. Single-mindedness of this Sartrean or Savonarolan sort is the quest for purity of heart – the attempt to will one thing – gone rancid. It is the attempt to see yourself as an incarnation of something larger than yourself (the Movement, Reason, the Good, the Holy) rather than accepting your finitude. The latter means, among other things, accepting that what matters most to you may well be something that may never matter much to most people. Your equivalent of my orchids may always seem merely weird, merely idiosyncratic, to practically everybody else. But that is no reason to be ashamed of, or downgrade, or try to slough off, your Wordsworthian moments, your lover, your family, your pet, your favourite lines of verse, or your quaint religious faith. There is nothing sacred about universality which makes the shared automatically better than the unshared. There is no automatic privilege of what you can get everybody to agree to (the universal) over what you cannot (the idiosyncratic).

This means that the fact that you have obligations to other people (not to bully them, to join them in overthrowing tyrants, to feed them when they are hungry) does not entail that what you share with other people is more important than anything else. What you share with them, when you are aware of such moral obligations, is not, I argued in *Contingency*, 'rationality' or 'human nature' or 'the fatherhood of God' or 'a knowledge of the Moral Law', or anything other than ability to sympathize with the pain of others. There is no particular reason to expect that your sensitivity to that pain, and your idiosyncratic loves, are going to fit within one big overall account of how everything hangs together. There is, in short, not much reason to hope for the sort of single vision that I went to college hoping to get.

So much for how I came to the views I currently hold. As I said earlier, most people find these views repellent. My *Contingency* book got a couple of good reviews, but these were vastly outnumbered by reviews which said that the book was frivolous, confused and irresponsible. The gist of the criticisms I get from both left and right is pretty much the same as the gist of the criticisms aimed at Dewey by the Thomists, the Straussians and the Marxists, back in the 1930s and 1940s. Dewey thought, as I now do, that there was nothing bigger, more permanent and more reliable, behind our sense of moral obligation to those in pain than a certain contingent historical phenomenon – the gradual spread of the sense that the pain of others matters, regardless of whether they are of the same family, tribe, colour, religion, nation or intelligence as oneself. This idea, Dewey thought, cannot be shown to be true by science, or religion or philosophy – at least if 'shown to be true' means 'capable of being made evident to anyone, regardless of background'. It can only be made evident to people whom it is not too late to acculturate into our own particular, late-blooming, historically contingent form of life.

This Deweyan claim entails a picture of human beings as children of their time and place, without any significant metaphysical or biological limits on their plasticity. It means that a sense of moral obligation is a matter of conditioning rather than of insight. It also entails that the notion of insight (in any area, physics as well as ethics) as a glimpse of what is *there*, apart from any human needs and desires, cannot be made coherent. As William James put it, 'The trail of the human serpent is over all.' More specifically, our conscience and our aesthetic taste are, equally, products of the cultural environment in which we grew up. We decent, liberal humanitarian types (representatives of the moral community to which both my reviewers and I belong) are just luckier, not more insightful, than the bullies with whom we struggle.

This view is often referred to dismissively as 'cultural relativism'. But it is not relativistic, if that means saying that every moral view is as good as every other. *Our* moral view is, I firmly believe, much better than any competing view, even though there are a lot of people whom you will never be able to convert to it. It is one thing to say, falsely, that there is nothing to choose between us and the Nazis. It is another thing to say, correctly, that there is no neutral, common ground to which an experienced Nazi philosopher and I can repair in order to argue out our differences. That Nazi and I will always strike one another as begging all the crucial questions, arguing in circles.

Socrates and Plato suggested that if we tried hard enough we should find beliefs which *everybody* found intuitively plausible, and that among these would be moral beliefs whose implications, when clearly realized, would make us virtuous as well as knowledgeable. To thinkers like Allan Bloom (on the Straussian side) and Terry Eagleton (on the Marxist side), there just *must* be such beliefs – unwobbling pivots that determine the answer to the question: Which moral or political alternative is *objectively* valid? For Deweyan pragmatists like me, history and anthropology are enough to show that there are no unwobbling pivots, and that seeking objectivity is just a matter of getting as much intersubjective agreement as you can manage.

Nothing much has changed in philosophical debates about whether objectivity is more than intersubjectivity since the time I went to college – or, for that matter, since the time Hegel went to seminary. Nowadays we philosophers talk about 'moral language' instead of 'moral experience', and about 'contextualist theories of reference' rather than about 'the relation between subject and object'. But this is just froth on the surface. My reasons for turning away from the anti-Deweyan views I imbibed at Chicago are pretty much the same reasons Dewey had for turning away from evangelical Christianity and from the neo-Hegelian pantheism which he embraced in his 20s. They are also pretty much the reasons which led Hegel to turn away from Kant, and to decide that both God and the Moral Law had to be temporalized and historicized to be believable. I do not think that I have more insight into the debates about our need for 'absolutes' than I had when I was 20, despite all the books I have read and arguments I have had in the intervening 40 years. All those years of reading and arguing did was to let me spell out my disillusionment with Plato – my conviction that philosophy was no help in dealing with Nazis and other bullies – in more detail, and to a variety of different audiences.

At the moment there are two cultural wars being waged in the United States. The first is the one described in detail by my colleague James Davison Hunter in his comprehensive and informative *Culture Wars: The Struggle to Define America*. This war – between the people Hunter calls 'progressivists' and those he calls 'orthodox' – is important. It will decide whether our country continues along the trajectory defined by the Bill of Rights, the Reconstruction Amendments, the building of the land-grant colleges, female suffrage, the New Deal, *Brown* v. *Board of Education*, the building of the community colleges, Lyndon Johnson's civil rights legislation, the feminist movement, and the gay rights movement. Continuing along this trajectory would mean that America might continue to set an example of increasing tolerance and increasing equality. But it may be that this trajectory could be continued only while Americans' average real income continued to rise. So 1973 may have been the beginning of the end: the end both of rising economic expectations and of the political consensus that emerged from the New Deal. The future of American politics may be just a series of increasingly blatant and increasingly successful variations on the Willie Horton spots. Sinclair Lewis's *It Can't Happen Here* may become an increasingly plausible scenario. Unlike Hunter, I feel no need to be judicious and balanced in my attitude toward the two sides in this first sort of culture war. I see the 'orthodox' (the people who think that hounding gays out of the military promotes traditional family values) as the same honest, decent, blinkered, disastrous people who voted for Hitler in 1933. I see the 'progressivists' as defining the only America I care about.

The second cultural war is being waged in magazines like *Critical Inquiry* and *Salmagundi*, magazines with high subscription rates and low circulations. It is between those who see modern liberal society as fatally flawed (the people handily lumped together as 'postmodernists') and typical left-wing Democrat professors like myself, people who see ours as a society in which technology and democratic institutions can, with luck, collaborate to increase equality and decrease suffering. This war is not very important. Despite the conservative columnists who pretend to view with alarm a vast conspiracy (encompassing both the postmodernists and the pragmatists) to politicize the humanities and corrupt the youth, this war is just a tiny little dispute within what Hunter calls the 'progressivist' ranks.

People on the postmodernist side of this dispute tend to share Noam Chomsky's view of the United States as run by a corrupt élite which aims at enriching itself by immiserating the Third World. From that perspective, our country is not so much in danger of slipping into fascism as it is a country which has always been quasi-fascist. These people typically think that nothing will change unless we get rid of 'humanism', 'liberal individualism', and 'technologism'. People like me see nothing wrong with any of these -isms, nor with the political and moral heritage of the Enlightenment – with the least common denominator of Mill and Marx, Trotsky and Whitman, William James and Václav Havel. Typically, we Deweyans are sentimentally patriotic about America – willing to grant that it could slide into fascism at any time, but proud of its past and guardedly hopeful about its future.

Most people on my side of this second, tiny, upmarket cultural war have, in the light of the history of nationalized enterprises and central planning in central and eastern Europe, given up on socialism. We are willing to grant that welfare state capitalism is the best we can hope for. Most of us who were brought up Trotskyite now feel forced to admit that Lenin and Trotsky did more harm than good, and that Kerensky has gotten a bum rap for the past 70 years. But we see ourselves as still faithful to everything that was good in the socialist movement. Those on the other side, however, still insist that nothing will change unless there is some sort of total revolution. Postmodernists who consider themselves post-Marxists still want to preserve the sort of purity of heart which Lenin feared he might lose if he listened to too much Beethoven.

I am distrusted by both the 'orthodox' side in the important war and the 'postmodern' side in the unimportant one, because I think that the 'postmoderns' are philosophically right though politically silly, and that the 'orthodox' are philosophically wrong as well as politically dangerous. Unlike both the orthodox and the postmoderns, I do not think that you can tell much about the worth of a philosopher's views on topics such as truth, objectivity and the possibility of a single vision by discovering his politics, or his irrelevance to politics. So I do not think it counts in favour of Dewey's pragmatic view of truth that he was a fervent social democrat, nor against Heidegger's criticism of Platonic notions of objectivity that he was a Nazi, nor against Derrida's view of linguistic meaning that his most influential American ally, Paul de Man, wrote a couple of anti-Semitic articles when he was young. The idea that you can evaluate a writer's philosophical views by reference to their political utility seems to me a version of the bad Platonic-Straussian idea that we cannot have justice until philosophers become kings or kings philosophers.

Both the orthodox and the postmoderns still want a tight connection between people's politics and their views on large theoretical (theological, metaphysical, epistemological, metaphilosophical) matters. Some postmodernists who initially took my enthusiasm for Derrida to mean that I must be on their political side decided, after discovering that my politics were pretty much those of Hubert Humphrey, that I must have sold out. The orthodox tend to think that people who, like the postmodernists and me, believe neither in God nor in some suitable substitute, should think that everything is permitted, that everybody can do what they like. So they tell us that we are either inconsistent or self-deceptive in putting forward our moral or political views.

I take this near unanimity among my critics to show that most people – even a lot of purportedly liberated postmodernists – still hanker for something like what I wanted when I was 15: a way of holding reality and justice in a single vision. More specifically, they want to unite their sense of moral and political responsibility with a grasp of the ultimate determinants of our fate. They want to see love, power and justice as coming together deep down in the nature of things, or in the human soul, or in the structure of language, or *somewhere*. They want some sort of guarantee that their intellectual acuity, and those special ecstatic moments which that acuity sometimes affords, are of some relevance to their moral convictions. They still think that virtue and knowledge are somehow linked – that being right about philosophical matters is important for right action. I think this is important only occasionally and incidentally.

I do not, however, want to argue that philosophy is socially useless. Had there been no Plato, the Christians would have had a harder time selling the idea that all God really wanted from us was fraternal love. Had there been no Kant, the nineteenth century would have had a harder time reconciling Christian ethics with Darwin's story about the descent of man. Had there been no Darwin, it would have been harder for Whitman and Dewey to detach the Americans from their belief that they were God's chosen people, to get them to start standing on their own feet. Had there been no Dewey and no Sidney Hook, American intellectual leftists of the 1930s would have been as buffaloed by the Marxists as were their counterparts in France and in Latin America. Ideas do, indeed, have consequences.

But the fact that ideas have consequences does not mean that we philosophers, we specialists in ideas, are in a key position. We are not here to provide principles or foundations or deep theoretical diagnoses, or a synoptic vision. When I am asked (as, alas, I often am) what I take contemporary philosophy's 'mission' or 'task' to be, I get tonguetied. The best I can do is to stammer that we philosophy professors are people who have a certain familiarity with a certain intellectual tradition, as chemists have a certain familiarity with what happens when you mix various substances together. We can offer some advice about what will happen when you try to combine or to separate certain ideas, on the basis of our knowledge of the results of past experiments. By doing so, we may be able to help you hold your time in thought. But we are not the people to come to if you want confirmation that the things you love with all your heart are central to the structure of the universe, or that your sense of moral responsibility is 'rational and objective' rather than 'just' a result of how you were brought up.

There are still, as C. S. Peirce put it, 'philosophical slop-shops on every corner' which *will* provide such confirmation. But there is a price. To pay the price you have to turn your back on intellectual history and on what Milan Kundera calls 'the fascinating imaginative realm where no one owns the truth and everyone has the right to be understood . . . the wisdom of the novel'. You risk losing the sense of finitude, and the tolerance, which result from realizing how very many synoptic visions there have been, and how little argument can do to help you choose among them. Despite my relatively early disillusion-ment with Platonism, I am very glad that I spent all those years reading philosophy books. For I learned something that still seems very important: to distrust the intellectual snobbery which originally led me to read them. If I had not read all those books, I might never have been able to stop looking for what Derrida calls 'a full presence beyond the reach of play', for a luminous, self-justifying, self-sufficient synoptic vision.

By now I am pretty sure that looking for such a presence and such a vision is a bad idea. The main trouble is that you might succeed, and your success might let you imagine that you have something more to rely on than the tolerance and decency of your fellow human beings. The democratic community of Dewey's dreams is a community in which nobody imagines that. It is a community in which everybody thinks that it is human solidarity, rather than knowledge of something not merely human, that really matters. The actually existing approxi-mations to such a fully democratic, fully secular community now seem to me the greatest achievements of our species. In comparison, even Hegel's and Proust's books seem optional, orchidaceous extras.

II

Hope in Place of Knowledge: A Version of Pragmatism

2. Truth without Correspondence to Reality

(1994)

Pragmatism is often said to be a distinctively American philosophy. Sometimes this is said in tones of contempt, as it was by Bertrand Russell. Russell meant that pragmatism is a shallow philosophy, suitable for an immature country. Sometimes, however, it is said in praise, by people who suggest that it would be un-American, and thus immoral, not to be a pragmatist – for to oppose pragmatism is to oppose the democratic way of life.

Although I think that Russell's contempt for both pragmatism and America was unjustified, I also think that this sort of praise of pragmatism is misguided. Philosophy and politics are not that tightly linked. There will always be room for a lot of philosophical disagreement between people who share the same politics, and for diametrically opposed political views among philosophers of the same school. In particular, there is no reason why a fascist could not be a pragmatist, in the sense of agreeing with pretty much everything Dewey said about the nature of truth, knowledge, rationality and morality. Nietzsche would have agreed with Dewey against Plato and Kant on all these specifically philosophical topics. Had they debated, the *only* substantial disagreement between Nietzsche and Dewey would have been about the value of egalitarian ideas, ideas of human brotherhood and sisterhood, and thus about the value of democracy.

It is unfortunate, I think, that many people hope for a tighter link between philosophy and politics than there is or can be. In particular, people on the left keep hoping for a philosophical view which cannot be used by the political right, one which will lend itself only to good causes.[1] But there never will be such a view; any philosophical view is a tool which can be used by many different hands. Just as you cannot learn much about the value of Heidegger's views on truth and rationality from the fact that he was a Nazi, so you cannot learn much about the value of Dewey's (quite similar)[2] views on the same subjects from the fact that he was a lifelong fighter for good, leftist political causes, nor from the fact that he shared Walt Whitman's sense that 'the United States are themselves the greatest poem'. Your opinion of pragmatism can, and should, be independent of your opinion of either democracy or America.

For all that, Dewey was not entirely wrong when he called pragmatism 'the philosophy of democracy'. What he had in mind is that both pragmatism and America are expressions of a hopeful, melioristic, experimental frame of mind. I think the most one can do by way of linking up pragmatism with America is to say that both the country and its most distinguished philosopher suggest that we can, in politics, substitute *hope* for the sort of knowledge which philosophers have usually tried to attain. America has always been a future-oriented country, a country which delights in the fact that it invented itself in the relatively recent past.

In what follows, I shall be arguing that it helps understand the pragmatists to think of them as saying that the distinction between the past and the future can substitute for all the old philosophical distinctions – the ones which Derrideans call 'the binary oppositions of Western metaphysics'. The most important of these oppositions is that between reality and appearance. Others include the distinctions between the unconditioned and the conditioned, the absolute and the relative, and the properly moral as opposed to the merely prudent.

As I shall be using the term 'pragmatism', the paradigmatic pragmatists are John Dewey and Donald Davidson. But I shall be talking mostly about Dewey, and will bring in Davidson only occasionally (to help out in the clinches, so to speak). It is customary to distinguish the 'classical pragmatists' – Peirce, James and Dewey – from such living 'neopragmatists' as Quine, Goodman, Putnam and Davidson. The break between the two is the so-called 'linguistic turn'. This was the turn philosophers took when, dropping the topic of experience and picking up that of language, they began taking their cue from Frege rather than from Locke. In the US, this turn was taken only in the 1940s and 1950s, and it was as a result of this turn that James and Dewey ceased to be read in American philosophical departments.

When people try to associate Americanism and pragmatism, it is usually only the classical pragmatists whom they have in mind. The so-called neopragmatists do not concern themselves much with moral and social philosophy, nor do they see themselves as representing anything distinctively American. As a student of Carnap, Quine was taught that philosophy should stay close to logic, and keep its distance from politics, literature and history. Quine's students, Goodman and Davidson, take this Carnapian view for granted. Of the neopragmatists I have listed, only Putnam has, in his later writings, stepped beyond the limits Carnap set.

Of the three classical pragmatists, only James and Dewey deliberately and self-consciously related their philosophical doctrines to the country of which they were prominent citizens. Peirce thought of himself as part of an international community of inquirers, working on technical and specialized problems which had little to do with historical developments or national cultures.[3] When he referred to political issues and social trends, it was in the same left-handed way in which Quine refers to them – as topics which have little to do with philosophy.

James and Dewey, however, took America seriously; both reflected on the world-historical significance of their country. Both were influenced by Emerson's evolutionary sense of history, and in particular by his seminal essay on 'The American Scholar'. This essay rejoices in the difference between the Old World and the New, and Oliver Wendell Holmes called it 'our national Declaration of Intellectual Independence'. Both men threw themselves into political movements – especially anti-imperialist movements – designed to keep America true to itself, to keep it from falling back into bad old European ways. Both used the word 'democracy' – and the quasi-synonymous word 'America' – as Whitman had: as names of something sacred. In an essay of 1911, Dewey wrote:

> Emerson, Walt Whitman and Maeterlinck are thus far, per-
> haps, the only men who have been habitually, and, as it were,

instinctively aware that democracy is neither a form of government nor a social expediency, but a metaphysic of the relation
of man and his experience in nature . . .[4]

As Cornel West has made clear,[5] one needs to have read some
Emerson in order to understand the source of the 'instinctive awareness' which James and Dewey shared. West says that Emerson

associates a mythic self with the very content and character
of America. His individualism pertains not simply to discrete
individuals but, more important, to a normative and exhortative
conception of the individual *as* America. His ideological projec-
tion of the first new nation is in terms of a mythic self . . . a
heroic American Scholar, one who has appropriated God-like
power and might and has acquired the confidence to use this
power and might for 'the conversion of the world'.[6]

At bottom, however, Emerson, like his disciple Nietzsche, was not a
philosopher of democracy but of private self-creation, of what he
called 'the infinitude of the private man'. Godlike power was never
far from Emerson's mind. His America was not so much a community
of fellow citizens as a clearing in which Godlike heroes could act out
self-written dramas.

In contrast, Whitman's tone, like James's and Dewey's, is more
secular and more communal than Emerson's. So perhaps the best
way to grasp the attitude towards America which James and Dewey
took for granted, and shared with the audiences who heard their
lectures, is to reread Whitman's *Democratic Vistas*, written in 1867. That
book opens by saying:

As the greatest lessons of Nature through the universe are
perhaps the lessons of variety and freedom, the same present
the greatest lessons also in New World politics and progress . . .
America, filling the present with greatest deeds and problems,
cheerfully accepting the past, including feudalism (as indeed,
the present is but the legitimate birth of the past, including
feudalism) counts, as I reckon, for her justification and success,
(for who, as yet, dare claim success?) almost entirely on the

future . . . For our New World I consider far less important for what it has done, or what it is, than for results to come.[7]

In this essay I shall focus on Whitman's phrase 'counts . . . for her justification and success . . . almost entirely upon the future'. As I see it, the link between Whitmanesque Americanism and pragmatist philosophy – both classical and 'neo-' – is a willingness to refer all questions of ultimate justification to the future, to the substance of things hoped for. If there is anything distinctive about pragmatism it is that it substitutes the notion of a better human future for the notions of 'reality', 'reason' and 'nature'. One may say of pragmatism what Novalis said of Romanticism, that it is 'the apotheosis of the future'.

As I read Dewey, what he somewhat awkwardly called 'a new metaphysic of man's relation to nature', was a generalization of the moral of Darwinian biology. The only justification of a mutation, biological or cultural, is its contribution to the existence of a more complex and interesting species somewhere in the future. Justification is always justification from the point of view of the survivors, the victors; there is no point of view more exalted than theirs to assume. This is the truth in the ideas that might makes right and that justice is the interest of the stronger. But these ideas are misleading when they are construed metaphysically, as an assertion that the present status quo, or the victorious side in some current war, stand in some privileged relation to the way things really are. So 'metaphysic' was an unfortunate word to use in describing this generalized Darwinism which is democracy. For that word is associated with an attempt to replace appearance by reality.

Pragmatists – both classical and 'neo-' – do not believe that there is a way things really are. So they want to replace the appearance–reality distinction by that between descriptions of the world and of ourselves which are less useful and those which are more useful. When the question 'useful for what?' is pressed, they have nothing to say except 'useful to create a better future'. When they are asked, 'Better by what criterion?', they have no detailed answer, any more than the first mammals could specify in what respects they were better than the dying dinosaurs. Pragmatists can only say something as vague as:

Better in the sense of containing more of what we consider good and less of what we consider bad. When asked, 'And what exactly do you consider good?', pragmatists can only say, with Whitman, 'variety and freedom', or, with Dewey, 'growth'. 'Growth itself,' Dewey said, 'is the only moral end.'[8]

They are limited to such fuzzy and unhelpful answers because what they hope is not that the future will conform to a plan, will fulfil an immanent teleology, but rather that the future will astonish and exhilarate. Just as fans of the avant garde go to art galleries wanting to be astonished rather than hoping to have any particular expectation fulfilled, so the finite and anthropomorphic deity celebrated by James, and later by A. N. Whitehead and Charles Hartshorne, hopes to be surprised and delighted by the latest product of evolution, both biological and cultural. Asking for pragmatism's blueprint of the future is like asking Whitman to sketch what lies at the end of that illimitable democratic vista. The vista, not the endpoint, matters.

So if Whitman and Dewey have anything interesting in common, it is their principled and deliberate fuzziness. For principled fuzziness is the American way of doing what Heidegger called 'getting beyond metaphysics'. As Heidegger uses it, 'metaphysics' is the search for something clear and distinct, something fully present. That means something that does not trail off into an indefinite future, something like what Aristotle called 'the now', *to nun*, a *nunc stans*, a plenitude of present being. Heidegger thought of pragmatism as part of such a search, and thereby got it completely backwards. He thought of Americanism as the reduction of the world to raw material, and of the reduction of thinking to planning, and of pragmatism as the juvenile 'American interpretation of Americanism'.[9] That reduction was the exact opposite of his own attempt to sing a new song. But Heidegger never read Whitman's new song. Had he done so, he might conceivably have come to see America as Hegel (if only briefly) did: as the further westering of the spirit, the next evolutionary stage beyond Europe.

If one thinks of the metaphysics of presence as the metaphysics of Europe, then one can see the contrast between this metaphysics and the 'new metaphysic' which is democracy as the contrast between old

Europe and new America. Just as Mark Twain was convinced that everything bad in European life and society could be corrected by adopting the American attitudes and customs which his Connecticut Yankee brought to King Arthur's Court, so Dewey was convinced that everything that was wrong with traditional European philosophy was the result of clinging to a world picture which arose within, and met the needs of, an inegalitarian society. He saw all the baneful dualisms of the philosophical tradition as remnants and figurations of the social division between contemplators and doers, between a leisure class and a productive class.[10] He explains the origin of philosophy as the attempt to reconcile 'the two kinds of mental product' – the products of the priests and the poets with those of the artisans.[11] Such reconciliation is needed when the myths and customs of the society can no longer be taken on faith, but must be defended by the sort of causal reasoning which artisans use to explain why things are to be done in one way rather than in another.

Dewey argues that so far the thrust of philosophy has been conservative; it has typically been on the side of the leisure class, favouring stability over change. Philosophy has been an attempt to lend the past the prestige of the eternal. 'The leading theme of the classic philosophy of Europe,' he says, has been to make metaphysics 'a substitute for custom as the source and guarantor of higher moral and social values'.[12] Dewey wanted to shift attention from the eternal to the future, and to do so by making philosophy an instrument of change rather than of conservation, thereby making it American rather than European. He hoped to do so by denying – as Heidegger was to deny later on – that philosophy is a form of knowledge. This means denying that there is or could be an extra-cultural foundation for custom, and acknowledging openly that, 'In philosophy, "reality" is a term of value or choice.'[13] He wanted to get rid of what he called 'the notion, which has ruled philosophy ever since the time of the Greeks, that the office of knowledge is to uncover the antecedently real, rather than, as is the case with our practical judgments, to gain the kind of understanding which is necessary to deal with problems as they arise'.[14] In saying that democracy is a 'metaphysic of the relation of man and his experience in nature', he is saying that the institutions of a truly nonfeudal society would produce, and be produced by, a nondualistic way of thinking about reality and knowledge. This way of thinking would, for the first time, put the intellectuals at the service of the productive class rather than the leisure class. Pragmatism would, for the first time, treat theory as an aid to practice, rather than seeing practice as a degradation of theory.

If all this sounds vaguely reminiscent of Marx, that is because both Marx and Dewey were steeped in Hegel, and because both rejected everything nonhistoricist in Hegel, especially his idealism. They also rejected his preference for understanding the world rather than changing it. Both kept only those parts of Hegel which could easily be reconciled with Darwin. Dewey described Hegel as 'a triumph in material content of the modern secular and positivistic spirit . . . an invitation to the human subject to mastery of what is already contained in the here and now of the world . . .'[15] He viewed Darwin and Hegel as two aspects of a single antidualistic movement of thought – a movement which, by rejecting the essence–accident distinction and blurring the line between spirit and matter, emphasized continuity over disjunction, and production of the novel over contemplation of the eternal.[16]

Habermas has said that Marx, Kierkegaard and American pragmatism were the three productive responses to Hegel, and that pragmatism was 'the social-democratic branch of Young Hegelianism'.[17] The effect of Hegel on both Marx and Dewey was to switch attention from the Kantian question, 'What are the ahistorical conditions of possibility?' to the question, 'How can we make the present into a richer future?' But whereas Marx thought that he could see the shape of world history as a whole, and could see the present as a transitional stage between feudalism and communism, Dewey was content to say that the present was a transitional stage to something which might, with luck, be unimaginably better.

When, rather late in life, he eventually got around to reading Marx, Dewey concluded that Marx had been taken in by the bad, Greek, side of Hegel – the side which insisted on necessary laws of history. He saw Marx, Comte and Spencer as having succumbed to the lure of a pseudoscience which could extrapolate from the present to the future. He concluded that

Marxism is 'dated' in the matter of its claims to be peculiarly scientific. For just as *necessity* and search for a *single* all-comprehensive law was typical of the intellectual atmosphere of the forties of the last century, so *probability* and *pluralism* are the characteristics of the present state of science.[18]

This view of Marx is reminiscent of Karl Popper's *The Poverty of Historicism* and also of E. P. Thompson's anti-Althusserian polemic *The Poverty of Theory*. Of the two, however, Dewey is much closer to Thompson, whose *Making of the English Working Class* he would have read with enthusiasm and delight. Had he read Popper, he would have applauded Popper's fallibilism while deploring the dualisms which Popper, like Carnap, took for granted. For the logical empiricist movement, of which Carnap and Popper were representatives – the movement which was to shove pragmatism brusquely aside, in American departments of philosophy, after the Second World War – reinvented the sharp Kantian distinctions between fact and value, and between science on the one hand and ideology, metaphysics and religion on the other. These were distinctions which both James and Dewey had done their best to blur. The logical empiricists had, with the help of Frege and Russell, linguistified all the old Kantian distinctions which Dewey thought Hegel had helped us to overcome. The history of the re-dissolution of those distinctions by the neopragmatists, under the leadership of Quine, is the story of the re-pragmatization – and thus the de-Kantianizing and the re-Hegelianizing – of American philosophy.[19]

So far I have been trying to give an overview of Dewey's place in the intellectual scheme of things by saying something about his relation to Emerson, Whitman, Kant, Hegel and Marx. Now I want to become a bit more technical, and to offer an interpretation of the most famous pragmatist doctrine – the pragmatist theory of truth. I want to show how this doctrine fits into a more general programme: that of replacing Greek and Kantian dualisms between permanent structure and transitory content with the distinction between the past and the future. I shall try to show how the things which James and Dewey said about truth were a way of replacing the task of justifying past custom and tradition by reference to unchanging structure with the task of replacing an unsatisfactory present with a more satisfactory future, thus replacing certainty with hope. This replacement would, they thought, amount to Americanizing philosophy. For they agreed with Whitman that America is the country which counts for its 'reason and justification' upon the future, and *only* upon the future.

Truth is what is supposed to distinguish knowledge from well-grounded opinion – from justified belief.[20] But if the true is, as James said, 'the name of whatever proves itself to be good in the way of belief, and good, too, for definite, assignable, reasons',[21] then it is not clear in what respects a true belief is supposed to differ from one which is merely justified. So pragmatists are often said to confuse truth, which is absolute and eternal, with justification, which is transitory because relative to an audience.

Pragmatists have responded to this criticism in two principal ways. Some, like Peirce, James and Putnam, have said that we can retain an absolute sense of 'true' by identifying it with 'justification in the ideal situation' – the situation which Peirce called 'the end of inquiry'. Others, like Dewey (and, I have argued, Davidson),[22] have suggested that there is little to be said about truth, and that philosophers should explicitly and self-consciously *confine* themselves to justification, to what Dewey called 'warranted assertibility'.

I prefer the latter strategy. Despite the efforts of Putnam and Habermas to clarify the notion of 'ideal epistemic situation', that notion seems to me no more useful than that of 'correspondence to reality', or any of the other notions which philosophers have used to provide an interesting gloss on the word 'true'. Furthermore, I think that any 'absoluteness' which is supposedly ensured by appeal to such notions is equally well ensured if, with Davidson, we insist that human belief cannot swing free of the nonhuman environment and that, as Davidson insists, most of our beliefs (most of *anybody's* beliefs) must be true.[23] For this insistence gives us everything we wanted to get from 'realism' without invoking the slogan that 'the real and the true are "independent of our beliefs" ' – a slogan which, Davidson rightly says, it is futile either to accept or to reject.[24]

Davidson's claim that a truth theory for a natural language is nothing more or less than an empirical explanation of the causal relations which hold between features of the environment and the holding true of sentences, seems to me all the guarantee we need that we are, always and everywhere, 'in touch with the world'. If we have such a guarantee, then we have all the insurance we need against 'relativism' and 'arbitrariness'. For Davidson tells us that we can never be more arbitrary than the world lets us be. So even if there is no Way the World Is, even if there is no such thing as 'the intrinsic nature of reality', there are still causal pressures. These pressures will be described in different ways at different times and for different purposes, but they are pressures none the less.

The claim that 'pragmatism is unable to account for the absoluteness of truth' confuses two demands: the demand that we explain the relation between the world and our claims to have true beliefs and the specifically epistemological demand either for present certainty or for a path guaranteed to lead to certainty, if only in the infinitely distant future. The first demand is traditionally met by saying that our beliefs are made true by the world, and that they correspond to the way things are. Davidson denies both claims. He and Dewey agree that we should give up the idea that knowledge is an attempt to *represent* reality. Rather, we should view inquiry as a way of using reality. So the relation between our truth claims and the rest of the world is causal rather than representational. It causes us to hold beliefs, and we continue to hold the beliefs which prove to be reliable guides to getting what we want. Goodman is right to say that there is no one Way the World Is, and so no one way it is to be accurately represented. But there are lots of ways to act so as to realize human hopes of happiness. The attainment of such happiness is not something distinct from the attainment of justified belief; rather, the latter is a special case of the former.

Pragmatists realize that this way of thinking about knowledge and truth makes certainty unlikely. But they think that the quest for certainty – even as a long-term goal – is an attempt to escape from the world. So they interpret the usual hostile reactions to their treatment of truth as an expression of resentment, resentment at being deprived of something which earlier philosophers had mistakenly promised. Dewey urges that the quest for certainty be replaced with the demand for imagination – that philosophy should stop trying to provide reassurance and instead encourage what Emerson called 'self-reliance'. To encourage self-reliance, in this sense, is to encourage the willingness to turn one's back both on the past and on the attempt of 'the classical philosophy of Europe' to ground the past in the eternal. It is to attempt Emersonian self-creation on a communal scale. To say that one should replace knowledge by hope is to say much the same thing: that one should stop worrying about whether what one believes is well grounded and start worrying about whether one has been imaginative enough to think up interesting alternatives to one's present beliefs. As West says, 'For Emerson, the goal of activity is not simply domination, but also provocation; the telos of movement and flux is not solely mastery, but also stimulation.'[25]

In the context of post-Kantian academic philosophy, replacing knowledge by hope means something quite specific. It means giving up the Kantian idea that there is something called 'the nature of human knowledge' or 'the scope and limits of human knowledge' or 'the human epistemic situation' for philosophers to study and describe. A recent book by Michael Williams, *Unnatural Doubts*, makes clear how much can be gained by giving up this idea. For, once we drop it, we shall not be able to make sense of Descartes' claim that the fact that we might be dreaming casts doubt on all our knowledge of the external world. This is because we shall recognize no such thing as 'our knowledge of the external world', nor any such order as 'the natural order of reasons' – an order which, for example, starts with the 'deliverances of the senses' and works up from there in the time-honoured manner imagined by empiricists from Locke to Quine. These two notions are interlocked since, as Williams says, 'the threat of scepticism is indissolubly linked to a foundational conception of knowledge'[26] and that conception is indissolubly linked to that of context-free justification. To give up the idea of context-free justification is to give up the idea of 'knowledge' as a suitable object of study – the idea which Descartes and Kant inherited from Plato's *Theaetetus*.

Once one has said, as Plato did in that dialogue, that S knows that p is true if and only if p is true, and if S both believes that p and is justified in believing that p, there is nothing epistemological to be said *unless* one can find something general and interesting to say either about justification or about truth. Philosophers have hoped to find something interesting to say about both by finding some connection between the two – thereby linking the temporal with the eternal, the transitory human subject with what is there *anyway*, whether there are humans around or not.[27] That can be done if philosophy can show that the better justified a belief is, the more likely it is to be true. Failing that, it might try to show that a certain procedure for justifying belief is more likely to lead to truth than some other procedure. Dewey hoped to show that there was such a procedure; Davidson, and more pragmatists, seem to me right in suggesting that there is not.

As I see the history of pragmatism, there are two great differences between the classical pragmatists and the neopragmatists. The first I have already mentioned: it is the difference between talking about 'experience', as James and Dewey did, and talking about 'language', as Quine and Davidson do. The second is the difference between assuming that there is something called 'the scientific method', whose employment increases the likelihood of one's beliefs being true, and tacitly abandoning this assumption. Peirce, in his essay on 'The Fixation of Belief', one of the founding documents of pragmatism, tried to describe what he called 'the method of science'.[28] Dewey and his students, notably Hook, insisted on the importance of this method. That insistence was the principal area of overlap between Deweyan pragmatism and the logical empiricism which briefly replaced it in American philosophy departments. But as American philosophy moved into its postpositivistic stage, less and less was heard about the scientific method, and about the distinction between science and nonscience.

That distinction was undermined by the most influential English language philosophical treatise of the past half-century: Kuhn's *Structure of Scientific Revolutions*, published in 1962. Although Kuhn did not explicitly attack the notion of 'scientific method' (as Feyerabend later did), the effect of his book was to let that notion quietly fade away. It has been helped to do so by Davidson's insistence that truth is the same thing in physics and ethics, and by Putnam's polemics against the scientism which Carnap taught him. From within the non-representationalist picture of knowledge common to Davidson and Dewey, there is no easy way to reconstruct the distinction between science and nonscience in terms of a difference in *method*.[29] Everything that has happened in philosophy of language since Quine makes it difficult to reconstruct the foundationalist assumptions which are required to take the notion of 'method' seriously. I have urged elsewhere that all that remains of Peirce's, Dewey's and Popper's praise of science is praise of certain moral virtues – those of an open society – rather than any specifically epistemic strategy.[30]

As I see the present situation of pragmatism, postpositivistic analytic philosophy has made it clearer to us than it was to Peirce and Dewey that we should no longer try to follow up on the *Theaetetus* by trying to find something interesting to say about the connection between justification and truth. We should agree with William James on just the point on which he differed from Peirce and Dewey, namely that science and religion are *both* respectable paths for acquiring respectable beliefs, albeit beliefs which are good for quite different purposes. What we have learned, principally from Kuhn and from Davidson, is that there is nothing like Descartes' 'natural order of reasons' to be followed when we justify beliefs. There is no activity called 'knowing' which has a nature to be discovered, and at which natural scientists are particularly skilled. There is simply the process of justifying beliefs to audiences. None of these audiences is closer to nature, or a better representative of some ahistorical ideal of rationality, than any other. The idea of a subject of study called 'rationality' goes at the same time, and for the same reasons, as the idea of a subject of study called 'knowledge'.

A Dewey who had let himself be persuaded by James to give up on scienticism and methodolatry could agree with Davidson that there is nothing to be said about truth of the sort epistemologists want said. Once one has said, with Peirce, that beliefs are rules of action rather than attempts to represent reality, and, with Davidson, that 'belief is in its nature veridical',[31] one can take the moral of naturalism to be that knowledge is not a natural kind needing study and description, rather than that we must provide a naturalized epistemology. Such a reformed Dewey could also have welcomed Davidson's point that truth is not an epistemic concept.[32] This point entails, among other things, that no interesting connection will ever be found between the concept of truth and the concept of justification.[33] The only connection between these two notions is that, for the same reason that most beliefs are true, most beliefs are justified.

For, a believer who is (unlike a child or a psychotic) a fully fledged member of her community will always be able to produce justification for most of her beliefs – justification which meets the demands of that community. There is, however, no reason to think that the beliefs she is best able to justify are those which are most likely to be true, nor that those she is least able to justify are those which are most likely to be false. The fact that most beliefs are justified is, like the fact that most beliefs are true, merely one more consequence of the holistic character of belief-ascription. That, in turn, is a consequence of the fact that beliefs which are expressed as meaningful sentences necessarily have lots of predictable inferential connections with lots of other meaningful sentences.[34] We cannot, no matter how hard we try, continue to hold a belief which we have tried, and conspicuously failed, to weave together with our other beliefs into a justificatory web. No matter how much I want to believe an unjustifiable belief, I cannot will myself into doing so. The best I can do is distract my own attention from the question of why I hold certain beliefs. For most matters of common concern, however, my community will insist that I attend to this question. So such distraction is only feasible for private obsessions, such as my conviction that some day my lucky number will win the jackpot.

It may seem strange to say that there is no connection between justification and truth. This is because we are inclined to say that truth is the aim of inquiry. But I think we pragmatists must grasp the nettle and say that this claim is either empty or false. Inquiry and justification have lots of mutual aims, but they do not have an overarching aim called truth. Inquiry and justification are activities we language-users cannot help engaging in; we do not need a goal called 'truth' to help us do so, any more than our digestive organs need a goal called health to set them to work. Language-users can no more help justifying their beliefs and desires to one another than stomachs can help grinding up foodstuffs. The agenda for our digestive organs is set by the particular foodstuffs being processed, and the agenda for our justifying activity is provided by the diverse beliefs and desires we encounter in our fellow language-users. There would only be a 'higher' aim of inquiry called 'truth' if there were such a thing as *ultimate* justification – justification before God, or before the tribunal of reason, as opposed to any merely finite human audience.

But, given a Darwinian picture of the world, there can be no such tribunal. For such a tribunal would have to envisage all the alternatives to a given belief, and know everything that was relevant to criticism of every such alternative. Such a tribunal would have to have what Putnam calls a 'God's eye view' – a view which took in not only every feature of the world as described in a given set of terms, but that feature under every other possible description as well. For if it did not, there would remain the possibility that it was as fallible as the tribunal which sat in judgment on Galileo, a tribunal which we condemn for having required justification of new beliefs in old terms. If Darwin is right, we can no more make sense of the idea of such a tribunal than we can make sense of the idea that biological evolution has an aim. Biological evolution produces ever new species, and cultural evolution produces ever new audiences, but there is no such thing as the species which evolution has in view, nor any such thing as the 'aim of inquiry'.

To sum up, my reply to the claim that pragmatists confuse truth and justification is to turn this charge against those who make it. They are the ones who are confused, because they think of truth as something towards which we are moving, something we get closer to the more justification we have. By contrast, pragmatists think that there are a lot of detailed things to be said about justification to any given audience, but nothing to be said about justification in general. That is why there is nothing general to be said about the nature or limits of human knowledge, nor anything to be said about a connection between justification and truth. There is nothing to be said on the latter subject not because truth is atemporal and justification temporal, but because *the **only** point in contrasting the true with the merely justified is to contrast a possible future with the actual present.*

*   *   *   *

NOTES

1 Otto Neurath is reputed to have said that 'no one can use logical empiricism to ground a totalitarian argument', and certainly the members of the Vienna Circle, like many contemporary writers, saw Heidegger's philosophy and Hitler's politics as bound up with each other. But one should remember that no one can use logical empiricism, or pragmatism, to ground an *anti*totalitarian argument. No argumentative roads from epistemological or semantic premises will take one to political conclusions, any more than to conclusions about the relative value of literary works. But it is nevertheless obvious why those who favour a pragmatist account of the nature of human knowledge tend to admire Whitman and Jefferson more than they do Baudelaire or Hitler.

2 For a discussion of the similarities between the Heidegger of *Being and Time* and pragmatism, see Mark Okrent, *Heidegger's Pragmatism* (Ithaca, N.Y.: Cornell University Press, 1988). For an attempt to relate the same elements in Heidegger to Davidson's work, see the final chapter of J. E. Malpas, *Donald Davidson and the Mirror of Meaning* (Cambridge: Cambridge University Press, 1992).

3 Peirce had little use for Emerson, but in his later period, when he was developing a 'metaphysics of evolutionary love', he confessed that though he was 'not conscious of having contracted any of that virus' of 'Concord transcendentalism', it was probable that 'some benignant form of the disease was implanted in my soul unawares' (C. S. Peirce, *Collected Papers*, Hartshorne and Weiss, eds. (Cambridge, Mass.: Harvard University Press, 1936), vol. VI, section 102).

4 John Dewey, 'Maeterlinck's Philosophy of Life' in *The Middle Works of John Dewey* (Carbondale, Ill.: Southern Illinois University Press, 1978), vol. VI.

5 See West's *The American Evasion of Philosophy: A Genealogy of Pragmatism* (Madison: University of Wisconsin Press, 1989), ch. i. West explains his title, which refers to Emerson's having set aside the Cartesian problematic which had dominated European philosophy, at p. 36.

6 West, pp. 12–13.

7 Walt Whitman, *Complete Poetry and Selected Prose* (New York: The Library of America, 1982), p. 929.

8 John Dewey, *Reconstruction in Philosophy, The Middle Works of John Dewey*, vol. XII, p. 181.

9 ' "Americanism" is something European. It is an as-yet-uncomprehended species of the gigantic, the gigantic that is itself inchoate and does not as yet originate at all out of the complete and gathered metaphysical essence of the modern age. The American interpretation of Americanism by means of pragmatism still remains outside the metaphysical realm' (Heidegger, 'The Age of the World Picture' in William Lovitt, ed. and trans., *The Question Concerning Technology* (New York: Harper & Row, 1977), p. 15. There is some reason to think that Heidegger's knowledge of pragmatism was confined to the material presented in the dissertation of Edouard Baumgarten, a Heidegger student who had studied with Dewey.

10 See Dewey's *The Quest for Certainty, The Later Works of John Dewey*, vol. IV, ch. i, for a clear statement of this claim. Dewey says, for example, 'Work has been onerous, toilsome, associated with a primeval curse . . . On account of the unpleasantness of practical activity, as much of it as possible has been put upon slaves and serfs. Thus the social dishonor in which this class was held was extended to the work they do. There is also the age-long association of knowing and thinking with immaterial and spiritual principles, and of the arts, of all practical activity in doing and making, with matter . . . The disrepute which has attended the thought of material things in comparison with immaterial thought has been transferred to everything associated with practice' (p. 4). Later he says, 'If one looks at the foundations of the philosophies of Plato and Aristotle as an anthropologist looks at his material, it is clear that these philosophies were systematizations in rational terms of the content of Greek religious and artistic beliefs. The systematization involved a purification . . . Thus, along with the elimination of myths and grosser superstitions, there were set up the ideals of science and of a life of reason . . . But with all our gratitude for these enduring gifts, we cannot forget the conditions which attended them. For they brought with them the idea of a higher realm of fixed reality of which alone true science is possible and of an inferior world of changing things with which experience and practical matters are concerned . . .' (p. 14).

11 See Dewey, *Reconstruction in Philosophy*, p. 86.

12 Dewey, *Reconstruction in Philosophy*, p. 89.

13 Dewey, 'Philosophy and Democracy', *The Middle Works of John Dewey*, vol. XI, p. 45.

14 Dewey, *The Quest for Certainty*, p. 14.

15 Dewey, *The Quest for Certainty*, p. 51.

16 For more on this topic, see my 'Dewey Between Hegel and Darwin' included in *Truth and Progress* (Cambridge: Cambridge University Press, 1998).

17 See Peter Dews, ed., *Habermas: Autonomy and Solidarity* (London: Routledge, 1992), p. 151.

18 Dewey, *Freedom and Culture, The Later Works of John Dewey*, vol. XIII, p. 123.

19 I have sketched a version of this story in my *Philosophy and the Mirror of Nature*, and have discussed the attempt by Sidney Hook (Dewey's favourite, and most gifted, student) to reconcile pragmatism with logical empiricism in my 'Pragmatism without Method' (included in *Objectivity, Relativism and Truth* (Cambridge: Cambridge University Press, 1991)).

20 For present purposes I can neglect the so-called 'fourth condition of knowledge' proposed by Edmund Gettier – that a belief be brought about in appropriate ways, in addition to being held, justified and true.

21 William James, *Pragmatism* (Cambridge, Mass.: Harvard University Press, 1978), p. 43.

22 Davidson has said that 'true' should be taken as transparently clear, and as primitive and indefinable. In my writings on Davidson, I have interpreted this to mean that Davidson agreed with Dewey that there is little for philosophers to say about truth. Davidson repudiated this interpretation, and the suggestion that he was a 'disquotationalist' about truth, in his 'The Structure and Content of Truth' (*Journal of Philosophy* (June, 1990), vol. 87, p. 288; see also p. 302). In his recent *Donald Davidson and the Mirror of Meaning* (Cambridge: Cambridge University Press, 1992), J. E. Malpas cites this repudiation of my interpretation, and suggests that it shows what is wrong with my repeated attempts to add Davidson to the list of contemporary neopragmatists. (See Malpas, p. 357, and ch. 7 passim.) The heart of Davidson's claim that there is more to be said about truth than Tarski says, and that truth is an explanatory concept (my argument to the contrary in 'Pragmatism, Davidson and Truth'

notwithstanding), is that 'a theory of truth [for a given natural language, such as English or French] is a theory for describing, explaining, understanding, and predicting a basic aspect of verbal behavior' ('Structure and Content', p. 313). This fact, Davidson continues, shows that 'truth is a crucially important explanatory concept'.

My response is that the fact that an empirical theory which correlates verbal behaviour with situation and environment, as well as with the linguistic behaviour of the person propounding the theory (thus ensuring the 'triangulation' of speaker, hearer and environment which Davidson describes as 'the ultimate source of both objectivity and communication' (p. 325)) is genuinely explanatory does not mean that the concept of truth is genuinely explanatory. Calling such a theory a 'theory of truth' rather than a 'theory of meaning' or, simply, 'a theory of the linguistic behaviour of a certain group', does not show what Malpas calls the 'centrality' of the concept of truth. It merely shows the need to possess such a theory in order to make effective use of *any* semantic concept. See, on this point, Davidson's indifference, in his 1967 essay 'Truth and Meaning' to the question of whether a theory which generates the T-sentences for a language L is to be called 'a theory of meaning' or 'a theory of truth' (*Inquiries into Truth and Interpretation* (Oxford: Oxford University Press, 1984), p. 24). In that essay, the question of what a theory which produces the relevant T-sentences is a theory *of* is treated as of negligible importance – as I think it in fact is. So when Davidson ends 'Structure and Content' by saying, 'The conceptual underpinning of interpretation is a theory of truth', I wish that he had said instead, 'The explanation of our ability to interpret is our ability to triangulate' and let it go at that.

Be that as it may, all that matters for my version of pragmatism, and my claim that there is less to be said about truth than philosophers have traditionally thought, is a point on which Davidson, Malpas and I heartily concur: that, as Davidson puts it, 'We should not say that truth is correspondence, coherence, warranted assertability, ideally justified assertibility, what is accepted in the conversation of the right people, what science will end up maintaining, what explains the convergence on single theories in science, or the success of our ordinary beliefs. To the extent that realism and antirealism depend on one or another of these views of truth we should refuse to endorse either' ('Structure and Content', p. 309).

23 See Davidson's 'A Coherence Theory of Truth and Knowledge' (in *Truth* *and Interpretation: Perspectives on the Philosophy of Donald Davidson* (Oxford: Blackwell, 1986)) for his argument for this claim. Despite Malpas's strictures (cited in the previous note), and Davidson's refusal to call himself a pragmatist on the ground that it is definatory of pragmatism to define truth as warranted assertibility, I still think it fruitful to see Davidson as carrying through on the classical pragmatists' project. One justification for describing him in these terms can be gleaned from Robert Brandom's 'Pragmatism, Phenomenalism, and Truth Talk' (*Midwest Studies in Philosophy*, vol. 12, pp. 75–94). There Brandom suggests that we think of the basic insight of the classical pragmatists as what he calls 'phenomenalism' about truth – defined as the denial 'that there is more to the phenomenon of truth than the proprieties of such takings [i.e., of holding true, treating as true, etc.]' (p. 77). If one substitutes 'than the sort of explanation of the proprieties of such takings provided by an empirical T-theory for a language', then Davidson too counts as 'phenomenalist' in the relevant sense.

24 See Davidson, 'Structure and Content', p. 305. I regret that Malpas resuscitates the term 'realism' to describe Davidson's (and Heidegger's) view at the conclusion of his book (pp. 276–7). As Malpas says, this is not the sense of the term 'used by Nagel, Putnam or Dummett'. I think it is needlessly confusing to invent a new sense to fit Davidson and Heidegger. I would prefer something like 'anti-scepticism' or 'anti-Cartesianism' to designate the inescapability of *in-der-Welt-sein* affirmed by both philosophers. For what is involved is not a positive thesis, but simply the abjuration of a particular picture which has held us captive – the picture I have called (in the introduction to my *Objectivity, Relativism and Truth*) 'representationalism', and which Michael Williams (whose work I discuss below) calls 'epistemological realism'.

25 West, p. 26.

26 Michael Williams, *Unnatural Doubts: Epistemological Realism and the Basis of Scepticism* (Oxford: Blackwell, 1991), p. xx.

27 The phrase 'what is there anyway' is Bernard Williams' way of explicating what he calls 'the absolute notion of reality' – a notion which the pragmatists did their best to get rid of.

28 His description of this method in that essay of 1877 is foundationalist in spirit, and not easy to reconcile with the antifoundationalism of the 1868 essays 'Questions Concerning Certain Faculties Claimed for Man' and 'Some Consequences of Four Incapacities'.

29 This is not to say that the notion of 'methods of reaching truth' has gone altogether out of fashion within contemporary analytic philosophy. On the contrary, there is a flourishing movement called 'naturalistic epistemology' (a term of Quine's), which sets its face against the pragmatism of Kuhn's approach to science, and tries to rehabilitate the notion of 'method'. It is able to do so, however, only because it takes a representationalist account of knowledge for granted.

The aims and assumptions of this movement are well set out in Philip Kitcher's 'The Naturalists Return', *Philosophical Review* (January 1992) vol. 101, pp. 53–114, an article which ends by seeing naturalized epistemology as needed to counteract the baleful influence of people like Feyerabend and myself. Kitcher says that, 'Traditional naturalism finds an objective standard for epistemological principles by seeing the project of inquiry as one which cognitively limited beings, set in the actual world, seek a particular kind of representation of that world. Given the nature of the world, of the beings in question, and the kind of representation that is sought, there will be determinate answers to questions about how it is best to proceed, and hence an objective epistemological standard' (p. 101). At p. 93 Kitcher deplores Kuhnian accounts which make the history of science 'resemble a random walk' rather than 'an undirectional progress', and at p. 96 he deplores the way in which 'radical naturalists' 'abandon the meliorative venture of Bacon and Descartes, letting epistemology fall into place as chapters of psychology, sociology and the history of science'. I applaud exactly what Kitcher deplores, but exploring the differences between his representationalism and my Davidsonian anti-representationalism is beyond the scope of this essay.

30 See 'Science as Solidarity' and 'Is Natural Science a Natural Kind?' in my *Objectivity, Relativism and Truth*.

31 In 'A Coherence Theory of Truth and Knowledge', p. 314. Davidson continues: 'Belief can be seen to be veridical by considering what determines the existence and contents of a belief. Belief, like the other so-called propositional attitudes, is supervenient on facts of various sorts, behavioral, neuro-physiological, biological and physical.' This naturalism about belief (one which James and Dewey would have applauded, and which I have tried to expound in my 'Non-Reductive Physicalism') is why belief cannot swing free of the world, in the way in which dreams do. It is important for seeing the relation of Davidson's thesis to Cartesian scepticism, to remember how much the dreamer knows, and how little of his knowledge the realization that he is dreaming impugns – e.g., all those commonplace platitudes which are not about the way the dreamer's environment is presently arranged. Those who think that Descartes' First Meditation made scepticism an urgent philosophical topic typically brush over this point. Thus Barry Stroud, in his *The Significance of Philosophical Scepticism* (Oxford: Clarendon Press, 1984), says that the dreamer 'might be a physicist who knows a great deal about the way things are which the child does not know . . . There is therefore no incompatibility with knowing and dreaming' (p. 16). But he then goes on to say that this point 'does not affect Descartes' argument' because the physicist cannot know what he knows 'on the basis of the senses'. Indeed he cannot, but this idea that physics is 'based on the senses' is precisely the idea of 'a natural order of reasons' which Williams (following Sellars) rightly criticizes in chapter 2 of *Unnatural Doubts*. This passage in Stroud is a good illustration of the fact that the notion of such an order does *all* the work in the First Meditation. The possibility that one is dreaming does none.

32 See Davidson, 'Structure and Content', p. 298.

33 Had Dewey taken not only this point, but also Davidson's point that 'relativism about truth is perhaps always a symptom of infection by the epistemological virus', I think that he would have said fewer of the relativistic-sounding things for which he was constantly attacked by Lovejoy, Russell and others. Had he taken Williams' point, he would have realized that he could say most of what he wanted to say about what was wrong with traditional epistemological discussions of truth by talking about the context-dependent character of justification. Unlike Davidson, who takes a necessary condition of being a pragmatist to be precisely the infection by the virus in question, I take the only necessary condition to be the one Brandom offers: believing that there is nothing to said about truth which cannot be said on the basis of facts about, and explanations of, the proprieties of holding true. On such proprieties, see the closing pages of 'Structure and Content', in which Davidson expatiates on the role of norms and affects in belief-ascription, and thus in constructing T-theories.

34 And, of course, of the fact that if you don't speak a language you don't have many beliefs. Davidson thinks that you cannot have *any* beliefs. But for present purposes it is enough to say that dogs and infants can't have most of the ones we can have, unless we separate the having of a belief from our ability to ascribe it accurately to the believer (thereby permitting dogs, or amoebae for that matter, to have, for all we know, views about cosmology, transubstantiation, etc.).

3. A World without Substances or Essences

(1994)

Philosophers in the English-speaking world usually do not take the work of philosophers in the non-English-speaking world very seriously, and conversely. The gap between so-called 'analytic' and so-called 'Continental' philosophy shows no signs of being bridged. This seems to me a pity, because I think that the best work being done in these two traditions overlaps to an important extent. In this essay I shall try to sketch a way of looking at things which is common to the philosophers I most admire on both sides of the gap.

The quickest way of expressing this commonality is to say that philosophers as diverse as William James and Friedrich Nietzsche, Donald Davidson and Jacques Derrida, Hilary Putnam and Bruno Latour, John Dewey and Michel Foucault, are antidualists. This does not mean that they are against binary oppositions; it is not clear that thought is possible without using such oppositions. It means rather that they are trying to shake off the influences of the peculiarly metaphysical dualisms which the Western philosophical tradition inherited from the Greeks: those between essence and accident, substance and property, and appearance and reality. They are trying to replace the world pictures constructed with the aid of these Greek oppositions with a picture of a flux of continually changing relations. One effect of this panrelationalism is that it lets us put aside the distinction between subject and object, between the elements in human knowledge contributed by the mind and those contributed by the world, and thereby helps us put aside the correspondence theory of truth.

Various labels and slogans are associated with this antiessentialistic, antimetaphysical movement in various Western traditions. Among them are pragmatism, existentialism, deconstructionism, holism, process philosophy, poststructuralism, postmodernism, Wittgensteinianism, antirealism, and hermeneutics. Perhaps for merely patriotic reasons, my own preferred term is pragmatism; among the slogans are 'Everything is a social construction' and 'All awareness is a linguistic affair'. The former is a characteristically European slogan, and those who use it often take their point of departure from Foucault. The latter slogan was coined by the great American thinker Wilfrid Sellars, and the epithet he chose for the system of thought which embodied this slogan was 'psychological nominalism'.

As a first illustration of the convergence between analytic and Continental philosophy, I want to show how these two slogans come to much the same thing. Both are ways of saying that we shall never be able to step outside of language, never be able grasp reality unmediated by a linguistic description. So both are ways of saying that we should be suspicious of the Greek distinction between appearance and reality, and that we should try to replace it with something like the distinction between 'less useful description of the world' and 'more useful description of the world'. To say that everything is a social construction is to say that our linguistic practices are so bound up with our other social practices that our descriptions of nature, as well as of ourselves, will always be a function of our social needs.[1] To say that all awareness is a linguistic affair is to say that we have no knowledge of the kind which Bertrand Russell, working in the tradition of British empiricism, called 'knowledge by acquaintance'. All our knowledge is of the sort which Russell called 'knowledge by description'. If you put the two slogans together, you get the claim that all our knowledge is under descriptions suited to our current social purposes.

This claim is antimetaphysical in the large sense of the term 'metaphysics' in which Heidegger said that all Platonism is metaphysics and all metaphysics is Platonism. Platonism, in this large sense, attempts to get free of society, of *nomos*, convention, and to turn to *physis*, to nature. But if the two slogans I have just cited are right, there is no such thing as *physis* to be known. The *nomos–physis*, convention–nature distinction goes for the same reason that the appearance–reality distinction goes. For once you have said that all our awareness is under a description, and that descriptions are functions of social needs, then 'nature' and 'reality' can only be names of something unknowable – something like Kant's 'Thing-in-Itself.' The whole movement of Western philosophical thought since Hegel has been an attempt to avoid such an unknowable.

Kant was a turning point in the history of Western philosophy because he was a *reductio ad absurdum* of the attempt to distinguish between the role of the subject and the role of the object in constituting knowledge. Hegel realized this, and realized that the distinctions between the subjective and the objective have to be transcended. Unfortunately, Hegel himself used the terms 'subjective' and 'objective' to describe the sequence of successive descriptions which successive social needs made necessary as moral and intellectual progress continued, and used the term 'union of subject and object' to describe the end of history. This was a mistake, because it took an outdated dualism too seriously. It would have been better if Hegel had done what Dewey did later: describe intellectual and moral progress simply as the growth of freedom, as leading to democracy rather than to Absolute Knowledge. Dewey was the philosopher who most clearly and explicitly set aside the goal common to the Greeks and the German Idealists (accurate representation of the intrinsic nature of reality) in favour of the political goal of increasingly free societies and increasingly diverse individuals within them. That is why he seems to me the most useful and most significant figure in twentieth-century philosophy.

Before one can take Dewey and pragmatism seriously, however, one must be convinced that the Platonic quest, the attempt to get behind appearance to the intrinsic nature of reality, is hopeless. So now I want to recapitulate the dialectic which leads up to Sellars's psychological nominalism, and thus, indirectly, to the social constructionism common to Foucault and Dewey.

Ever since the seventeenth century, philosophers have been suggesting that we may never know reality, because there is a barrier between us and it – a veil of appearances produced by the interaction between subject and object, between the constitution of our own sense organs or our minds and the way things are in themselves. Since the nineteenth century, philosophers have been suggesting that *language* may form such a barrier – that our language imposes categories on objects which may not be intrinsic to them. Pragmatists reply to seventeenth-century arguments about the veil of appearances by saying that we need not model knowledge on vision. So there is no need to think of the sense organs or our ideas as intervening between a mental eye and its object. Instead, pragmatists say, we can think of both as tools for manipulating the object. They reply to nineteenth-century arguments about the distorting effect of language by saying that language is not a medium of representation. Rather, it is an exchange of marks and noises, carried out in order to achieve specific purposes. It cannot fail to represent accurately, for it never represents at all.

Pragmatists insist on nonocular, nonrepresentational ways of describing sensory perception, thought and language, because they would like to break down the distinction between knowing things and using them. Starting from Bacon's claim that knowledge is power, they proceed to the claim that power is all there is to knowledge – that a claim to know X is a claim to be able to do something with or to X, to put X into relation with something else. To make this claim plausible, however, they have to attack the notion that knowing X is a matter of being related to something *intrinsic* to X, whereas using X is a matter of standing in an *extrinsic*, accidental, relation to X.

In order to attack that notion, they need to break down the distinction between intrinsic and extrinsic – between the inner core of X and a peripheral area of X which is constituted by the fact that X stands in certain relations to the other items which make up the universe. The attempt to break down this distinction is what I shall call antiessentialism. For pragmatists, there is no such thing as a nonrelational feature of X, any more than there is such a thing as the intrinsic nature, the essence, of X. So there can be no such thing as a description which matches the way X really is, apart from its relation to human needs or consciousness or language. Once the distinction between intrinsic and extrinsic goes, so does the distinction between reality and appearance, and so do worries about whether there are barriers between us and the world.

The term 'objective' is defined by antiessentialists not in terms of a relation to intrinsic features of objects but rather by reference to relative ease of attaining consensus among inquirers. Just as the appearance–reality distinction is replaced by distinctions between relative utility of descriptions, so the objective–subjective distinction is replaced by distinctions between relative ease in getting agreement. To say that values are more subjective than facts is just to say that it is harder to get agreement about which things are ugly or which actions evil than about which things are rectangular. To say that X is *really* blue even though it appears yellow from a certain angle and under a certain light, is to say that the sentence 'X is blue' is more useful – that is, can be employed more frequently – than the sentence 'X is yellow.' The latter sentence is useful only for occasional, evanescent purposes.

A typical first reaction to antiessentialism is that it is too anthropocentric, too much inclined to treat humanity as the measure of all things. To many people, antiessentialism seems to lack humility, a sense of mystery, a sense of human finitude. It seems to lack a common-sensical appreciation of the obdurate otherness of the things of this world. The antiessentialist reply to this common-sensical reaction is that common sense is itself no more than the habit of using a certain set of descriptions. In the case at hand, what is called common sense is simply the habit of using language inherited from the Greeks, and especially from Plato and Aristotle. Their descriptions of our relation to the rest of the universe – descriptions which incorporate the intrinsic–extrinsic distinction – are no longer good enough for us. We can do better.

Plato, Aristotle and orthodox monotheism all insist on a sense of mystery and wonder in regard to anthropomorphic but nonhuman powers. On a pragmatist view, this undesirable sense of wonder should not be confused with a desirable awareness that there are some things which human beings cannot control. Nor should it be confused with the desirable awe which we feel in the presence of the great works of the human imagination – redescriptions of the universe which make all things seem new and wonderful. The big difference between an undesirable sense of humility and a desirable sense of finitude is that the former presupposes that there is, already in existence, something better and greater than the human. The latter presupposes only that there are lots of things which are different from the human. A Greek sense of wonder requires us to think that there is something sufficiently like us to be enviable but so superior to us as to be barely intelligible. A pragmatic sense of limits requires us only to think that there are some projects for which our tools are presently inadequate, and to hope that the future may be better than the past in this respect.

Another difference is that Greek descriptions of our situation presuppose that humanity itself has an intrinsic nature – that there is something unchangeable called 'the human' which can be contrasted with the rest of the universe. Pragmatism sets that presupposition aside and urges that humanity is an open-ended notion, that the word 'human' names a fuzzy but promising project rather than an essence. So, pragmatists transfer to the human future the sense of awe and mystery which the Greeks attached to the non-human; it is transformed into a sense that the humanity of the future will be, although linked with us by a continuous narrative, superior to present-day humanity in as yet barely imaginable ways. It coalesces with the awe we feel before works of imagination, and becomes a sense of awe before humanity's ability to become what it once merely imagined, before its capacity for self-creation.

In the rest of this essay I shall be trying to sketch how things look when described in antiessentialist terms. I hope to show that such terms are more useful than terminologies which presuppose what Dewey called 'the whole brood and nest of dualisms' which we inherit from the Greeks. The panrelationalism I advocate is summed up in the suggestion that we think of everything as if it were a *number*.

The nice thing about numbers, from my point of view, is simply that it is very hard to think of them as having intrinsic natures, as having an essential core surrounded by a penumbra of accidental relationships. Numbers are an admirable example of something which it is difficult to describe in essentialist language.

To see my point, ask what the essence of the number 17 is – what it is *in itself*, apart from its relationships to other numbers. What is wanted is a description of 17 which is different *in kind* from the following descriptions: less than 22, more than 8, the sum of 6 and 11, the square root of 289, the square of 4.123105, the difference between 1,678,922 and 1,678,905. The tiresome thing about all *these* descriptions is that none of them seems to get closer to the number 17 than do any of the others. Equally tiresomely, there are obviously an infinite number of other descriptions which you could offer of 17, all of which would be equally 'accidental' and 'extrinsic'. None of these descriptions seems to give you a clue to the intrinsic seventeenness of 17 – the unique feature which makes it the very number that it is. For your choice among these descriptions is obviously a matter of what purpose you have in mind – the particular situation which caused you to think of the number 17 in the first place.

If we want to be essentialist about the number 17, we have to say, in philosophical jargon, that *all* its infinitely many different relations to infinitely many other numbers are *internal* relations – that is, that none of these relations could be different without the number 17 being different. So there seems to be no way to define the essence of seventeenhood short of finding some mechanism for generating *all* the true descriptions of 17, specifying all its relations to *all* the other numbers. Mathematicians can in fact produce such a mechanism by axiomatizing arithematic, or by reducing numbers to sets and axiomatizing set theory. But if the mathematician then points to his neat little batch of axioms and says, 'Behold the essence of 17!' we feel gypped. There is nothing very seventeenish about those axioms, for they are equally the essence of 1, or 2, of 289, and of 1,678,922.

I conclude that, whatever sorts of things may have intrinsic natures, numbers do not – that it simply does not pay to be an essentialist about numbers. We antiessentialists would like to convince you that it also does not pay to be essentialist about tables, stars, electrons, human beings, academic disciplines, social institutions, or anything else. We suggest that you think of all such objects as resembling numbers in the following respect: there is nothing to be known about them except an initially large, and forever expandable, web of relations to other objects. Everything that can serve as the term of a relation can be dissolved into another set of relations, and so on for ever. There are, so to speak, relations all the way down, all the way up, and all the way out in every direction: you never reach something which is not just one more nexus of relations. The system of natural numbers is a good model of the universe because in that system it is obvious, and obviously harmless, that there are no terms of relations which are not simply clusters of further relations.

To say that relations go all the way down is a corollary of psychological nominalism: of the doctrine that there is nothing to be known about anything save what is stated in sentences describing it. For every sentence about an object is an explicit or implicit description of its relation to one or more other objects. So if there is no knowledge by acquaintance, no knowledge which does not take the form of a sentential attitude, then there is nothing to be known about anything save its relations to other things. To insist that there is a difference between a nonrelational *ordo essendi* and a relational *ordo cognoscendi* is, inevitably, to recreate the Kantian Thing-in-Itself. To make that move is to substitute a nostalgia for immediacy, and a longing for a salvatory relation to a nonhuman power, for the utopian hope which pragmatism recommends. It is to reinvent what Heidegger called 'the onto-theological tradition'.

For psychological nominalists, no description of an object is more a description of the 'real', as opposed to the 'apparent', object than any other, nor are any of them descriptions of, so to speak, the object's relation to itself – of its identity with its own essence. Some of them are, to be sure, better descriptions than others. But this betterness is a matter of being more useful tools – tools which accomplish some human purpose better than do competing descriptions. All these purposes are, from a philosophical as opposed to a practical point of view, on a par. There is no over-riding purpose called 'discovering the truth' which takes precedence. As I have said before, pragmatists do not think that truth is the aim of inquiry. The aim of inquiry is utility, and there are as many different useful tools as there are purposes to be served.

Common sense – or at least Western common sense – has trouble with the claim that numbers are good models for objects in general because it seems counterintuitive to say that physical, spatiotemporal objects dissolve into webs of relations in the way that numbers do.

When numbers are analysed away into relations to other numbers, nobody mourns the loss of their substantial, independent, autonomous reality. But things are different with tables and stars and electrons. Here common sense is inclined to stick in its toes and say that you cannot have relations without things to be related. If there were not a hard, substantial autonomous table to stand in relation to, e.g., you and me and the chair, or to be constituted out of hard, substantial, elementary particles, there would be nothing to get related and so no relations. There is, common sense insists, a difference between relations and the things that get related, and philosophy cannot break that distinction down.

The antiessentialist reply to this bit of common sense is pretty much the one Berkeley made to Locke's attempt to distinguish primary from secondary qualities – the reply which Peirce called the first invocation of the pragmatist principle. The contemporary, linguistified form of Berkeley's reply is: All that we know about this hard, substantial table – about the thing that gets related as opposed to its relations – is that certain sentences are true of it. It is that of which the following statements are true: It is rectangular, it is brown, it is ugly, made out of a tree, smaller than a house, larger than a mouse, less luminous than a star, and so on and on. There is nothing to be known about an object except what sentences are true of it. The antiessentialist's argument thus comes down to saying that since all sentences can do is relate objects to one another, every sentence which describes an object will, implicitly or explicitly, attribute a relational property to it.[2] We antiessentialists try to substitute the picture of language as a way of hooking objects up to one another for the picture of language as a veil interposed between us and objects.

Essentialists typically rejoin, at this point, that psychological nominalism is a mistake, that we should retrieve what was true in empiricism, and not admit that language provides our only cognitive access to objects. They suggest that we must have some prelinguistic knowledge of objects, knowledge that cannot be caught in language. This knowledge, they say, is what prevents the table or the number or the human being from being what they call a 'mere linguistic construct'. To illustrate what he means by nonlinguistic knowledge, the essentialist, at this point in the argument, usually bangs his hand on the table and flinches. He thereby hopes to demonstrate that he has acquired a bit of knowledge, and a kind of intimacy with the table, which escapes the reach of language. He claims that that knowledge of the table's *intrinsic causal powers*, its sheer brute *thereness*, keeps him in touch with reality in a way in which the antiessentialist is not.

Unfazed by this suggestion that he is out of touch, the antiessentialist reiterates that if you want to know what the table really, intrinsically, is, the best answer you are going to get is 'that of which the following statements are true: it is brown, ugly, painful to banging heads, capable of being stumbled over, made of atoms, and so on and on'. The painfulness, the solidity, and the causal powers of the table are on all fours with its brownness and its ugliness. Just as you do not get on more intimate terms with the number 17 by discovering its square root, you do not get on more intimate terms with the table, closer to its intrinsic nature, by hitting it than by looking at it or talking about it. All that hitting it, or decomposing it into atoms, does is to enable you to relate it to a few more things. It does not take you out of language into fact, or out of appearance into reality, or out of a remote and disinterested relationship into more immediate and intense relationship.

The point of this little exchange is, once again, that the anti-essentialist denies that there is a way to pick out an object from the rest of the universe *except* as the object of which a certain set of sentences are true. With Wittgenstein, he says that ostention only works against the backdrop of a linguistic practice, and that the self-identity of the thing picked out is itself description-relative.[3] Anti-essentialists think that the distinction between things related and relations is just an alternative way of making the distinction between what we are talking about and what we say about it. The latter distinction is, as Whitehead said, just a hypostatization of the relation between linguistic subject and linguistic predicate.[4]

Just as the utterance of a noun conveys no information to people who are unfamiliar with adjectives and verbs, so there is no way to convey information except by relating something to something else. Only in the context of a sentence, as Frege told us, does a word have meaning. But that means that there is no way of getting behind language to some more immediate nonlinguistic form of acquaintance with what we are talking about. Only when linked up with some other parts of speech does a noun have a use, and only as the term of a relation is an object an object of knowledge. There is no knowledge of the subject without knowledge of what sentences referring to it are true, just as there is no knowledge of a number without knowledge of its relations to other numbers.

Our sense that we can know a thing without knowing its relations to other things is explained away by antiessentialist philosophers as a reflection of the difference between being certain about some familiar, taken-for-granted, obvious relations in which the thing stands and being uncertain about its other relations. Seventeen, for example, starts out by being the sum of 17 ones, the number between 16 and 18, and so on. Enough such familiar statements, and we begin to think of 17 as a thing waiting to get related to other things. When we are told that 17 is also the difference between 1,678,922 and 1,678,905 we feel that we have learned about a rather remote, inessential, connection between it and something else, rather than more about *17 itself*. But when pressed we have to admit that the relation between 17 and 1,678,922 is no more or less intrinsic than that between 16 and 17. For, in the case of numbers, there is no clear sense to be given to term 'intrinsic'. We do not really want to say that 17, in the secret depths of its heart, *feels* closer to 16 than to numbers further down the line.

Antiessentialists suggest that we also brush aside the question of whether the hardness of the table is more intrinsic to the table than its colour, or whether the atomic constitution of the star Polaris is more intrinsic to it than its location in a constellation. The question of whether there really are such things as constellations, or whether they are merely illusions produced by the fact that we cannot visually distinguish the distance of stars, strikes antiessentialists as being as bad as the question of whether there really are such things as moral values, or whether they are merely projections of human wishes. They suggest we brush aside all questions about where the thing stops and its relations begin, all questions about where its intrinsic nature starts and its external relations begin, all questions about where its essential core ends and its accidental periphery begins. Antiessentialists like to ask, with Wittgenstein, whether a chessboard is *really* one thing or 64 things. To ask that question, they think, is to expose its foolishness – its lack of any interesting point. Questions which have a point are those which meet William James's requirement that any difference must *make* a difference. Other questions – such as those about the ontological status of constellations or of moral values – are 'merely verbal' or, worse yet, 'merely philosophical'.

The residual essentialism of common sense may rejoin to all this that antiessentialism is a sort of linguistic idealism: a way of suggesting that there was really nothing there to be talked about before people began talking – that objects are artefacts of language. But this rejoinder is a confusion between the question, 'How do we pick out objects?' and, 'Do objects antedate being picked out by us?' The antiessentialist has no doubt that there were trees and stars long before there were statements about trees and stars. But the fact of antecedent existence is of no use in giving sense to the question, 'What are trees and stars apart from their relations to other things – apart from our statements about them?' Nor is it of any help in giving sense to the sceptic's claim that trees and stars have non-relational, intrinsic, essences which may, alas, be beyond our ken. If that claim is to have a clear meaning, we have to be able to say something more about *what* is beyond our ken, what we are deprived of. Otherwise, we are stuck with Kant's unknowable Thing-in-Itself. From the antiessentialist's point of view, the Kantian lament that we are for ever trapped behind the veil of subjectivity is merely the pointless, because tautologous, claim that something we define as being beyond our knowledge is, alas, beyond our knowledge.

The essentialist's picture of the relation between language and world drives him back on the claim that the world is identifiable independently of language. This is why he has to insist that the world is initially known to us through a kind of nonlinguistic encounter – through banging into it, or letting it bounce some photons off our retinas. This initial encounter is an encounter with the very world itself – the world as it intrinsically is. When we try to recapture what we learned in this encounter in language, however, we are frustrated by the fact that the sentences of our language merely relate things to other things. The sentences, 'This is brown', or 'This is square', or 'This is hard', tell us something about how our nervous system deals with stimuli emanating from the neighbourhood of the object. Sentences like, 'It is located at the following space–time coordinates' are, even more obviously, sentences which tell us about what the essentialist mournfully calls 'merely relational, merely accidental, properties'.

Confronted with this impasse, the essentialist is tempted to turn for help to natural science. He is tempted to say that a sentence like, 'It is made up of the following sorts of elementary particles arranged in the following ways' gets us inside the object as it truly is. The last line of defence for essentialist philosophers is the belief that physical science gets us outside ourselves, outside our language and our needs and our purposes to something splendidly nonhuman and nonrelational. Essentialists who retreat to this line argue that seventeenth-century corpuscularians like Hobbes and Boyle were right to distinguish between the features of things which are really 'in' them and those which it is useful, for human purposes, to describe them as having.

To us antiessentialists, descriptions of objects in terms of elementary particles are useful in many different ways – as many ways as particle physics can contribute to either technological advances or imaginative, astrophysical, redescriptions of the universe as a whole. But that sort of utility is their *only* virtue. To the essentialist philosophers, and to many natural scientists who do not otherwise concern themselves with philosophy, this pragmatic view of physics as the handmaiden of technology and of the poetic imagination is offensive. These people share a sense that particle physics – and more generally, whatever scientific vocabulary could, in principle, serve to redescribe any phenomenon whatever – is an example of a kind of truth which pragmatism does not recognize. This kind of truth is not a matter of the utility of a description for a human purpose, but rather of a transcendence of the merely human. Particle physics has, so to speak, become the last refuge of the Greek sense of wonder – the sense of an encounter with the almost Wholly Other.[5]

Why does particle physics seem to give the notion of 'intrinsic nature' a new lease on life? I think the answer is that the vocabulary of this branch of physics seems to offer a special kind of mastery and self-assurance, in that it can ('in principle') explain the utility of all other descriptions, as well as its own. An ideal psychophysics would treat human beings as themselves swirls of particles, and would provide explanations of why these organisms have developed certain linguistic habits – why they have described the world as they have. So it seems as if such an ideal physics could treat utility to human beings as itself something explicable, subsumable, capable of being distanced and being put in perspective. When we think of the universe in terms of the dispersion and interaction of particles, we seem to rise above human needs and look down upon them. We seem to have become slightly more than human, to have distanced ourselves from our own humanity and seen ourselves from nowhere.

For us antiessentialists, this temptation to think that we have eluded our human finitude by seeing ourselves under the aspect of elementary particles is just one more attempt to create a divinity and then claim a share in the divine life. The trouble with all such attempts is that the need to be God is just one more human need. Or, to put the point less invidiously, the project of seeing all our needs from the point of view of someone without any such needs is just one more human project. Stoic absence of passion, Zen absence of will, Heideggerian *Gelassenheit*, and physics-as-the-absolute-conception-of-reality are, from this angle, just so many variations on a single project – the project of escaping from time and chance.[6]

We antiessentialists, however, cannot afford to sneer at this project. For we cannot afford to sneer at *any* human project, any chosen form of human life. In particular, we should not allow ourselves to say what I have just said: that by taking this view of physical science we *seem* to see ourselves as more than human. For an antiessentialist cannot invoke the appearance–reality distinction. We cannot say that our opponents' way of looking at physics gets physics wrong, mistakes its intrinsic nature, substitutes an accidental and inessential use of it for what it is in itself. In our view, physical science no more has an intrinsic nature than does the number 17. Like 17, it is capable of being described in an infinity of ways, and none of these ways is the 'inside' way. Seeing ourselves as participating in the divine life by describing ourselves under the aspect of eternity is not an illusion or a confusion; it is just one more attempt to satisfy one more human need. Seeing ourself as at last in touch, through physical science, with the ultimate nature of reality, is also not an illusion or a confusion; it is one more human project which may, like all human projects, eclipse the possibility of other, more desirable but incompatible projects.

Nor can we antiessentialists let ourselves get away with saying that our essentialist opponents mistakenly think that they have 'eluded human finitude'. It is not as if human finitude is the ultimate truth of the matter, as if human beings are *intrinsically* finite. On our view, human beings are what they make themselves, and one of the things they have wanted to make themselves is a divinity – what Sartre calls a 'being in and for itself'. We antiessentialists cannot say, with Sartre, that this attempt is a 'futile passion'. The metaphysical systems of Aristotle and Spinoza are not exercises in futility, any more than are the antimetaphysical systems of William James, Nietzsche and Sartre himself. There is no inescapable truth which either metaphysicians or pragmatists are trying to evade or capture, for any candidate for truth can be escaped by a suitable choice of description and can be underwritten by another such choice.

What about the Sartrean proposition that 'human beings are what they make themselves', which I have just put forward as antiessentialist doctrine? Is that proposition true? Well, it is true in the same way that Peano's axioms for arithmetic are true. These axioms sum up the implications of the use of a certain vocabulary, the vocabulary of numbers. But suppose you have no interest in using that vocabulary. Suppose that you are willing to forgo the advantages of counting and calculating, and, perhaps because of a morbid fear of technology, are willing and eager to speak a language in which no mention of the number 17 occurs. For you, those axioms are not candidates for truth – they have no relevance to your projects.

So it is for the Sartrean proposition. This proposition sums up a certain view about what sorts of projects it is best to pursue. If, however, your own projects are religious or metaphysical, and if you are therefore willing to forgo the advantages of the kinds of egalitarian politics and Romantic art whose implications Sartre sums up, Sartre's proposition is not even a candidate for truth. You may call it false if you like, but the falsity is not like the falsity of a candidate for truth which has been tested and found wanting. It is rather a matter of obvious *irrelevance* – obvious inability to be of use for your purposes. Putting a Sartrean description before a Spinozist is like putting a bicycle pump in the hands of a ditch digger, or a yardstick in the hands of a brain surgeon – it is not even a candidate for utility.[7]

Is there then no argument possible between Sartre and Spinoza, no communication between Peano and the antitechnologist? It makes all the difference here whether we are talking about 'argument' or about 'communication'. We can have communication and disagreement without an argument ever having been joined. Indeed, we often do. That is what happens whenever we find ourselves unable to find common premises, when we have to agree to differ, when we begin to talk about 'differences of taste'. Communication requires no more than agreement to use the same tools to pursue shared needs. Argument requires agreement about which needs take priority over others. The language, and the common sense, which the Spinozist and the Sartrean share reflects the fact that both need food, sex, shelter, books and quite a lot of other things – and that they go about getting those things in much the same ways. Their inability to *argue* fruitfully on philosophical questions reflects the fact that neither gives much weight to the particular needs which led the other to philosophize. Similarly, the inability of two painters to agree on how to paint reflects the fact that neither gives much weight to the needs which led the other to the easel. To say that such disagreements are 'merely philosophical' or 'merely artistic' is to say that, when they agree to put philosophy or painting aside, the participants can agree to collaborate on common projects.[8] To say that their philosophical or artistic disagreements are nevertheless profound and important is to say that neither considers those *other* projects central to their lives.

This way of putting things may seem to neglect the fact that Sartreans sometimes turn Spinozist, atheists Catholic, antiessentialists essentialist, metaphysicians pragmatist, and vice versa. More generally, it seems to neglect the fact that people change their central projects, change those parts of their self-image which they had previously found most precious. The question is, however, whether this ever happens as a result of *argument*. Perhaps sometimes it does, but this is surely the exception. Such conversions are typically as much a surprise to the person herself as to her friends. The phrase 'she has become a new person – you would not recognize her' typically means 'she no longer sees the point or relevance or interest of the arguments which she once deployed on the other side'.

Common sense, however, like Greek philosophy, thinks that conversions *should* come about by argument. Common sense hopes that these conversions will not be like suddenly falling in love with an utterly different sort of person but rather like gradually coming to recognize the shape of one's own mind. The Socratic assumption that desirable conversions are a matter of self-discovery rather than self-transformation necessitates the Platonic doctrine that every human mind has, in broad outlines, the same shape: the shape given by memory of the Forms. In later philosophers, this becomes the belief in 'reason', either as a faculty for penetrating through appearances to reality or as a set of elementary truths which lie deep within each of us, waiting for argument to bring them to light. To believe in reason, in either sense, is to believe not only that there is such a thing as human nature, but that this nature is unique and not a matter of what we share with the other animals. This unique ingredient in human beings makes us knowers rather than simply users, and thus makes us capable of being converted by argument rather than bowled over by irrational forces.

We antiessentialists, of course, do not believe that there is such a faculty. Since nothing has an intrinsic nature, neither do human beings. But we are happy to admit that human beings are unique in a certain respect: that normal, adult, properly socialized and trained human beings stand in a unique set of relations. For these human beings are able to *use language*, and so are able to describe things. As far as we know, nothing else is able to describe things. Numbers and physical forces can be greater than each other, but they do not describe each other as greater. *We* so describe them. Plants and the other animals can interact, but their success in these interactions is not a matter of their finding increasingly more profitable redescriptions of each other. Our success *is* largely a matter of finding such redescriptions.

Darwin made it hard for essentialists to think of the higher anthropoids as having suddenly acquired an extra added ingredient called 'reason' or 'intelligence', rather than simply more of the sort of cunning which the lower anthropoids had already manifested. This is why, since Darwin, essentialist philosophers have tended to talk less about 'mind' and more about 'language'. Words like 'sign', 'symbol', 'language' and 'discourse' have become philosophical buzzwords in our century in the way in which 'reason', 'science' and 'mind' were buzzwords in the previous century. The development of symbolizing abilities is, indeed, susceptible to an evolutionary account in terms of increasing cunning. But essentialist philosophers have tended to forget that they substituted 'language' for 'mind' in order to accommodate Darwin, and have gone on to raise exactly the same problems about the former as their predecessors raised about the latter.

As I said earlier, these problems arise from thinking of language as a third thing, intruding between subject and object and forming a barrier to human knowledge of how things are in themselves. To keep faith with Darwin, however, we should think of the word 'language' not as naming a thing with an intrinsic nature of its own, but as a way of abbreviating the kinds of complicated interactions with the rest of the universe which are unique to the higher anthropoids. These interactions are marked by the use of strings of noises and marks to facilitate group activities, as tools for coordinating the activities of individuals.

The new relations in which these anthropoids stand to other objects are signalized not simply by the use of the mark X to direct the attention of the rest of the group to the object A, but by the use of several different marks to direct attention to A, corresponding to the several different purposes which A may serve. In philosophical jargon, one can say that behaviour becomes properly linguistic only when organisms start using a semantical metalanguage and become capable of putting words in intensional contexts. More plainly: it only becomes properly linguistic when we can say things like, 'It is also called "Y"', but for your purposes you should describe it as X' or, 'You have every reason to call it an X, but nevertheless it is not an X.' For only at that point do we need to use specifically linguistic notions like 'meaning', 'truth', 'reference' and 'description'. Only now does it become not only useful, but almost indispensable, to describe the anthropoids as 'meaning A by X' or 'believing falsely that all As are Bs'.

Looking at language in this Darwinian way, as providing tools for coping with objects rather than representations of objects, and as providing different sets of tools for different purposes, obviously makes it hard to be an essentialist. For it becomes hard to take seriously the idea that one description of A can be more 'objective' or 'closer to the intrinsic nature of A' than another. The relation of tools to what they manipulate is simply a matter of utility for a particular purpose, not of 'correspondence'. A stomach pump is no closer to human nature than a stethoscope, and a voltage tester is no closer to the essence of an electrical appliance than a screwdriver. Unless one believes, with Aristotle, that there is a difference between knowing and using, that there is a purpose called 'knowing the truth' distinct from all other purposes, one will not think of one description of A as 'more accurate' than another *sans phrase*. For accuracy, like utility, is a matter of adjusting the relation between an object and other objects, a matter of putting an object in a profitable context. It is not a matter of getting the object right, in the Aristotelian sense of seeing it as it is apart from all relations.

An evolutionary description of the development of linguistic ability gives essentialist thinking no foothold, just as an Aristotelian account of human knowledge leaves no room for a Darwinian understanding of the growth of such knowledge. But, once again, you should notice that it would be inconsistent with my own antiessentialism to try to convince you that the Darwinian way of thinking of language – and, by extension, the Deweyan, pragmatist way of thinking of truth – is the objectively true way. All I am entitled to say is that it is a useful way, useful for particular purposes. All I can claim to have done here is to offer you a redescription of the relation between human beings and the rest of the universe. Like every other redescription, this one has to be judged on the basis of its utility for a purpose.

So it seems appropriate to end now by turning to the following question: For what purpose does the antiessentialist think that his description of knowledge and inquiry, of human culture, is a better tool than the Aristotelian, essentialist description? My answer has already been suggested several times, but it may be as well to make it explicit. Pragmatists think that there are two advantages to antiessentialism. The first is that adopting it makes it impossible to formulate a lot of the traditional philosophical problems. The second is that adopting it makes it easier to come to terms with Darwin. Since I have in previous books (particularly *Philosophy and the Mirror of Nature*) said a lot about the sort of philosophical therapy which an antiessentialist description of things makes possible, I shall concentrate here on the second advantage.

I agree with Dewey that the function of philosophy is to mediate between old ways of speaking, developed to accomplish earlier tasks, with new ways of speaking, developed in response to new demands. As he put it:

> When it is acknowledged that under disguise of dealing with ultimate reality, philosophy has been occupied with the precious values embedded in social traditions, that it has sprung from a clash of social ends and from a conflict of inherited institutions with incompatible contemporary tendencies, it will be seen that the task of future philosophy is to clarify men's ideas as to the social and moral strifes of their own day.[9]

The social and moral strife incited by the publication of Darwin's *The Descent of Man* has been largely forgotten. But it seems to me that philosophy has still not caught up with Darwin – still not faced up to the challenge which he presents. There is still, I think, a lot of work to be done in reconciling the precious values embedded in our traditions with what Darwin had to say about our relation to other animals. Dewey and Davidson seem to me the philosophers who have done most to help us accomplish this reconciliation.

To see the work of these men in this light, it helps to compare what they have done with what Hume and Kant did. The latter philosophers faced the task of assimilating the New Science of the seventeenth century with the moral vocabulary which Europe inherited from, among other sources, the Stoics and the Christians. Hume's solution to the problem consisted of assimilating human reason to that of animals and assimilating human morality to the kind of benevolent interest in fellow members of the species which animals also display. Hume was a protopragmatist, in the sense that, when he has finished with it, the distinction between knowing reality and coping with reality has become very fuzzy indeed. But, notoriously, Hume's solution struck most readers – especially German readers – as a cure worse than the disease. They thought that human knowledge – and in particular claims to universal and necessary truth – had to be saved from Hume.

Kant offered an alternative solution, one which Hegel considered still far too sceptical and defeatist – far too Humean and proto-pragmatic. But philosophers less ambitious than Hegel have been, for the most part, willing to settle for some form of Kant's solution. Kant saved the claim to unconditionality, in the form of universality and necessity, by distinguishing between the transcendental phenomenal-world-creating scheme, and the empirical and merely phenomenal content which fills up that scheme. He immunized our traditional moral vocabulary, and in particular our claim to be under *unconditional* moral obligations, by sheltering it behind the wall which separates the moral and noumenal from the phenomenal and empirical. By creating this system, he earned the wholehearted thanks of people who, like the protagonist of Fichte's *The Vocation of Man*, had been afraid that their self-image as moral agents could not survive corpuscularian mechanics.

Kant thus helped us hang on to the idea of something nonrelational because unconditional. Universal and necessary a priori synthetic truths and unconditional moral commands were safe because the world of corpuscularian mechanics was not the real world. The real world was the world in which we, behind our empirical backs, so to speak, had constituted the phenomenal world – the same world in which we were nonempirical, nonpragmatic, moral agents. Kant thereby helped us hang on to the idea that there is a great big difference between us and the other animals. For them, poor phenomenal things that they are, everything is relative and pragmatic. But we have a noumenal and transcendental side, a side which escapes relationality. So we may hope to know the truth, in a non-Baconian sense of knowing, a sense in which knowing is not reducible to using. We may hope to do right, in a sense of right which is not reducible to the pursuit of pleasure or to the gratification of benevolent instincts.

Darwin, however, made it much harder to be a Kantian than it had previously been. Once people started experimenting with a picture of themselves as what Darwin's apt pupil, Nietzsche, called 'clever animals', they found it very hard to think of themselves as having a transcendental or a noumenal side. Further, when Darwinian evolutionary theory was brought together with the suggestion, mooted by Frege and Peirce and anticipated by Herder and Humboldt, that it is *language*,[10] rather than consciousness or mind, which is the distinguishing feature of our species, Darwinian evolutionary theory made it possible to see all of human behaviour – including that 'higher' sort of behaviour previously interpreted as fulfilment of the desire to know the unconditionally true and do the unconditionally right – as continuous with animal behaviour. For the origin of language, unlike the origin of consciousness, or of a faculty called 'reason' capable of grasping the intrinsic nature of things, is intelligible in naturalistic terms. We can give what Locke called a 'plain historical account' of how animals came to talk. However, we cannot give a plain historical account of how they stopped coping with reality and began representing it, much less of how they stopped being merely phenomenal beings and began to constitute the phenomenal world.

We can, of course, stick with Kant and insist that Darwin, like Newton, is merely a story about phenomena, and that transcendental stories have precedence over empirical stories. But the hundred-odd years spent absorbing and improving on Darwin's empirical story have, I suspect and hope, unfitted us for listening to transcendental stories. In the course of those years we have gradually substituted the making of a better future for ourselves, constructing a utopian, democratic society, for the attempt to see ourselves from outside of time and history. Antiessentialism is one expression of that shift. The willingness to see philosophy as an aid to creating ourselves rather than to knowing ourselves is another.

* * * *

NOTES

1 This point can be put in Foucault's language by saying that truth will never be separated from power, but that power is not something bad in itself. The power of a utopian egalitarian community to create good citizens via biopower is a good thing. Officially, Foucault does not believe in a good Rousseauvian subject, unshaped by discourses of power. But his tendency towards distrust of all forms of authority occasionally led him to toy with this pleasing fiction.

2 The properties usually called 'nonrelational' (e.g., 'red', as opposed to 'on the left-hand side') are treated by psychological nominalists as properties signified by predicates which are, for some purpose or another, being treated as primitive. But the primitiveness of a predicate is not intrinsic to the predicate; it is relative to a way of teaching, or otherwise exhibiting, a use of the predicate. The putative nonrelationality of a property signified by a predicate is relative to a certain way of describing a certain range of objects having the predicate. One way of putting the lessons taught by both Saussure and Wittgenstein is to say that no predicate is intrinsically primitive.

For a firm statement, of the contrasting, antinominalist, antipragmatist view, see John Searle, *The Rediscovery of the Mind* (Cambridge, Mass.: MIT Press, 1992), p. 211. The contrast which Searle draws there between intrinsic features of the world, such as molecules, and observer-relative features, such as it being a nice day for a picnic, is, for pragmatists, an arbitrary preference for the human purposes served by physicists over those served by picnickers.

3 On the fundamental importance of this latter Wittgensteinian point, see Barry Allen, *Truth in Philosophy* (Cambridge, Mass.: Harvard University Press, 1993).

4 It is useful to think of this Whiteheadian criticism of Aristotle (a criticism found in other early twentieth-century philosophers – e.g., Peirce and Russell – who tried to formulate a non subject-predicate logic) as paralleling Derrida's

criticism of logocentrism. Derrida's picture of a word as a node in an infinitely flexible web of relationships with other words is obviously reminiscent of Whitehead's account, in *Process and Reality*, of every actual occasion as consti- tuted by relations to all other actual occasions. My hunch is that the twentieth century will be seen by historians of philosophy as the period in which a kind of neo-Leibnizian panrelationalism was developed in various different idioms – a panrelationism which restates Leibniz's point that each monad is nothing but all the other monads seen from a certain perspective, each substance nothing but its relations to all the other substances.

5 For examples of the sort of glorification of elementary particles which I have in mind, see the passage from John Searle referred to in note 2, and also David Lewis, 'Putnam's Paradox', *Australasian Journal of Philosophy*, 1983. I discuss this article briefly at pp. 7 *ff.* of my *Objectivity, Relativism and Truth*.

6 As I have said elsewhere, I think that Derrida is importantly right in seeing Heideggerian renunciation as just one more attempt to affiliate oneself with power.

7 The best account of the contrast between propositions which are truth candidates and those which are not is William James's discussion of the difference between 'live' and 'dead' intellectual options in his famous essay 'The Will to Believe'.

8 This analogy should not be construed as an 'aesthetic' theory of the nature of philosophy, any more than as a 'philosophical' theory of the nature of painting. Pragmatists do not have much use for Kant's distinctions between the cognitive, the moral and the aesthetic. I am not trying to say that philosophy is less 'cognitive' than has been thought, but merely to point to the difference between situations in which there is sufficient agreement about ends to make possible fruitful argument about alternative means, and situations in which there is not. But this difference is of course not sharp. There is a continuum between unquestioning devotion to the same ends and inability to understand how one's interlocutor could be so crazy as not to share one's own ends.

9 John Dewey, *Reconstruction in Philosophy, The Middle Works of John Dewey* (Carbondale, Ill.: Southern Illinois University Press, 1982), vol. XII, p. 94.

10 See Manfred Frank, *What is Neostructuralism?* (Minneapolis: University of Minnesota Press, 1984), p. 217: 'the linguistic turn consists in the transferral of the philosophical paradigm of consciousness onto that of the sign'. Frank's book is very valuable in giving a sense of the continuity between Herder and

Humboldt's eighteenth-century view of language and the view common to Derrida and Wittgenstein. In particular, his comparison on p. 129 of Herder's claim that 'our reason is formed only *through fictions*' with Nietzsche's more famous claim that language is 'a mobile army of metaphors, metonymies, anthropomorphisms' makes one realize that antiessentialism is at least as old as the suggestion that there is no Adamic language, and that different languages, including our own, serve different social needs. Reading Frank leads one to wonder whether, if Hegel had followed Herder's lead, and thus had been led to talk more about social needs and less about Absolute Knowledge, Western philosophy might not have saved itself a century of nervous shuffles.

4. Ethics Without Principles

(1994)

I have been suggesting that we think of pragmatism as an attempt to alter our self-image so as to make it consistent with the Darwinian claim that we differ from other animals simply in the complexity of our behaviour. To adopt this image of ourselves as exceptionally clever animals is to set aside the Greek way of distinguishing ourselves from the brutes. Plato and Aristotle suggested that the other animals lived in a world of sensory appearance, that their lives consisted of adjusting to the changes of these appearances, and that they were thus incapable of *knowing*, for knowledge consists in penetrating behind appearance to reality. Pragmatists, in contrast, treat inquiry – in both physics and ethics – as the search for adjustment, and in particular for that sort of adjustment to our fellow humans which we call 'the search for acceptable justification and eventual agreement'. I have argued that we should substitute this latter search for the traditional descriptions of the quest for truth.

In the previous chapter, I portrayed pragmatism as a generalized form of antiessentialism – as an attempt to break down the distinction between the intrinsic and the extrinsic features of things. By thinking of everything as relational through and through, pragmatists attempt to get rid of the contrast between reality and appearance. Pragmatists hope to make it impossible for the sceptic to raise the question, 'Is our knowledge of things adequate to the way things really are?' They substitute for this traditional question the *practical* question, 'Are our ways of describing things, of relating them to other things so as to make them fulfil our needs more adequately, as good as possible? Or can we do better? Can our future be made better than our present?'

In this chapter I turn to the distinction between morality and prudence. This distinction is traditionally drawn by opposing un-conditional and categorical obligations to conditional and hypo-thetical ones. Pragmatists have doubts about the suggestion that anything is unconditional, because they doubt that anything is, or could be, nonrelational. So they need to reinterpret the distinctions between morality and prudence, morality and expediency, and morality and self-interest, in ways which dispense with the notion of unconditionality.

Dewey suggested that we reconstruct the distinction between pru-dence and morality in terms of the distinction between routine and non-routine social relationships. He saw 'prudence' as a member of the same family of concepts as 'habit' and 'custom'. All three words describe familiar and relatively uncontroversial ways in which indi-viduals and groups adjust to the stresses and strains of their non-human and human environments. It is obviously prudent both to keep an eye out for poisonous snakes in the grass and to trust strangers less than members of one's own family. 'Prudence', 'expediency' and 'efficiency' are all terms which describe such routine and uncontroversial adjust-ments to circumstance.

Morality and law, on the other hand, begin when controversy arises. We invent both when we can no longer just do what comes naturally, when routine is no longer good enough, or when habit and custom no longer suffice. These will no longer suffice when the individual's needs begin to clash with those of her family, or her family's with those of the neighbours', or when economic strain begins to split her community into warring classes, or when that community must come to terms with an alien community. On Dewey's account, the prudence–morality distinction is, like that between custom and law, a distinction of degree – the degree of need for conscious deliberation and explicit formulation of precepts – rather than a distinction of kind. For pragma-tists like Dewey, there is no distinction of kind between what is useful and what is right. For, as Dewey said, 'Right is only an abstract name for the multitude of concrete demands in action which others impress upon us, and of which we are obliged, if we would live, to take some account.'[1] The utilitarians were right when they coalesced the moral and the useful, even though they were wrong in thinking that utility is simply a matter of getting pleasure and avoiding pain. Dewey agrees with Aristotle, against Bentham, that human happiness cannot be reduced to the accumulation of pleasures.

From Kant's point of view, however, Aristotle, Bentham and Dewey are equally blind to the true nature of morality. To identify moral obligation with the need to adjust one's behaviour to the needs of other human beings is, for Kantians, either vicious or simple-minded. Dewey seems to Kantians to have confused duty with self-interest, the intrinsic authority of the moral law with the banausic need to bargain with opponents whom one cannot overcome.

Dewey was well aware of this Kantian criticism. Here is one of the passages in which he attempted to answer it:

> Morals, it is said, imply the subordination of fact to ideal con-
> sideration, while the view presented [Dewey's own view]
> makes morals secondary to bare fact, which is equal to depriving
> them of dignity and jurisdiction ... The criticism rests upon a
> false separation. It argues in effect that either ideal standards
> antecede customs and confer their moral quality upon them, or
> that in being subsequent to custom[s] and evolved from them,
> they are mere accidental by-products. But how does it stand
> with language? ... Language grew out of unintelligent bab-
> blings, instinctive motions called gestures, and the pressure
> of circumstance. But nevertheless language once called into
> existence is language and operates as language.[2]

The point of Dewey's analogy between language and morality is that there was no decisive moment at which language stopped being a series of reactions to the stimuli provided by the behaviour of other humans and started to be an instrument for expressing beliefs. Similarly, there was no point at which practical reasoning stopped being prudential and became specifically moral, no point at which it stopped being merely useful and started being authoritative.

Dewey's reply to those who, like Kant, think of morality as stemming from a specifically human faculty called 'reason', and of prudence as something shared with the brutes, is that the *only* thing that is specifically human is language. But the history of language is a seamless story of gradually increasing complexity. The story of how we got from Neanderthal grunts and nudges to German philosophical treatises is no more discontinuous than the story of how we got from the amoebae to the anthropoids. The two stories are parts of one larger story. Cultural evolution takes over from biological evolution without a break. From an evolutionary point of view, there is no difference between the grunts and the treatises, save complexity. Yet the difference between language-using and dumb animals, and the difference between cultures which do not engage in conscious, collective moral deliberation and cultures which do, are as important and obvious as ever, even though both are differences of degree. On Dewey's view, philosophers who have sharply distinguished reason from experience, or morality from prudence, have tried to turn an important difference of degree into a difference of metaphysical kind. They have thereby constructed problems for themselves which are as insoluble as they are artificial.

Dewey saw Kant's moral philosophy as taking 'the doctrine that the essence of reason is complete universality (and hence necessity and immutability) with the seriousness becoming the professor of logic'.[3] He interpreted Kant's attempt to get advice about what to do out of the mere idea of universalizability as offering not an impossible disregard of consequences but merely 'a broad impartial view of consequences'. All that the categorical imperative does, Dewey said, is to commend 'the habit of asking how we should be willing to be treated in a similar case'.[4] The attempt to do more, to get 'ready-made rules available at a moment's notice for settling any kind of moral difficulty', seemed to Dewey to have been 'born of timidity and nourished by love of authoritative prestige'. Only such a tendency to sado-masochism, Dewey thought, could have led to the idea that 'absence of immutably fixed and universally applicable ready-made principles is equivalent to moral chaos'.[5]

So much for the standard Deweyan criticism of the Kantian way of viewing the distinction between morality and prudence. I want now to turn to another distinction, that between reason and sentiment, thinking and feeling. Doing so will let me relate Dewey's views to those of Annette Baier. Baier, one of the leading feminist philosophers of the present day, takes David Hume as her model. She praises Hume as the 'woman's moral philosopher' because of his willingness to take sentiment, and indeed sentimentality, as central to the moral consciousness. She also praises him for 'de-intellectualizing and de-sanctifying the moral endeavor . . . presenting it as the human equivalent of various social controls in animal or insect populations'.[6] Though Baier rarely mentions Dewey, and Dewey rarely discusses Hume's moral philosophy at any length, these three militantly anti-Kantian philosophers are on the same side of most arguments. All three share the same distrust of the notion of 'moral obligation'. Dewey, Baier and Hume can all agree with Nietzsche that the pre-Socratic Greeks were free from the 'timidity', the fear of having to make hard choices, which led Plato to search for immutable moral truth. All three see the temporal circumstances of human life as difficult enough without sado-masochistically adding immutable, unconditional obligations.

Baier has proposed that we substitute the notion of 'appropriate trust' for that of 'obligation' as our central moral concept. She has said that

> there is no room for moral theory as something which is more philosophical and less committed than moral deliberation, and which is not simply an account of our customs and styles of justification, criticism, protest, revolt, conversion, and resolution.[7]

In words that echo some of Dewey's, Baier says that 'the villain is the rationalist, law-fixated tradition in moral philosophy',[8] a tradition which assumes that 'behind every moral intuition lies a universal rule'.[9] That tradition assumes that Hume's attempt to think of moral progress as a progress of sentiments fails to account for moral obligation. But, on Baier's view, as on Dewey's, there is nothing to account for: moral obligation does not have a nature, or a source, different from tradition, habit and custom. Morality is simply a new and controversial custom. Our sense that prudence is unheroic and morality heroic is merely the recognition that testing out the relatively untried is more dangerous, more risky, than doing what comes naturally.

Baier and Dewey agree that the central flaw in much traditional moral philosophy has been the myth of the self as nonrelational, as capable of existing independently of any concern for others, as a cold psychopath needing to be constrained to take account of other people's needs. This is the picture of the self which philosophers since Plato have expressed in terms of the division between 'reason' and 'the passions' – a division which Hume unfortunately perpetuated in his notorious inversion of Plato, his claim that 'reason is, and should be, the slave of the passions'. Ever since Plato, the West has construed the reason–passion distinction as paralleling the distinction between the universal and the individual, as well as that between unselfish and selfish actions. The religious, Platonic and Kantian traditions have thus saddled us with a distinction between the true self and the false self, the self which hears the call of conscience and the self which is merely 'self-interested'. The latter self is merely prudential, and not yet moral.

Baier and Dewey both argue that this notion of the self as cold, self-interested, calculating, psychopath should be set aside. If we really were such selves, the question 'Why should I be moral?' would be forever unanswerable. Only when we masochistically picture ourselves as such selves do we feel the need to punish ourselves by quailing before divine commands, or before Kant's tribunal of pure practical reason. But if we follow the pragmatists' advice to see everything as constituted by its relations to everything else, it is easy to detect the fallacy which Dewey described as 'transforming the (truistic) fact of acting *as* a self into the fiction of acting always *for* self'.[10] We shall commit this fallacy, and continue to think of the self as a psychopath in need of restraint, as long as we accept what Dewey called the 'belief in the fixity and simplicity of the self'. Dewey associated this belief with 'the theologians' . . . dogma of the unity and ready-made completeness of the soul'.[11] But he might equally well have associated it with the argument of Plato's *Phaedo*, or with Kant's doctrine that the moral self is a nonempirical self.

If we put such notions of unity and readymade completeness to one side, we can say, with Dewey, that 'selfhood (except insofar as it has encased itself in a shell of routine) is in process of making, and that any self is capable of including within itself a number of inconsistent selves, of unharmonized dispositions'.[12] This notion of multiple inconsistent selves is, as Donald Davidson has shown, a good way of naturalizing and demystifying the Freudian notion of the unconscious.[13] But the most important link between Freud and Dewey is the one which Baier emphasizes: the role of the family, and in particular of maternal love, in creating nonpsychopaths, that is, human selves who find concern for others entirely natural. Baier says, in words which Dewey might have written, that 'the secular equivalent of faith in God . . . is faith in the human community and its evolving procedures – in the prospects for many-handed cognitive ambitions and moral hopes'.[14] But she sees that faith as rooted in the faith most of us have in our parents and siblings. The trust which holds a family together is Baier's model for the secular faith which may hold together modern, posttraditional societies.

Freud helped us to see that we get psychopaths – people whose self-conception involves no relations to others – only when parental love, and the trust which such love creates in the child, are absent. To see the point Baier wants us to appreciate, consider the question: Do I have a moral obligation to my mother? My wife? My children? 'Morality' and 'obligation' here seem inapposite. For doing what one is obliged to do contrasts with doing what comes naturally, and for most people responding to the needs of family members is the most natural thing in the world. Such responses come naturally because most of us define ourselves, at least in part, by our relations to members of our family. Our needs and theirs largely overlap; we are not happy if they are not. We would not wish to be well fed while our children go hungry; that would be unnatural. Would it also be immoral? It is a bit strange to say so. One would only employ this term if one encountered a parent who was also a pathological egoist, a mother or father whose sense of self had nothing to do with her or his children – the sort of person envisaged by decision theory, someone whose identity is constituted by 'preference rankings' rather than by fellow feeling.

By contrast, I may feel a specifically *moral* obligation to deprive both my children and myself of a portion of the available food because there are starving people outside the door. The word 'moral' is appropriate here because the demand is less *natural* than the demand to feed my children. It is less closely connected with my sense of who I am. But the desire to feed the hungry stranger may of course *become* as tightly woven into my self-conception as the desire to feed my family. Moral development in the individual, and moral progress in the human species as a whole, is a matter of re-marking human selves so as to enlarge the variety of the relationships which constitute those selves. The ideal limit of this process of enlargement is the self envisaged by Christian and Buddhist accounts of sainthood – an ideal self to whom the hunger and suffering of *any* human being (and even, perhaps, that of any other animal) is intensely painful.

Should this progress ever be completed, the term 'morality' would drop out of the language. For there would no longer be any way, nor any need, to contrast doing what comes naturally with doing what is moral. We should all have what Kant calls a 'holy will'. The term 'moral obligation' becomes increasingly less appropriate to the degree to which we identify with those whom we help: the degree to which we mention them when telling ourselves stories about who we are, the degree to which their story is also our story.[15] It comes fairly naturally to share what one has with an old friend, or a near neighbour, or a close business associate, who has been left destitute by a sudden disaster. It comes less naturally to share with a casual acquaintance, or a complete stranger, who is in the same unfortunate situation. In a world in which hunger is common, it does not come naturally to take food from one's children's mouth in order to feed a hungry stranger and her children. But if the stranger and her children are on your doorstep, you may well feel obliged to do just that. The terms 'moral' and 'obligation' become even more appropriate when it is a matter of depriving your children of something they want in order to send money to the victims of a famine in a country you have never seen, to people whom you might well find repellent if you ever encountered them, people whom you might not want as friends, might not want your children to marry, people whose *only* claim on your attention is that you have been told that they are hungry. But Christianity has taught the West to look forward to a world in which there are no such people, a world in which all men and women are brothers and sisters. In such a world, there would never be any occasion to speak of 'obligation'.

When moral philosophers in the Kantian tradition put sentiment on a par with prejudice, and tell us that 'from a strictly moral point of view' there is no difference between one's own hungry child and a randomly selected hungry child on the other side of the world, they are contrasting this so-called 'moral point of view' with a point of view they call 'mere self-interest'. The idea behind this way of speaking is that morality and obligation start where self-interest stops. The problem with this way of speaking, Dewey insisted, is that the boundaries of the self are fuzzy and flexible. So philosophers in this tradition try to obscure this fuzziness by fixing those boundaries. They do so by saying that the self is constituted by a preference ranking – one which divides people up according to whom one would prefer to be fed first, for example. Then they either contrast moral obligation with preference, or else 'subjectivize' feelings of moral obligation by taking them as just further preferences.

There are difficulties with both of these alternatives. If you contrast moral obligation with preference, you have trouble with the question of moral motivation: what sense does it make, after all, to say that a person acts against her own preferences? On the other hand, if you no longer distinguish between morality and self-interest, and say that what we call morality is simply the self-interest of those who have been acculturated in a certain way, then you will be accused of 'emotivism', of having failed to appreciate Kant's distinction between dignity and value. One way leads to the question Plato tried to answer, 'Why should I be moral?' The other way leads to the question, 'Is there any difference between a taste for feeding hungry strangers and a taste for vanilla ice cream?' More generally, one way seems to lead to a dualistic metaphysics to splitting the human self, and possibly the universe as a whole, into higher and lower segments. The other seems to lead to a wholesale abnegation of our aspirations to something 'higher' than mere animality.

Pragmatists are often accused of just such an abnegation. They are lumped with reductionists, behaviourists, sensualists, nihilists and other dubious characters. I think that the pragmatist's best defence against this sort of charge is to say that she too has a conception of our difference from the animals. However, hers does not involve a sharp difference – a difference between the infinite and the finite – of the sort illustrated by Kant's distinction between dignity and value, between the unconditioned and the conditioned, the nonrelational and the relational. Rather, the pragmatist sees our difference as a much greater degree of flexibility – in particular, a much greater flexibility in the boundaries of selfhood, in the sheer quantity of relationships which can go to constitute a human self. She sees the ideal of human brotherhood and sisterhood not as the imposition of something nonempirical on the empirical, nor of something nonnatural on the natural, but as the culmination of a process of adjustment which is also a process of recreating human beings.

From this point of view, moral progress is not a matter of an increase of rationality – a gradual diminution of the influence of prejudice and superstition, permitting us to see our moral duty more clearly. Nor is it what Dewey called an increase of intelligence, that is, increasing one's skill at inventing courses of action which simultaneously satisfy many conflicting demands. People can be very intelligent, in this sense, without having wide sympathies. It is neither irrational nor unintelligent to draw the limits of one's moral community at a national, or racial, or gender border. But it is undesirable – morally undesirable. So it is best to think of moral progress as a matter of increasing *sensitivity*, increasing responsiveness to the needs of a larger and larger variety of people and things. Just as the pragmatists see scientific progress not as the gradual attenuation of a veil of appearance which hides the intrinsic nature of reality from us, but as the increasing ability to respond to the concerns of ever larger groups of people – in particular, the people who carry out ever more acute observations and perform ever more refined experiments – so they see moral progress as a matter of being able to respond to the needs of ever more inclusive groups of people.

Let me pursue this analogy between science and morals a bit further. I said in the first chapter in this section that pragmatists do not think of scientific, or any other inquiry, as aimed at truth, but rather at better justificatory ability – better to deal with doubts about what we are saying, either by shoring up what we have previously said or by deciding to say something different. The trouble with aiming at truth is that you would not know when you had reached it, even if you had in fact reached it. But you *can* aim at ever more justification, the assuagement of ever more doubt. Analogously, you cannot aim at 'doing what is right', because you will never know whether you have hit the mark. Long after you are dead, better informed and more sophisticated people may judge your action to have been a tragic mistake, just as they may judge your scientific beliefs as intelligible only by reference to an obsolete paradigm. But you *can* aim at ever more sensitivity to pain, and ever greater satisfaction of ever more various needs. Pragmatists think that the idea of something nonhuman luring us human beings on should be replaced with the idea of getting more and more human beings into our community – of taking the needs and interests and views of more and more diverse human beings into account. Justificatory ability is its own reward. There is no need to worry about whether we will also be rewarded with a sort of immaterial medal labelled 'Truth' or 'Moral Goodness'.[16]

The idea of a 'God's eye view' to which science continually approximates is of a piece with the idea of 'the moral law' to which social custom, in periods of moral progress, continually approximates. The ideas of 'discovering the intrinsic nature of physical reality' and of 'clarifying our unconditional moral obligations' are equally distasteful to pragmatists, because both presuppose the existence of something nonrelational, something exempt from the vicissitudes of time and history, something unaffected by changing human interests and needs. Both ideas are to be replaced, pragmatists think, by metaphors of width rather than of height or depth. Scientific progress is a matter of integrating more and more data into a coherent web of belief – data from microscopes and telescopes with data obtained by the naked eye, data forced into the open by experiments with data which have always been lying about. It is not a matter of penetrating appearance until one comes upon reality. Moral progress is a matter of wider and wider sympathy. It is not a matter of rising above the sentimental to the rational. Nor is it a matter of appealing from lower, possibly corrupt, local courts to a higher court which administers an ahistorical, incorruptible, transcultural moral law.

This switch from metaphors of vertical distance to metaphors of horizontal extent ties in with the pragmatists' insistence on replacing traditional distinctions of kind with distinctions in degree of complexity. Pragmatists substitute the idea of a maximally efficient explanation of a maximally wide range of data for that of the theory which cuts reality at the joints. They substitute the idea of a maximally warm, sensitive and sympathetic human being for the Kantian idea of a Good Will. But though maximality cannot be aimed at, you can aim at explaining more data or being concerned about more people. You cannot aim at being at the end of inquiry, in either physics or ethics. That would be like aiming at being at the end of biological evolution – at being not merely the latest heir of all the ages but the creature in which all the ages were destined to culminate. Analogously, you cannot aim at moral perfection, but you can aim at taking more people's needs into account than you did previously.

So far in this chapter I have been suggesting in rather general terms why the pragmatist wants to get rid of the notion of 'unconditional moral obligation'. In the hope of greater concreteness and vividness, I turn now to another example of unconditionality: the notion of unconditional human rights. Such rights are said to form the fixed boundaries of political and moral deliberation. In American jurisprudence, Ronald Dworkin tells us, rights 'trump' every consideration of social expediency and efficiency. In much political discussion, it is taken for granted that the rights which the US courts have interpreted the US Constitution to bestow, and those universal human rights enumerated in the Helsinki Declaration, are beyond discussion. They are the unmoved movers of much of contemporary politics.

From a pragmatist's point of view, the notion of 'inalienable human rights' is no better and no worse a slogan than that of 'obedience to the will of God'. Either slogan, when invoked as an unmoved mover, is simply a way of saying that our spade is turned – that we have exhausted our argumentative resources. Talk of the will of God or of the rights of man, like talk of 'the honour of the family' or of 'the fatherland in danger' are not suitable targets for philosophical analysis and criticism. It is fruitless to look behind them. None of these notions should be analyzed, for they are all ways of saying, 'Here I stand: I can do no other.' These are not reasons for action so much as announcements that one has thought the issue through and come to a decision.

Philosophers who see morals as resting on metaphysics, press such notions too hard when they ask questions like, 'But *is* there a God?' or, 'Do human beings really *have* these rights?' Such questions presuppose that moral progress is at least in part a matter of increasing moral knowledge, knowledge about something independent of our social practices: something like the will of God or the nature of humanity. This metaphysical suggestion is vulnerable to Nietzschean suggestions that both God and human rights are superstitions – contrivances put forward by the weak to protect themselves against the strong. Whereas metaphysicians reply to Nietzsche by asserting that there is a 'rational basis' for belief in God or in human rights, pragmatists reply by saying that there is nothing wrong with contrivances. The pragmatist can cheerfully agree with Nietzsche that the idea of human brotherhood would only occur to the weak – to the people being shoved around by the brave, strong, happy warriors whom Nietzsche idolizes. But for pragmatists this fact no more counts against the idea of human rights than Socrates' ugliness counts against his account of the nature of love, or Freud's little private neuroses count against *his* account of love, or Newton's theologicoastrological motivations count against his mechanics. Once you drop the distinction between reason and passion, you no longer discriminate against a good idea because of its origins. You classify ideas according to their relative utility rather than by their sources.

Pragmatists think that the quarrel between rationalist metaphysicians and Nietzsche is without interest.[17] They grant to Nietzsche that reference to human rights is merely a convenient way of summarizing certain aspects of *our* real or proposed practices. Analogously, to say that the intrinsic nature of reality consists of atoms and the void is, for a pragmatist, a way of saying that *our* most successful scientific explanations interpret macrostructural change as a result of microstructural change. To say that God wills us to welcome the stranger within our gates is to say that hospitality is one of the virtues upon which *our* community most prides itself. To say that respect for human rights demanded our intervention to save the Jews from the Nazis, or the Bosnian Muslims from the Serbs, is to say that a failure to intervene would make *us* uncomfortable with ourselves, in the way in which knowledge that our neighbours are hungry while we have plenty on the table ourselves makes us unable to continue eating. To speak of human rights is to explain our actions by identifying ourselves with a community of like-minded persons – those who find it natural to act in a certain way.

Claims of the sort I have just made – claims which have the form 'To say such-and-such is to say so-and-so' – are often interpreted in terms of the reality–appearance distinction. So, metaphysically inclined thinkers, obsessed by the distinction between knowledge and opinion or between reason and passion, will interpret my claims as 'irrationalist' and 'emotivist'. But pragmatists do not intend these as claims about what is *really* going on – claims that what appeared to be a fact is actually a value, or what appeared to be a cognition is actually an emotion. Rather, these claims are practical recommendations on what to talk about, suggestions about the terms in which controversy on moral questions is best conducted. On the subject of atoms, the pragmatist thinks that we should not debate the issue of whether unobservable microstructure is a reality or just a convenient fiction. On the subject of human rights, the pragmatist thinks that we should not debate whether human rights have been there all the time, even when nobody recognized them, or are just the social construction of a civilization influenced by Christian doctrines of the brotherhood of man.

Of course they are social constructions. So are atoms, and so is everything else. For, as I suggested in chapter 3, to be a social construction is simply to be the intentional object of a certain set of sentences – sentences used in some societies and not in others. All that it takes to be an object is to be talked about in a reasonably coherent way, but not everybody needs to talk in all ways – nor, therefore, about all objects. Once we give up the idea that the point of discourse is to represent reality accurately, we will have no interest in distinguishing social constructs from other things. We shall confine ourselves to debating the utility of alternative constructs.

To debate the utility of the set of social constructs we call 'human rights' is to debate the question of whether inclusivist societies are better than exclusivist ones. That is to debate the question of whether communities which encourage tolerance of harmless deviance should be preferred to those communities whose social cohesion depends on conformity, on keeping outsiders at a distance and on eliminating people who try to corrupt the youth. The best single mark of our progress toward a fully fledged human rights culture may be the extent to which we stop interfering with our children's marriage plans because of the national origin, religion, race, or wealth of the intended partner, or because the marriage will be homosexual rather than heterosexual.

Those who wish to supply rational, philosophical foundations for a human rights culture say that what human beings have in common outweighs such adventitious factors as race or religion. But they have trouble spelling out what this commonality consists of. It is not enough to say that we all share a common susceptibility to pain, for there is nothing distinctively human about pain. If pain were all that mattered, it would be as important to protect the rabbits from the foxes as to protect the Jews from the Nazis. If one accepts a naturalistic, Darwinian account of human origins, it is not helpful to say that we all have reason in common, for on this account to be rational is simply to be able to use language. But there are many languages, and most of them are exclusionist. The language of human rights is no more or less characteristic of our species than languages which insist on racial or religious purity.[18]

Pragmatists suggest that we simply give up the philosophical search for commonality. They think that moral progress might be accelerated if we focused instead on our ability to make the particular little things that divide us seem unimportant – not by comparing them with the one big thing that unites us but by comparing them with other little things. Pragmatists think of moral progress as more like sewing together a very large, elaborate, polychrome quilt, than like getting a clearer vision of something true and deep. As I remarked earlier, they like to replace traditional metaphors of depth or height with metaphors of breadth and extent. Convinced that there is no subtle human essence which philosophy might grasp, they do not try to replace superficiality with depth, nor to rise above the particular in order to grasp the universal. Rather, they hope to minimize one difference at a time – the difference between Christians and Muslims in a particular village in Bosnia, the difference between blacks and whites in a particular town in Alabama, the difference between gays and straights in a particular Catholic congregation in Quebec. The hope is to sew such groups together with a thousand little stitches – to invoke a thousand little commonalities between their members, rather than specify one great big one, their common humanity.

This picture of moral progress makes us resist Kant's suggestion that morality is a matter of reason, and makes us sympathetic to Hume's suggestion that it is a matter of sentiment. If we were limited to these two candidates, we should side with Hume. But we would prefer to reject the choice, and to set aside faculty psychology once and for all. We recommend dropping the distinction between two separately functioning sources of beliefs and desires. Instead of working within the confines of this distinction, which constantly threatens us with the picture of a division between a true and real self and a false and apparent self, we once again resort to the distinction with which I began the first essay in this section: the distinction between the present and the future.

More specifically, we see both intellectual and moral progress not as a matter of getting closer to the True or the Good or the Right, but as an increase in imaginative power. We see imagination as the cutting edge of cultural evolution, the power which – given peace and prosperity – constantly operates so as to make the human future richer than the human past. Imagination is the source both of new scientific pictures of the physical universe and of new conceptions of possible communities. It is what Newton and Christ, Freud and Marx, had in common: the ability to redescribe the familiar in unfamiliar terms.

Such redescription was practised by the early Christians when they explained that the distinction between Jew and Greek was not as important as had been thought. It is being practised by contemporary feminists, whose descriptions of sexual behaviour and marital arrangements seem as strange to many men (and, for that matter, many women) as St Paul's indifference to traditional Judaic distinctions seemed to the scribes and the pharisees. It is what the Founding Fathers of my country attempted when they asked people to think of themselves not so much as Pennsylvanian Quakers or Catholic Marylanders but as citizens of a tolerant, pluralistic, federal republic. It is being attempted by those passionate advocates of European unity who hope that their grandchildren will think of themselves as European first and French or German second. But an equally good example of such redescription is Democritus' and Lucretius' suggestion that we try thinking of the world as rebounding atoms, and Copernicus' suggestion that we try thinking of the sun as at rest.

I hope that what I have been saying has helped make clear what I meant by urging that we substitute hope for knowledge. The difference between the Greek conception of human nature and the post-Darwinian, Deweyan conception is the difference between closure and openness – between the security of the unchanging and the Whitmanesque and Whiteheadian romance of unpredictable change. This element of romantic hope, this willingness to substitute imagination for certainty, and curiosity for pride, breaks down the Greek distinction between contemplation and action. Dewey saw that distinction as the great incubus from which intellectual life in the West needed to escape. His pragmatism was, as Hilary Putnam has said, an 'insistence on the supremacy of the agent point of view'. I have interpreted this supremacy as the priority of the need to create new ways of being human, and a new heaven and a new earth for these new humans to inhabit, over the desire for stability, security and order.

* * * *

NOTES

1 John Dewey, *Human Nature and Conduct, The Middle Works of John Dewey* (Carbondale, Ill.: Southern Illinois University Press, 1983), vol. XIV, p. 224.
2 Dewey, pp. 56–7.

3 Dewey, p. 168.

4 Dewey, p. 169.

5 Dewey, p. 164.

6 Annette Baier, *Postures of the Mind* (Minneapolis: University of Minnesota Press, 1985), p. 147.

7 Baier, p. 232.

8 Baier, p. 236.

9 Baier, p. 208.

10 Dewey, p. 95.

11 Dewey, p. 96.

12 Dewey, p. 96.

13 See Donald Davidson, 'Paradoxes of Irrationality' in *Philosophical Essays on Freud*, Richard Wollheim and James Hopkins, eds. (Cambridge: Cambridge University Press, 1982). Davidson's view of Freud is expanded and developed by Marcia Cavell in her *The Psychoanalytic Mind: From Freud to Philosophy* (Cambridge, Mass.: Harvard University Press, 1993).

14 Baier, p. 293.

15 Here I draw upon Daniel Dennett's very enlightening account of the self as a 'center of narrative gravity', in his *Consciousness Explained* (Cambridge, Mass.: MIT Press, 1990). I have attempted to develop the antiessentialism of the second chapter in this section in an article on Dennett, in which I suggest that what goes for selves goes for objects in general, and that a pragmatist should think of all objects as centres of descriptive gravity ('Holism, Intentionality, and the Ambition of Transcendence' in my *Truth and Progress* (Cambridge: Cambridge University Press, 1998).

16 As I see it, the notion of a 'universal validity claim', as used by Habermas and Apel, is just the claim to such a medal, and is thus dispensable. Although I entirely agree with Habermas about the desirability of substituting what he calls 'communicative reason' for 'subject-centred reason', I think of his insistence on universality, and his dislike for what he calls 'contextualism' and 'relativism', as leftovers from a period of philosophical thought in which it seemed that an appeal to the universal was the only alternative to immersion in the contingent status quo.

17 This is a point which I emphasize in my 'Human Rights, Rationality, and Sentimentality', included in *Of Human Rights: Oxford Amnesty Lectures, 1993* (New York: Basic Books, 1993) and reprinted in my *Truth and Progress* (Cambridge:

Cambridge University Press, 1998). That paper offers a more extended version of the view of human rights which I am summarizing here.

18 Here again I agree with Habermas about the linguistic character of rationality. But I try to use this doctrine to show that we do not need to think in universalist terms. Habermas's universalism forbids him to adopt the view of human rights I am offering here.

III

Some Applications
of Pragmatism

5. The Banality of Pragmatism and the Poetry of Justice

(1990)

Thomas Grey, in his *Holmes and Legal Pragmatism*, says: 'From a certain philosophical perspective, Holmes' pragmatist theory of law is ... essentially banal. At its most abstract level it concludes in truisms: Law is more a matter of experience than of logic, and experience is tradition interpreted with one eye on coherence and another on policy.'[1]

I think it is true that by now pragmatism is banal in its application to law. I also suspect that Grey is right when he claims that 'pragmatism is the implicit working theory of most good lawyers'.[2] To that extent, at least, everybody seems now to be a legal realist. Nobody wants to talk about a 'science of law' any longer. Nobody doubts that what Morton White called 'the revolt against formalism'[3] was a real advance, both in legal theory and in American intellectual life generally.

It is true that Ronald Dworkin still bad-mouths pragmatism and insists that there is 'one right answer' to hard legal questions. On the other hand, Dworkin says that he does not want to talk about 'objectivity' any more. Further, Dworkin's description of 'law as integrity' in *Law's Empire*[4] seems to differ only in degree of elaboration from Cardozo's account of 'the judge as legislator' in *The Nature of the Judicial Process*.[5] So I find it hard to see what the force of the phrase 'one right answer' is supposed to be. Dworkin's polemics against legal realism appear as no more than an attempt to sound a note of Kantian moral rigorism as he continues to do exactly the sort of thing the legal realists wanted done.[6] I think Margaret Radin is right when she says that Dworkin's criticism of pragmatism amounts to little more than 'gerrymandering the word "pragmatism" to mean crass instrumentalism'.[7]

Since neither Dworkin nor Richard Posner nor Roberto Unger has any use for what Posner calls 'formalism' – namely 'the idea that legal questions can be answered by inquiry into the relation between concepts'[8] – it seems plausible to claim that the battles that the legal realists fought in alliance with Dewey have essentially been won.[9] The interesting issues now seem to cluster around formalism in a wider sense, one that Unger defines as 'a commitment to . . . a method of legal justification that contrasts with open-ended disputes about the basic terms of social life, disputes that people call ideological, philosophical, or visionary'.[10]

Even under this broader definition of formalism, however, it is not so easy to find a good example of a formalist among legal theorists. Dworkin sometimes suggests that judges are prevented by their office from being open-ended in this way, although theorists are not. Dworkin proposes that helping the law work itself pure by means of an ever more radical egalitarianism is a matter not for 'the princes of law's empire' – the judges – but rather for philosophers, the 'seers and prophets of that empire'.[11] But Dworkin is ambiguous on the question of whether Hercules, in his official capacity, can take heed of open-ended disputes of the sort Unger has in mind. On the one hand, Dworkin says that the work of CLS theorists is 'useful to Hercules', but on the other, he warns that CLS may be merely 'an anachronistic attempt' to make legal realism – 'that dated movement' – reflower.[12] Yet surely CLS adherents like Allan Hutchinson and Peter Gabel are not interested in formulating a general theory of the sort exemplified by legal realism. Instead, they are, if you like, interested in being useful to Hercules. They want to open up the discourse of the legal profession to issues that Hercules will eventually find raised in half of the briefs he must read.

For myself, I find it hard to discern any interesting *philosophical* differences between Unger, Dworkin and Posner; their differences strike me as entirely political, as differences about how much change and what sort of change American institutions need. All three have visionary notions, but their visions are different. I do not think that one has to broaden the sense of 'pragmatist' very far to include all three men under this accommodating rubric.

The very ease by which these three men are accommodated under this rubric illustrates the banality of pragmatism. Pragmatism was reasonably shocking 70 years ago, but in the ensuing decades it has gradually been absorbed into American common sense. Nowadays, Allan Bloom and Michael Moore seem to be the only people who still think pragmatism is dangerous to the moral health of our society.[13] Posner, therefore, raises a good question when he asks whether the so-called 'new' pragmatists have anything to contribute – anything that we have not already internalized as a result of being taught by people who were raised on Dewey.[14]

My own answer to this question is that the new pragmatism differs from the old in just two respects, only one of which is of much interest to people who are not philosophy professors. The first is that we new pragmatists talk about language instead of experience, or mind, or consciousness, as the old pragmatists did. The second respect is that we have all read Kuhn, Hanson, Toulmin and Feyerabend, and have thereby become suspicious of the term 'scientific method'.[15] New pragmatists wish that Dewey, Sidney Hook and Ernest Nagel had not insisted on using this term as a catchphrase, since we are unable to provide anything distinctive for it to denote.[16]

As far as I can determine, it is only these doubts about scientific method, and thus about method in general, that might matter for legal theory. The first respect in which the new pragmatism is new – its switch from experience to language – has offered philosophy professors some fruitful new ways to pose old issues of atomism-vs.-holism and representationalism-vs.-anti-representationalism (as in the controversies between Hilary Putnam and David Lewis, Donald Davidson and Michael Dummett, Daniel Dennett and Jerry Fodor). But these issues are pretty remote from the concerns of nonphilosophers.[17] By contrast, as Judge Posner's article shows,[18] *method* can still seem important.

Posner says that 'lack of method' was 'a great weakness' of legal realism.[19] He distinguishes between 'scientific philosophy' and 'social science . . . the application of scientific method to social behavior' and says that his own economic approach to law is 'rooted in and inspired by a belief in the intellectual power and pertinence of economics'.[20]

My own Kuhnian–Feyerabendian doubts about scientific method make me wish that Posner had been content with this last remark and not added the sentences about method. Social scientists, like novelists, poets, and politicians, occasionally come up with good ideas that judges can use. For all I know, the brand of economics that centres on considerations of efficiency may provide Hercules with some very useful ideas. But I am fairly certain that it would be hard for Posner to explain what was especially scientific about either the genesis or the application of these ideas.[21] My assurance on this point is the result of watching many philosophers try and fail to find an epistemic or methodological, as opposed to a sociological or moral, distinction between science and nonscience.[22]

I agree with Grey that one advantage of pragmatism is freedom from theory-guilt.[23] Another advantage is freedom from anxiety about one's scientificity. So I think it is in the spirit of Dewey to say that the test of the power and pertinence of a given social science is how it works when you try to apply it. The test of law and economics is whether judges agree in finding Posner's ideas useful when, as Grey puts it, 'interpreting tradition with one eye on coherence and the other on policy'.[24]

On the other hand, I agree with Posner that judges will probably not find pragmatist philosophers – either old or new – useful. Posner is right in saying that pragmatism clears the underbrush and leaves it to others to plant the forest.[25] I would add that the underbrush in question is mostly specifically philosophical underbrush. The 'new' pragmatism should, I think, be viewed merely as an effort to clear away some alder and sumac, which sprang up during a 30-year spell of wet philosophical weather – the period that we now look back on as 'positivistic analytic philosophy'. This clearance will restore the appearance of the terrain that Dewey landscaped, but it will not do more than that.

To accomplish more, and in particular to avoid the complacency that Radin rightly sees as the danger of coherence theories of know-ledge,[26] we have to turn to Dewey the prophet rather than Dewey the pragmatist philosopher. We have to read the Emersonian visionary rather than the contributor to *The Journal of Philosophy* who spent 40 years haggling over definitions of 'true' with McGilvary, Lovejoy, Russell, Lewis, Nagel and the rest. This is the Dewey whom Cornel West describes as calling for 'an Emersonian culture of radical democracy',[27] the Dewey who is grist for CLS mills. Like the 'prophetic pragmatism' for which West calls, this Dewey is 'a child of Protestant Christianity wedded to left romanticism'.[28]

No argument leads from a coherence view of truth, an anti-representationalist view of knowledge, and an antiformalist view of law and morals, to Dewey's left-looking social prophecies. The Heidegger of *Being and Time* shared all those views, but Heidegger looked rightward and dreamed different dreams.[29] These were anti-egalitarian, nostalgic dreams, which resembled those of T. S. Eliot and Allen Tate rather than the one that Dewey embodied in a quote from Keats:[30]

> [M]an should not dispute or assert, but whisper results to his neighbour, and thus, by every germ of spirit sucking the sap from mold etherial, every human being might become great, and Humanity instead of being a wide heath of Furze and briars with here and there a remote Pine or Oak, would become a grand democracy of Forest Trees![31]

This romantic side of Dewey is not banal. When one comes across such passages as this, one wakes out of the slumber induced by what Grey calls 'the good gray liberal expound[ing] the mild virtues of the theoretic middle way'.[32] But this side of Dewey is not distinctively *pragmatist* either. These passages do not let one know, as Grey rightly says Wallace Stevens does, what it *feels like* to be a pragmatist – what it feels like to have overcome the dualisms of fiction and reality, imagination and reason. The pragmatists provided good philosophical arguments against some of the philosophical presuppositions of formalism. Yet the success of the revolt against formalism that Morton White describes, the revolt whose success lets us find much of Dewey platitudinous, owed as much to visionary carrots as to argumentative sticks.

Dewey's Keatsian vision was shared by many social democrats in many countries at the turn of the century.[33] As Putnam rightly says, it is not a vision that can be successfully backed up by a Habermas–Apel style argument about the presuppositions of rational discourse.[34] But visions do not really need backup. To put forth a vision is always one of Fitzjames Stephen's 'leaps in the dark'.[35] Thus, insofar as we late-comers can get more than platitudes from Dewey, it will be because we are able to read our own specific egalitarian hopes into his generic ones, not because we can still use his antiformalist arguments as weapons.

As examples of attempts to actualize specific hopes, consider such debatable decisions as *Brown* v. *Board of Education*,[36] *Roe* v. *Wade*,[37] Judge Sand's recent decision that begging is a first amendment right,[38] various state supreme court decisions holding that all school districts within the state must have the same per-pupil expenditure, and some future Supreme Court decision that will strike down anti-sodomy laws. These are cases in which the courts have done, or might do, what Posner claims 'the pragmatic counsel . . . to the legal system' would warn them against.[39] They have 'roil[ed] needlessly the political waters'.[40] They have 'prematurely nationalized an issue [that many thought] best left to simmer longer at the state and local level until a consensus based on experience with a variety of approaches . . . emerged'.[41]

Undoubtedly, an ideally unromantic and bland pragmatist would offer such advice, but Dewey the visionary would not. Dewey the romantic would have been delighted that the courts sometimes tell the politicians and the voters to start noticing that there are people who have been told to wait for ever until a consensus emerges – a consensus within a political community from which these people are effectively excluded.[42] Dewey the pragmatist would not, I think, have accepted Dworkin's quasi-Kantian claim that in these cases the courts were simply 'taking rights seriously' rather than being visionary – for he would have thought 'rights' a good example of what Posner calls 'the law's metaphysical balloons'.[43] Unlike Dworkin, Dewey would not have attempted to formulate a general legal theory that justified the practice of making leaps in the constitutional dark.[44] Rather, I imagine Dewey would say that to suddenly notice previously existing but hitherto invisible constitutional rights is just the quaint way in which our courts are required to express a conviction that the political waters badly need roiling.

In the terms Radin uses, this conviction can be restated as the claim that a paradigm shift is needed in order to break up 'bad coherence'.[45] Such a shift can be initiated when visionary judges conspire to prevent their brother Hercules, the 'complacent pragmatist judge' whom Radin describes, from perpetuating such coherence. The cheer we egalitarians raise at such breakthroughs into romance – at such examples of the poetry of justice – is, I think, what justifies Posner's statement that although it was 'not . . . a good judicial opinion', Holmes's *Lochner* dissent was 'the greatest judicial opinion of the last hundred years'.[46] I read that dissent as saying, in part, 'Like it or not, gentlemen, trade unions are part of our country too.' I think of *Brown* as saying that, like it or not, black children are children too. I think of *Roe* as saying that, like it or not, women get to make hard decisions too, and of some hypothetical future reversal of *Bowers* v. *Hardwick*[47] as saying that, like it or not, gays are grown-ups too.

I can share Dworkin's and Ely's concerns over the 'unprincipled' character of such decisions – their concern at the possibility that equally romantic and visionary, yet morally appalling, decisions may be made by pragmatist judges whose dreams are Eliotic or Heideggerian rather than Emersonian or Keatsian. But as a pragmatist, I do not believe that legal theory offers us a defence against such judges – that it can do much to prevent another *Dred Scott* decision. In particular, I do not see that such judges will have more or less 'integrity' than those who decided *Brown* or *Roe*. I agree with Grey when he says: 'Pragmatism rejects the maxim that you can only beat a theory with a better theory . . . No rational God guarantees in advance that important areas of practical activity will be governed by elegant theories.'[48]

Further, I think that pragmatism's *philosophical* force is pretty well exhausted once this point about theories has been absorbed. But, in American intellectual life, 'pragmatism' has stood for more than just a set of controversial philosophical arguments about truth, knowledge, and theory. It has also stood for a visionary tradition to which, as it happened, a few philosophy professors once made particularly important contributions – a tradition to which some judges, lawyers, and law professors still make important contributions. These are the ones who, in their opinions, or briefs, or articles, enter into what Unger calls 'open-ended disputes about the basic terms of social life'.[49]

* * * *

NOTES

1 T. Grey, 'Holmes and Legal Pragmatism', *Stanford Law Review* (1989), vol. 41, pp. 787, 814.

2 T. Grey, 'Hear the Other Side: Wallace Stevens and Pragmatist Legal Theory', *Southern California Law Review* (1990), vol. 63, pp. 1569, 1590.

3 M. White, *Social Thought in America: The Revolt Against Formalism* (1949).

4 R. Dworkin, *Law's Empire* (1986), pp. 176–275.

5 B. Cardozo, *The Nature of the Judicial Process* (1921).

6 See Woozley, 'No Right Answer' in *Ronald Dworkin and Contemporary Jurisprudence*, M. Cohen, ed. (1983), p. 173. In a reply to Woozley, Dworkin echoes Dewey by saying that 'a concept of truth that somehow escapes the fact that all our concepts, including our philosophical concepts, take the only meaning they have from the function they play in our reasoning, argument, and conviction' is a 'mirage'. Dworkin, 'A Reply by Ronald Dworkin' in *Ronald Dworkin and Contemporary Jurisprudence*, pp. 247, 277. Dworkin's reply ends by saying that he is content with the statement that 'in hard cases at law one answer might be the most reasonable of all, even though competent lawyers will disagree about which answer is the most reasonable' (p. 278). This gloss neutralizes whatever antipragmatist and antilegal realist force there might have been in the 'one right answer' slogan.

On Dworkin's view (with which pragmatists heartily agree) that 'objectivity' (in a sense interestingly different from 'intersubjectivity') is an unnecessary notion for an accurate description of the decisionmaking process, see Dworkin, *Law's Empire*, p. 267.

7 M. Radin, 'The Pragmatist and the Feminist', *Southern California Law Review* (1990), vol. 63, pp. 1699, 1722.

8 R. Posner, 'What Has Pragmatism to Offer Law?', *Southern California Law Review* (1990), vol. 63, pp. 1653, 1663.

9 The battles have been won among theorists, if not among the more recently appointed members of the Supreme Court. The latter have not garnered much supporting theory for their views; E. D. Hirsch, Jr, the leading representative of intentionalism in the theory of interpretation, was quick to disassociate himself from their use of the concept of 'the Framers' intention'. See E. D. Hirsch, Jr, 'Counterfactuals in Interpretation' in *Interpreting Law and Literature*, S. Levinson and S. Mailloux, eds. (1988), pp. 55–68.

10 R. Unger, *The Critical Legal Studies Movement* (1986), vol. 1.

11 See Dworkin, *Law's Empire*, p. 407.

12 Dworkin, *Law's Empire*, pp. 272–3.

13 See A. Bloom, *The Closing of the American Mind* (1986); M. Moore, 'A Natural Law Theory of Interpretation', *Southern California Law Review* (1985), vol. 58, p. 277.

14 Posner, pp. 1658–9.

15 The two respects in which the new pragmatism differs from the old are connected, in that without the so-called 'linguistic turn', the question of 'theory-neutral observation language' would not have been posed. Without Carnap's and Hempel's attempts to develop logics of confirmation and explanation by treating theories and (potentially axiomatizable) as sets of propositions whose ultimate deductive consequences could be phrased in such an observation language, this question would not have seemed urgent. Also, without Quine's attack on the analytic-synthetic distinction, and Sellars's attack on the notion of 'pure sense-datum report', Kuhn's reception would have been colder than it was.

16 For reasons why Dewey's use of that phrase was misleading and unhelpful, see my own introduction to *The Later Works of John Dewey* (Carbondale, Ill.: Southern Illinois University Press, 1986), vol. VIII, pp. ix–xviii, and also my 'Pragmatism without Method' in *Sidney Hook: Philosopher of Democracy and Humanism*, P. Kurtz, ed. (1983), reprinted in my *Objectivism, Relativism, and Truth* (1991).

17 Insofar as concern with language as such has entered into legal theory, it has done so in the form of the 'deconstructionist' wing of the CLS movement. For some powerfully argued criticisms of the claim that deconstructionism has something to contribute to legal theory, see Williams, 'Critical Legal Studies: The Death of Transcendence and the Rise of the New Langdells', *New York University Legal Review* (1987), vol. 62, p. 429. Whereas Radin suggests that with Dewey you do not need Derrida, see Radin, p. 1719, Williams's point is that if you have Wittgenstein, you do not need Derrida. I think the latter claim is slightly more accurate, since the later Wittgenstein updates Dewey by working out a nonrepresentationalist approach to *language*, as opposed to a nonrepresentationalist approach to inquiry. Wittgenstein thus lets one meet the deconstructionists on their own turf.

18 Posner, pp. 1658–9.

19 Ibid., p. 1659.

20 Ibid., pp. 1668–9.

21 For some scepticism about the scientificity of economics, see D. McCloskey, *The Rhetoric of Economics* (1985).

22 See my own 'Natural Science a Natural Kind?' in *Construction and Constraint: The Shaping of Scientific Rationality*, E. McMullin, ed. (1988), p. 49, reprinted in my *Objectivity, Relativism and Truth*.

23 See Grey, 'Hear the Other Side', p. 1569.

24 Grey, 'Holmes and Legal Pragmatism'.

25 Posner, p. 1670.

26 Radin, p. 1710.

27 C. West, *The American Evasion of Philosophy: A Genealogy of Pragmatism* (1989), p. 104.

28 West, p. 227.

29 See M. Heidegger, *Auf der Erfahrung des Denkens* (1954).

30 On the overlap between Dewey and Heidegger, see M. Okrent, *Heidegger's Pragmatism* (1988), pp. 3–10, 280–1.

31 J. Dewey, *Art as Experience* (1934), p. 347.

32 Grey, 'Hear the Other Side', p. 1592.

33 See J. Kloppenberg, *Uncertain Victory: Social Democracy and Progressivism in European and American Thought 1870–1920* (1986), pp. 26–7.

34 H. Putnam, 'A Reconsideration of Deweyan Democracy', *Southern California Legal Review* (1990), vol. 63, pp. 1671, 1687–8.

35 Putnam, pp. 1693–4.

36 347 US (1954), p. 483.

37 410 US (1973), p. 113.

38 *Young* v. *New York City Transit Authority*, 729 F. Supp. (SDNY 1970), p. 341, revised in part, vacated in part, 903 F. 2d (2d Cir. 1990), p. 146.

39 Posner, p. 1668.

40 Posner, p. 1668.

41 Posner, p. 1663.

42 It might be objected that this phrase is inapplicable to *Roe* v. *Wade*, since women are included in the relevant community. I am not sure they are, both on Ely-like grounds of under-representation and on the vaguer but more powerful ground that (as banners at a pro-choice demonstration recently put it) 'if men got pregnant, they would have made abortion a sacrament'.

43 See Posner, p. 1663.

44 See Farber, 'Legal Pragmatism and the Constitution', Minnesota Legal Review (1988, vol. 72), p. 1331. I agree with Farber that we do not need 'a unified principle that would provide the basis for judicial decisions' (p. 1334) and with Farber's criticism of Dworkin's attacks on pragmatism (pp. 1343–9). But I think that Farber concedes too much to the opposition when he says that a 'principled pragmatism is far from being an oxymoron' (p. 1337) and also when he contests John Hart Ely's claim that 'when a majority has chosen to invade an arguably fundamental right, courts have no principled way of determining whether the right should be considered fundamental' (p. 1355). Farber is right, of course, if what he means by 'principled' in these contexts is simply susceptible to being supported by a reasonable argument – but this is not what Dworkin and Ely mean. Dworkin and Ely want a distinction between principle and policy, which pragmatism must refuse them.

45 Radin, p. 1710.

46 R. Posner, *Law and Literature* (1988), p. 285. I am grateful to George Rutherglen for helping me see that Harlan's dissent in *Lochner* was, romance apart, a far better example of what one expects judicial opinions to look like. I am also grateful to him for looking over a draft of this article and saving me from some howlers.

47 478 US (1986), p. 186.

48 Grey, 'Holmes and Legal Pragmatism', pp. 814–15.

49 See Unger.

6. Pragmatism and Law: A Response to David Luban

(1996)

Judge Posner's 'Pragmatic Adjudication'[1] is enormously refreshing. It cuts through an immense amount of tiresome and pointless talk about 'the nature of law' and 'the relation of law to politics' and gets down to the question: how should appellate court judges in a particular country at a particular time do their work? It not only argues lucidly for a particular answer to that question, but it also gives a good sense of what it must be like to be in Judge Posner's shoes. Posner helps you understand what sorts of things judges have to worry about, and what sorts of self-doubt they experience. His frankness about the need – given certain specifically American conditions – for judicial rule-making is as cheering as it is infrequent. His claim that judges would be blameworthy if they failed to have emotional reactions to certain statutes, and his reminder that, in the end, every society has to trust its wise elders, are similarly illuminating.

If, having read Posner, you wish there were more judges like him, you might nevertheless agree (as I do) with Thomas Grey that these desirable judges need never have considered, and can forever remain in blithe ignorance of the pragmatist philosopher's critiques of metaphysics and epistemological foundationalism.[2] Though Posner himself has read lots of pragmatist and nonpragmatist philosophers, another judge, one who would endorse everything in Posner's paper, might well have read so little philosophy as to have no views whatever on such questions as:

(1) Should true beliefs be thought of (a) as accurate representations of reality, or (b) as useful rules of action?

(2) Does reality (a) have an intrinsic nature which we must try to discover, or (b) are all possible descriptions of it equally relational and

extrinsic, in the sense of having been chosen in order to gratify various human needs and interests?

(3) Are the traditional problems of metaphysics and epistemology (a) inevitably encountered by any reflective mind, or (b) do they arise only in certain sociocultural situations? Should we try (a) to solve them, or, (b) by altering our own sociocultural situation, to dissolve them?

(4) Do we think because (a) we take pleasure (as David Luban puts it) 'in the rapt, silent, yet active contemplation of truths, regardless of whether they pay'[3] or (b) in order to solve problems?

I think Grey is right to suggest that this philosophical ignoramus could, *ceteris paribus*, be just as good a judge as Posner. We want our judges to have read widely – to be cultivated men and women – but if one judge cannot read novels, another cannot read economics, and still another cannot read metaphysics and epistemology, that is no great matter. Somebody can be cultivated even if he or she has a few blind spots. Many useful political thinkers and agents seem to have found metaphysics and epistemology pretty silly. Thomas Jefferson professed himself unable to read Plato, despite repeated attempts. He showed no interest whatever in the epistemological works of Hume and Locke, though he sopped up their political writings. Some people just cannot hack metaphysics and epistemology (or even metaethics), but that does not prevent them from successfully fulfilling their sociopolitical functions.

What about the judge who does enjoy reading philosophy, but has bad philosophical taste? This judge answers 'a!' to each of the above questions. Would her commitment to these wrong answers make her less ready to accept Posner's description of how she should do her job? I cannot see why it should. Such a judge might be thoroughly sympathetic to Posner's account of what our country needs from its appellate courts, even though she is also thoroughly sympathetic to John Searle's warnings against the baneful influence if Kuhn, Derrida and Rorty.[4] If Posner had used some buzzword like 'holist' to contrast with 'positivist', instead of using 'pragmatist', his colleague might never have suspected that Posner would – or so I fondly imagine – answer 'b!' to all of the above test questions.

Suppose she finds out that she disagrees with Posner on all matters epistemological, metaphysical, metaethical and metaphilosophical. Once she recovers from the initial shock, I suspect this would matter as little to their collaboration on the bench as her discovery that Posner is an atheist (while she is a cradle Catholic who has never had any serious doubts about the faith, even though she regards the present pope as an old fuddyduddy). Few of Jefferson's contemporaries could have imagined that one day you would see atheistical and devout jurists sitting around the same table, arguing out, peaceably and fruitfully, the constitutionality of legal barriers to gay marriage. But one of the nice things about contemporary America is that such arguments take place all the time. The concluding section of Grey's paper helps one see how this is possible.

Like Grey, I have trouble 'seeing how . . . Rorty's metaphysical[5] anti-realism (or alternatively Putnam's "internal realism") – is supposed to help deal with those "real human problems" which the pragmatists say philosophers should work on'.[6] But, as Grey goes on to say, not all pragmatist philosophy professors should spend all their time on real human problems. Some of us are detailed to work part-time on, for example, Searle.[7] We carry out this assignment by refining still further the ever more complex and technical arguments for 'b' and against 'a'. Searle is to us as Cardinal Ratzinger is to Hans Küng and his allies. Küng hopes that his church will spend less time on theology and more on real human problems, and that the future will hold ever fewer Ratzingers. But, trained as a theologian, he serves a useful function by doing his little reactive thing – even while foreseeing that thing's eventual obsolescence.

David Luban and I disagree on this question of obsolescence. He is inclined to answer 'a' to question (3) above, though doubtless he would add some qualifications. Luban sees something like a natural order of argument stretching from jurisprudence to philosophy. He sees metaphysical and epistemological disputes not as optional, but as inevitable once one presses, Socratically, for justification of morally significant decisions. He says, for example:

> The Supreme Court's 'inviolability of the human personality'
> [a phrase the court used in deciding a case about the right to

self-incrimination] may best be understood as a secular counterpart of the immortal soul that concerned the Inquisition. It is a
philosophical concept, and it is hard to see how the legal argument can stand free of the philosophical arguments that support
the conclusion that human personality is inviolable.[8]

I agree that this phrase refers to a secular counterpart of the immortal
soul, but I am not sure I know what philosophical arguments Luban has
in mind. I think of Kant, for example, as having used this inviolability as
a premise rather than having deduced it as a conclusion. More generally, I think of Enlightenment thinkers as having said: the immortality
of the human soul needs argument, but the dignity of human beings
does not. We can peel off our moral intuitions from the theological
premises from which they were once deduced – intuitions which, had
we lacked a religious upbringing, we might not have had. We can
hold these intuitive truths to be self-evident.

Suppose the Court, when asked why it thought that the human
personality is inviolable, replied that this principle is embedded in the
beliefs of most Americans, that it is central to our moral and legal
tradition, and that the Court is not about to look behind it for premises
from which it might be inferred. This would be a move like the one
Rawls makes when he says that his conception of justice is 'political,
not metaphysical',[9] and when he responds to Habermas that

[j]ustice as fairness is substantive . . . in the sense that it springs
from and belongs to the tradition of liberal thought and the
larger community of political culture of democratic societies. It
fails then to be properly formal and truly universal, and thus to be
part of the quasi-transcendental presuppositions (as Habermas
sometimes says) established by the theory of communicative
action.[10]

Suppose that the Court, in response to a request for philosophical
backup, simply cited this passage, and similar passages in Rawls.
Suppose it just said: we don't have a philosophical argument, we just
have an appeal to American common sense. Would this be to make
the American legal system what Luban calls 'a regime of force imposed

on a domain of cynicism'?[11] Would it no longer be such a regime if the Court quoted, and convinced people by quoting, the parts of Rawls which offer what Luban calls 'the fair-play argument of Hart and Rawls'?[12] Is the difference between the indirect appeal to intuition made by the premises of a fair-play argument and the direct appeal to common sense and tradition really that big a deal? Does the difference between the latter appeal and an appeal to the quasitranscendental, the difference between Rawls and Habermas (whose theory of communicative action is a sort of surrogate for metaphysics and epistemology), matter all that much?

My sense is that it does not, but Luban clearly differs, and I am not sure how to argue the point. I take Grey to have already answered, in the concluding section of his paper, the rhetorical question with which Luban ends his: '[H]ow can legal pragmatism stand free of first philosophy, of metaphysics, metaethics, and epistemology?'[13] Grey's account of the common ground which he and his evangelical friend manage to find, common ground which would enable them to work together as Posner-style judges, seems to me perfectly plausible.

All I can add to what Grey has already done is to remark that the kind of religious believer Luban and Grey have in mind – the kind whose appeal to Scripture is backed up with what Luban calls 'a handful of beliefs that are straightforwardly philosophical'[14] – is pretty rare. Even Thomists do not try to give an argument from unaided natural reason for including *Leviticus* in the scriptural canon, much less for coming down hard on 18:22 while weaselling out of obedience to all those other divine commandments (the dress code, for example). Kierkegaardians and Tillichians, and most listeners to the televangelists, would not dream of trying to give such arguments, even for belief in the existence of God. They have *faith*, and do not think they need to answer Socratic questions (nor that Euthyphro needed to). The Grey/Luban philosophy buff who is also a fundamentalist is a helpful fantasy, but I have never run into anybody much like her.

Let me conclude with some more general remarks on the relation between philosophy and the rest of culture. Luban offers three conceptions of philosophy to choose from: intellectual hygiene, '*strengere Wissenschaft* aimed at formulating, analyzing, and once and for all settling questions',[15] and Arendt's Heidegger-like view that 'philosophy doesn't aim to solve problems and doesn't seek to make progress'.[16] Luban assimilates this third view to Wilfrid Sellars's definition of philosophy as 'how things in the broadest possible sense of the term hang together in the broadest sense of the term'.[17]

I favour a fourth conception, one which also incorporates Sellars's definition. My conception entails neither that philosophy does not seek to make progress, nor Arendt's suggestion that 'the aim of philosophy is not an increase in knowledge, but an attempt to understand the *meaning* of whatever it is that the philosopher is thinking about'.[18]

This emphasis on *meaning* goes hand-in-hand with the view – currently held by Stanley Cavell, Thomas Nagel and Barry Stroud, among others – that the deepest and most important philosophical problems come naturally to the human mind, and arise independently of that mind's sociohistorical circumstances.[19] It also goes along with Luban's claim that

> [p]hilosophical problems ... begin with a distinction that we use in everyday life, for example the distinction between voluntary and involuntary action, or between justified and unjustified belief. A philosophical problem arises because it turns out that natural arguments show that the distinction is specious or inexplicable.[20]

Contrast this view, which tempts people to answer 'a!' to question (3) above, with Dewey's view that

> [w]hen it is acknowledged that under disguise of dealing with ultimate reality philosophy has been occupied with the precious values embedded in social traditions, that it has sprung from a clash of social ends and from a conflict of inherited institutions with incompatible contemporary tendencies, it will be seen that the task of future philosophy is to clarify men's ideas as to the social and moral strifes of their own day.[21]

The sort of clarification of ideas that Dewey recommends is not the same as Arendt's 'attempt to understand the *meaning* of whatever it is that the philosopher is thinking about'.[22] Arendt thought that she and

Socrates were both thinking about a lot of the same things: justice, for example. For Dewey, we and Socrates can't really think about many of the same things, because the problems we are trying to solve are so different. We live in different times, believe a lot of different things, and have different senses of what is relevant to what. There are some abstract similarities between justice then and justice now, but these similarities neither help formulate the current problems, nor provide much help in solving them. (Analogously, there are some abstract similarities between Democritus' and Bohr's atoms, but there is an obvious sense in which these two scientists were not talking about the same things.)

I think Dewey's description of philosophy can be synthesized with Sellars's by saying that the 'things' which the philosopher wants to make hang together keep changing. Philosophy has and will make progress, at least if one agrees with Dewey, that we have been making a lot of moral, political and social progress in recent centuries. For philosophical progress piggybacks on this latter sort of progress. We philosophers do not have a *strengere Wissenschaft* nowadays, but the things we are trying to make hang together are bigger and better than the things Socrates talked about.

They are bigger in the sense that they are much more complicated. They are better in that we live in a better age of the world: one in which the idea of finding an authority to which to subject ourselves is gradually getting replaced by the idea of coming to an agreement among ourselves. Socrates, or at any rate the Socrates of Plato's *Republic*, wanted an unwobbling pivot, something that would stay fixed for ever and serve as a guiding star. So did St Thomas and Luther, and so did the thinkers of the Enlightenment who made much of the notions of 'Reason' and 'Science' and 'Nature'.

We are better off than these intellectual ancestors because we have a lot of historical knowledge about how and why such stars first blazed, and then faded out – knowledge which has made us wonder whether we might not be able to get along without any such stars. The switch in modern philosophy from what Habermas calls 'subject-centred reason' to what he calls 'communicative reason' – a change which Dewey embodies best – is a recognition of the historical contingency

of philosophical problems, and of sociopolitical vocabularies and institutions. That switch is the most recent version of the revolt against
authority which found expression first in the Reformation, and then
in the Enlightenment.

For Deweyans, the whole idea of 'authority' is suspect. We can still
say, if we like, that the American legal system possesses a legitimate
authority, and that we have an obligation to obey our country's laws.
But we should not press either point. Dewey preferred to skip talk of
'authority', 'legitimacy' and 'obligation' and to talk instead about
'applied intelligence' and 'democracy'. He hoped we would stop
using the juridical vocabulary which Kant made fashionable among
philosophers, and start using metaphors drawn from town meetings
rather than from tribunals. He wanted the first question of both
politics and philosophy to be not, 'What is legitimate?' or, 'What is
authoritative?' but, 'What can we get together and agree on?' This is
the strand in Dewey's thought which Rawls, especially in his later
writings, has picked up and developed.

Posner's vision of the function of American judges – his vision of
their ability to travel back and forth between the present and the
future and to try to fashion a moral unity out of our national history
– fits nicely into Dewey's way of thinking. Nor is Posner's vision very
different, I suspect, from that of most Americans who take an interest
in what the courts, and especially the Supreme Court, are up to – at
least those who are grateful for the Court's decision in *Brown* v. *Board
of Education*.[23] For those who believe that the Civil Rights Movement,
the movement which *Brown* initiated, was an enormous boost to
our national self-respect and a reassuring instance of our continuing
capacity for moral progress, the thought that the courts do not just
apply rules, but make them, is no longer frightening. Nor is the
Deweyan suggestion that it is a waste of effort to try to figure out just
where, in *Brown* and in similar decisions, finding and applying old law
stops and making new law begins.

Luban is nostalgic for unwobbling pivots, for the kind of authority
which is supposed to be possessed by those raptly and silently contem-
plated truths of which he speaks. Luban uses the same language as
Kant, who thought that only the fixed and eternal could fill the mind

with awe (e.g. 'the starry heavens above, and the moral law within'[24]).
He fears that without respect for the authority of the fixed and eternal,
we shall become Trattenbachers: 'Take away Plato and you take away
Euclid. Take away Euclid and you find yourself in Trattenbach. Athens
or Trattenbach: there is no third way.'[25] This seems to me just wrong.
We have been inventing alternatives to both Athens and Trattenbach
for a long time. Of these, contemporary America, warts and all, is the
best so far discovered.

The wise elders whom Posner describes, doing their best to keep
America intact by keeping out political responses to surprising developments in harmony with our moral intuitions and our national traditions,
are, and deserve to be, revered. As our presidents, political parties
and legislators become ever more corrupt and frivolous, we turn to
the judiciary as the only political institution for which we can still feel
something like awe. This awe is not reverence for the Euclid-like
immutability of Law. It is respect for the ability of decent men and
women to sit down around tables, argue things out and arrive at a
reasonable consensus.

* * * *

NOTES

1 Richard Posner, 'Pragmatic Adjudication', *Cardozo Law Review* (1996), vol.
18, p. 1.

2 Thomas C. Grey, 'Freestanding Legal Pragmatism', *Cardozo Law Review*
(1996), vol. 18, p. 21.

3 David Luban, 'What's Pragmatic about Legal Pragmatism?', *Cardozo Law
Review* (1996), vol. 18, p. 43.

4 See John Searle, 'Rationality and Realism: What is at Stake', *Daedelus* (1992),
vol. 22, pp. 55–84.

5 I prefer Luban's description of me as a 'postphilosophical pragmatist' to
Grey's suggestion that I still hold a metaphysical view. But I see what Grey
means.

6 Grey, p. 32.

7 See Searle above and my reply, John Searle on Realism and Relativism in my *Truth and Progress*.

8 Luban, 'What's Pragmatic about Legal Pragmatism?', p. 64.

9 See John Rawls, 'Justice as Fairness: Political, not Metaphysical', *Philosophy and Public Affairs* (195), vol. 14, p. 225.

10 John Rawls, 'Reply to Habermas', *Journal of Philosophy* (1995), vol. 92, p. 179.

11 Luban, 'What's Pragmatic about Legal Pragmatism?', p. 65.

12 I am not quite sure what argument Luban has in mind here, but I think that it would be hard to find in Hart or Rawls an attempt to ground anything in 'a metaphysical conception of personality and human dignity'.

13 Luban, 'What's Pragmatic about Legal Pragmatism?', p. 73.

14 Luban, 'What's Pragmatic about Legal Pragmatism?', p. 73.

15 Luban, 'What's Pragmatic about Legal Pragmatism?', p. 51.

16 Luban, 'What's Pragmatic about Legal Pragmatism?', p. 52.

17 Luban, 'What's Pragmatic about Legal Pragmatism?', pp. 52–3 (quoting Wilfrid Sellars, *Science, Preception and Reality* (1963), vol. 1).

18 Luban, 'What's Pragmatic about Legal Pragmatism?', p. 52.

19 Luban cites Nagel's metaphilosophical view with approval in his long, complex and valuable article 'Doubts about the New Pragmatism', reprinted in David Luban, *Legal Modernism* (1994), p. 132. He also argues in that article that 'the neopragmatists have drastically misunderstood Wittgenstein' by treating him as one of themselves (p. 131). Luban has a point. Wittgenstein did, indeed, recoil in distaste from the realization that what he was saying sounded like pragmatism. So did Nietzsche. The question is whether it is these men's pragmatist-like views, or their last minute fears of turning into Trattenbachers, that most deserve our attention.

20 Luban, 'What's Pragmatic about Legal Pragmatism?', p. 54.

21 John Dewey, *Reconstruction in Philosophy, The Middle Works of John Dewey* (1982), vol. XI, p. 94. I have enlarged on this definition of Dewey's, and offered some examples of the strifes he was talking about, in Richard Rorty, 'Philosophy and the Future' in *Rorty and Pragmatism* (1994), pp. 197–205.

22 See Luban, 'What's Pragmatic about Legal Pragmatism?', p. 52.

23 347 US (1954), p. 483.

24 See the first sentence of the 'Conclusion' of *Immanuel Kant's Critique of Practical Reason*, Norman Kemp Smith, trans. (1929).

25 Luban, 'Doubts about the New Pragmatism', p. 129.

7. Education as Socialization and as Individualization

(1989)

When people on the political right talk about education, they immediately start talking about truth. Typically, they enumerate what they take to be familiar and self-evident truths and regret that these are no longer being inculcated in the young. When people on the political left talk about education, they talk first about freedom. The left typically views the old familiar truths cherished by the right as a crust of convention that needs to be broken through, vestiges of old-fashioned modes of thought from which the new generation should be freed.

When this opposition between truth and freedom becomes explicit, both sides wax philosophical and produce theories about the nature of truth and freedom. The right usually offers a theory according to which, if you have truth, freedom will follow automatically. Human beings, says this theory, have within them a truth-tracking faculty called 'reason', an instrument capable of uncovering the intrinsic nature of things. Once such obstacles as the passions or sin are overcome, the natural light of reason will guide us to the truth. Deep within our souls there is a spark that the right sort of education can fan into flame. Once the soul is afire with love of truth, freedom will follow – for freedom consists in realizing one's *true* self; that is, in the actualization of one's capacity to be rational. So, the right concludes, only the truth can make us free.

This Platonic picture of education as the awakening of the true self can easily be adapted to the needs of the left. The left dismisses Platonic asceticism and exalts Socratic social criticism. It identifies the obstacles to freedom that education must overcome not with the passions or with sin but with convention and prejudice. What the right calls 'overcoming the passions', the left calls 'stifling healthy animal instincts'. What the right thinks of as the triumph of reason, the left describes as the triumph of acculturation – acculturation engineered by the powers that be. What the right describes as civilizing the young, the left describes as alienating them from their true selves. In the tradition of Rousseau, Marx, Nietzsche and Foucault, the left pictures society as depriving the young of their freedom and of their essential humanity so that they may function as frictionless cogs in a vast, inhuman socioeconomic machine. So, for the left, the proper function of education is to make the young realize that they should not consent to this alienating process of socialization. On the leftist's inverted version of Plato, if you take care of freedom – especially political and economic freedom – truth will take care of itself. For truth is what will be believed once the alienating and repressive forces of society are removed.

On both the original, rightist and the inverted, leftist account of the matter, there is a natural connection between truth and freedom. Both argue for this connection on the basis of distinctions between nature and convention and between what is essentially human and what is inhuman. Both accept the identification of truth and freedom with the essentially human. The difference between them is simply over the question: Is the present socioeconomic set-up in accordance, more or less, with nature? Is it, on the whole, a realization of human potentialities, or rather a way of frustrating those potentialities? Will acculturation to the norms of our society produce freedom or alienation?

On abstract philosophical topics, therefore, the right and the left are largely in agreement. The interesting differences between right and left about education are concretely political. Conservatives think that the present set-up is, if not exactly good, at least better than any alternative suggested by the radical left. They think that at least some of the traditional slogans of our society, some pieces of its conventional wisdom, are the deliverances of 'reason'. That is why they think education should concentrate on resurrecting and re-establishing what they call 'fundamental truths which are now neglected or despised'. Radicals, in contrast, share Frank Lentricchia's view that the society in which we live is 'mainly unreasonable'. So they regard the conservative's 'fundamental truths' as what Foucault calls 'the discourse of power'. They think that continuing to inculcate the conventional wisdom amounts to betraying the students.

In the liberal democracies of recent times, the tension between these two attitudes has been resolved by a fairly simple, fairly satisfactory, compromise. The right has pretty much kept control of primary and secondary education and the left has gradually got control of non-vocational higher education. In America, our system of local school boards means that pre-college teachers cannot, in the classroom, move very far from the local consensus. By contrast, the success of the American Association of University Professors (AAUP) in enforcing academic freedom means that many college teachers set their own agendas. So education up to the age of 18 or 19 is mostly a matter of socialization – of getting the students to take over the moral and political common sense of the society as it is. It is obviously not only that, since sympathetic high school teachers often assist curious or troubled students by showing them where to find alternatives to this common sense. But these exceptions cannot be made the rule. For any society has a right to expect that, whatever else happens in the course of adolescence, the schools will inculcate most of what is generally believed.

Around the age of 18 or 19, however, American students whose parents are affluent enough to send them to reasonably good colleges find themselves in the hands of teachers well to the left of the teachers they met in high school. These teachers do their best to nudge each successive college generation a little more to the left, to make them a little more conscious of the cruelty built into our institutions, of the need for reform, of the need to be sceptical about the current consensus. Obviously this is not all that happens in college, since a lot of college is, explicitly or implicitly, vocational training. But our hope that colleges will be more than vocational schools is largely a hope that they will encourage such Socratic scepticism. We hope that the students can be distracted from their struggle to get into a high-paying profession, and that the professors will not *simply* try to reproduce themselves by preparing the students to enter graduate study in their own disciplines.

This means that most of the skirmishing about education between left and right occurs on the borders between secondary and higher education. Even ardent radicals, for all their talk of 'education for freedom', secretly hope that the elementary schools will teach the kids to wait their turn in line, not to shoot up in the johns, to obey the cop on the corner, and to spell, punctuate, multiply and divide. They do not really want the high schools to produce, every year, a graduating class of amateur Zarathustras. Conversely, only the most resentful and blinkered conservatives want to ensure that colleges hire only teachers who will endorse the status quo. Things get difficult when one tries to figure out where socialization should stop and criticism start.

This difficulty is aggravated by the fact that both conservatives and radicals have trouble realizing that education is not a continuous process from age five to age 22. Both tend to ignore the fact that the word 'education' covers two entirely distinct, and equally necessary, processes – socialization and individuation. They both fall into the trap of thinking that a single set of ideas will work for both high school and college education. That is why both have had trouble noticing the differences between Allan Bloom's *The Closing of the American Mind* and E. D. Hirsch's *Cultural Literacy*. The cultural left in America sees Bloom and Hirsch as examples of a single assault on freedom, twin symptoms of a fatuous Reaganite complacency. Conservatives, on the other hand, overlook the difference between Bloom's Straussian doubts about democracy and Hirsch's Deweyan hopes for a better educated democratic electorate: They think of both books as urging us to educate for truth, and to worry less about freedom.

Let me now put some of my own cards on the table. I think that Hirsch is largely right about the high schools and Bloom largely wrong about the colleges. I think that the conservatives are wrong in thinking that we have either a truth-tracking faculty called 'reason' or a true self that education brings to consciousness. I think that the radicals are right in saying that if you take care of political, economic, cultural and academic freedom, then truth will take care of itself. But I think the radicals are wrong in believing that there is a true self that will emerge once the repressive influence of society is removed. There is no such thing as human nature, in the deep sense in which Plato and Strauss use this term. Nor is there such a thing as alienation from one's essential humanity due to societal repression, in the deep sense made familiar by Rousseau and the Marxists. There is only the shaping of an animal into a human being by a process of socialization, followed (with luck) by the self-individualization and self-creation of that human being through his or her own later revolt against that very process. Hirsch is dead right in saying that we Americans no longer give our children a secondary education that enables them to function as citizens of a democracy. Bloom is dead wrong in thinking that the point of higher education is to help students grasp the 'natural' superiority of those who lead 'the theoretical life'. The point of non-vocational higher education is, instead, to help students realize that they can reshape themselves – that they can rework the self-image foisted on them by their past, the self-image that makes them competent citizens, into a new self-image, one that they themselves have helped to create.

I take myself, in holding these opinions, to be a fairly faithful follower of John Dewey. Dewey's great contribution to the theory of education was to help us get rid of the idea that education is a matter of either inducing or educing truth. Primary and secondary education will always be a matter of familiarizing the young with what their elders take to be true, whether it is true or not. It is not, and never will be, the function of lower-level education to challenge the prevailing consensus about what is true. Socialization has to come before individu-ation, and education for freedom cannot begin before some constraints have been imposed. But, for quite different reasons, non-vocational higher education is also not a matter of inculcating or educing truth. It is, instead, a matter of inciting doubt and stimulating imagination, thereby challenging the prevailing consensus. If pre-college education produces literate citizens and college education produces self-creating individuals, then questions about whether students are being taught the truth can safely be neglected.

Dewey put a new twist on the idea that if you take care of freedom, truth will take care of itself. For both the original Platonism of the right and the inverted Platonism of the left, that claim means that if you free the true self from various constraints it will automatically see truth. Dewey showed us how to drop the notion of 'the true self' and how to drop the distinction between nature and convention. He taught us to call 'true' whatever belief results from a free and open encounter of opinions, without asking whether this result agrees with something beyond that encounter. For Dewey, the sort of freedom that guarantees truth is not freedom from the passions or sin. Nor is it freedom from tradition or from what Foucault called 'power'. It is simply sociopolitical freedom, the sort of freedom found in bourgeois democracies. Instead of justifying democratic freedoms by reference to an account of human nature and the nature of reason, Dewey takes the desire to preserve and expand such freedoms as a starting point – something we need not look behind. Instead of saying that free and open encounters track truth by permitting a mythical faculty called 'reason' to function unfettered, he says simply that we have no better criterion of truth than that it is what results from such encounters.

This account of truth – the account that has recently been revived by Jürgen Habermas – amounts to putting aside the notion that truth is correspondence to reality. More generally, it puts aside the idea that inquiry aims at accurately representing what lies outside the human mind (whether this be conceived as the will of God, or the layout of Plato's realm of ideas, or the arrangement of atoms in the void). It thereby gets rid of the idea that sociopolitical institutions need to be 'based' on some such outside foundation.

For Dewey, as for Habermas, what takes the place of the urge to represent reality accurately is the urge to come to free agreement with our fellow human beings – to be full participating members of a free community of inquiry. Dewey offered neither the conservative's philosophical justification of democracy by reference to eternal values nor the radical's justification by reference to decreasing alienation. He did not try to justify democracy at all. He saw democracy not as founded upon the nature of man or reason or reality but as a promising experiment engaged in by a particular herd of a particular species of animal – our species and our herd. He asks us to put our faith in ourselves – in the utopian hope characteristic of a democratic community – rather than asking for reassurance or backup from outside.

This notion of a species of animals gradually taking control of its own evolution by changing its environmental conditions leads Dewey to say, in good Darwinian language, that 'growth itself is the moral end' and that to 'protect, sustain and direct growth is the chief *ideal* of education'. Dewey's conservative critics denounced him for fuzziness, for not giving us a criterion of growth. But Dewey rightly saw that any such criterion would cut the future down to the size of the present. Asking for such a criterion is like asking a dinosaur to specify what would make for a good mammal or asking a fourth-century Athenian to propose forms of life for the citizens of a twentieth-century industrial democracy.

Instead of criteria, Deweyans offer inspiring narratives and fuzzy utopias. Dewey had stories to tell about our progress from Plato to Bacon to the Mills, from religion to rationalism to experimentalism, from tyranny to feudalism to democracy. In their later stages, his stories merged with Emerson's and Whitman's descriptions of the democratic vistas – with their vision of America as the place where human beings will become unimaginably wonderful, different and free. For Dewey, Emerson's talent for criterionless hope was the essence of his value to his country. In 1903 Dewey wrote: '[T]he coming century may well make evident what is just now dawning, that Emerson is not only a philosopher, but that he is the Philosopher of Democracy.' Dewey's point was that Emerson did not offer truth, but simply hope. Hope – the ability to believe that the future will be unspecifiably different from, and unspecifiably freer than, the past – is the condition of growth. That sort of hope was all that Dewey himself offered us, and by offering it he became our century's Philosopher of Democracy.

Let me now turn to the topic of how a Deweyan conceives of the relation between pre-college and college education, between the need for socialization and the need to remove the barriers that socialization inevitably imposes. There is a standard caricature of Dewey's views that says Dewey thought that kids should learn to multiply or to obey the cop on the corner only if they have democratically chosen that lesson for the day, or only if this particular learning experience happens to meet their currently felt needs. This sort of nondirective nonsense was not what Dewey had in mind. It is true, as Hirsch says, that Dewey 'too hastily rejected "the piling up of information" '. But I doubt that it ever occurred to Dewey that a day would come when students could graduate from an American high school not knowing who came first, Plato or Shakespeare, Napoleon or Lincoln, Frederick Douglass or Martin Luther King, Jr. Dewey too hastily assumed that nothing would ever stop the schools from piling on the information and that the only problem was to get them to do other things as well.

Dewey was wrong about this. But he could not have foreseen the educationist establishment with which Hirsch is currently battling. He could not have foreseen that the United States would decide to pay its pre-college teachers a fifth of what it pays its doctors. Nor did he foresee that an increasingly greedy and heartless American middle class would let the quality of education a child receives become proportional to the assessed value of the parents' real estate. Finally, he did not foresee that most children would spend 30 hours a week watching televised fantasies, nor that the cynicism of those who produce these fantasies would carry over into our children's vocabularies of moral deliberation.

But Dewey's failures of prescience do not count against his account of truth and freedom. Nor should they prevent us from accepting his notion of the socialization American children should receive. For Dewey, this socialization consisted in acquiring an image of themselves as heirs to a tradition of increasing liberty and rising hope. Updating Dewey a bit, we can think of him as wanting the children to come to think of themselves as proud and loyal citizens of a country that, slowly and painfully, threw off a foreign yoke, freed its slaves, enfranchised its women, restrained its robber barons and licensed its trade unions, liberalized its religious practices, broadened its religious and moral tolerance, and built colleges in which 50 per cent of its population could enrol – a country that numbered Jefferson, Thoreau, Susan B. Anthony, Eugene Debs, Woodrow Wilson, Walter Reuther, Franklin

Delano Roosevelt, Rosa Parks and James Baldwin among its citizens. Dewey wanted the inculcation of this narrative of freedom and hope to be the core of the socializing process.

As Hirsch quite rightly says, that narrative will not be intelligible unless a lot of information gets piled up in the children's heads. Radical critics of Hirsch's books have assumed that he wants education to be a matter of memorizing lists rather than reading interesting books, but this does not follow from what Hirsch says. All that follows is that the students be examined on their familiarity with the people, things and events mentioned in those books. Hirsch's radical critics would sound more plausible if they offered some concrete suggestions about how to get such a narrative inculcated without setting examinations tailored to lists like Hirsch's or if they had some suggestions about how 18-year-olds who find *Newsweek* over their heads are to choose between political candidates.

Let us suppose, for a moment, that Hirsch's dreams came true. Suppose we succeed not only in inculcating such a narrative of national hope in most of our students but in setting it in the larger context of a narrative of world history and literature, all this against the background of the world picture offered by the natural scientists. Suppose, that is, that after pouring money into pre-college education, firing the curriculum experts, abolishing the licensing requirements, building brand new, magnificently equipped schools in the inner cities, and instituting Hirsch-like school-leaving examinations, it proves possible to make most American 19-year-olds as culturally literate as Dewey and Hirsch have dreamed they might be. What, in such a utopia, would be the educational function of American colleges? What would policymakers in higher education worry about?

I think all that they would then need to worry about would be finding teachers who were not exclusively concerned with preparing people to be graduate students in their various specialities and then making sure that these teachers get a chance to give whatever courses they feel like giving. They would still need to worry about making sure that higher education was not purely vocational – not simply a matter of fulfilling prerequisites for professional schools or reproducing current disciplinary matrices. They would not, however, have to worry about the integrity of the curriculum or about the challenge of connecting learning – any more than administrators in French and German universities worry about such things. That sort of worry would be left to secondary school administrators. If Hirsch's dreams ever come true, then the colleges will be free to get on with their proper business. That business is to offer a blend of specialized vocational training and provocation to self-creation.

The socially most important provocations will be offered by teachers who make vivid and concrete the failure of the country of which we remain loyal citizens to live up to its own ideals – the failure of America to be what it knows it ought to become. This is the traditional function of the reformist liberal left, as opposed to the revolutionary radical left. In recent decades, it has been the main function of American college teachers in the humanities and social sciences. Carrying out this function, however, cannot be made a matter of explicit institutional policy. For, if it is being done right, it is too complicated, controversial and tendentious to be the subject of agreement in a faculty meeting. Nor is it the sort of thing that can be easily explained to the governmental authorities or the trustees who supply the cash. It is a matter that has to be left up to individual college teachers to do or not do as they think fit, as their sense of responsibility to their students and their society inspires them. To say that, whatever their other faults, American colleges and universities remain bastions of academic freedom, is to say that the typical administrator would not dream of trying to interfere with a teacher's attempt to carry out such responsibilities.

In short, if the high schools were doing the job that lots of money and determination might make them able to do, the colleges would not have to worry about Great Books, or general education, or overcoming fragmentation. The faculty could just teach whatever seemed good to them to teach, and the administrators could get along nicely without much knowledge of what was being taught. They could rest content with making sure that teachers who want to teach a course that has never been taught before, or assign materials that have never been assigned before, or otherwise break out of the disciplinary matrix that some academic department has been perpetuating are free to do so –

as well as trying to ensure that teachers who might want to do such things get appointed to the faculty.

But, in the real world, the 19-year-olds arrive at the doors of the colleges not knowing a lot of the words on Hirsch's list. They still have to be taught a lot of memorizable conventional wisdom of the sort that gets dinned into the heads of their co-evals in other countries. So the colleges have to serve as finishing schools, and the administrators sometimes have to dragoon the faculty into helping with this task. As things unfortunately – and with luck only temporarily – are, the colleges have to finish the job of socialization. Worse yet, they have to do this when the students are already too old and too restless to put up with such a process. It would be well for the colleges to remind us that 19 is an age when young people should have finished absorbing the best that has been thought and said and should have started becoming suspicious of it. It would also be well for them to remind us that the remedial work that society currently forces college faculties to undertake – the kind of work that Great Books curricula are typically invented in order to carry out – is just an extra chore, analogous to the custodial functions forced upon the high school teachers. Such courses may, of course, be immensely valuable to students – as they were to Allan Bloom and me when we took them at the University of Chicago 40 years ago. Nevertheless, carrying out such remedial tasks is not the social function of colleges and universities.

We Deweyans think that the social function of American colleges is to help the students see that the national narrative around which their socialization has centred is an open-ended one. It is to tempt the students to make themselves into people who can stand to their own pasts as Emerson and Anthony, Debs and Baldwin, stood to *their* pasts. This is done by helping the students realize that, despite the progress that the present has made over the past, the good has once again become the enemy of the better. With a bit of help, the students will start noticing everything that is paltry and mean and unfree in their surroundings. With luck, the best of them will succeed in altering the conventional wisdom, so that the next generation is socialized in a somewhat different way than they themselves were socialized. To hope that this way will only be somewhat different is to hope that the society will remain reformist and democratic, rather than being convulsed by revolution. To hope that it will nevertheless be perceptibly different is to remind oneself that growth is indeed the only end that democratic higher education can serve and also to remind oneself that the direction of growth is unpredictable.

This is why we Deweyans think that, although Hirsch is right in asking, 'What should they know when they come out of high school?' and 'What remedial work remains, things being as they are, for the colleges to do?', the question, 'What should they learn in college?' had better go unasked. Such questions suggest that college faculties are instrumentalities that can be ordered to a purpose. The temptation to suggest this comes over administrators occasionally, as does the feeling that higher education is too important to be left to the professors. From an administrative point of view, the professors often seem self-indulgent and self-obsessed. They look like loose cannons, people whose habit of setting their own agendas needs to be curbed. But administrators sometimes forget that college students badly need to find themselves in a place in which people are not ordered to a purpose, in which loose cannons are free to roll about. The only point in having real live professors around instead of just computer terminals, videotapes and mimeoed lecture notes is that students need to have freedom enacted before their eyes by actual human beings. That is why tenure and academic freedom are more than just trade union demands. Teachers setting their own agendas – putting their individual, lovingly prepared specialities on display in the curricular cafeteria, without regard to any larger end, much less any institutional plan – is what non-vocational higher education is all about.

Such enactments of freedom are the principal occasions of the erotic relationships between teacher and student that Socrates and Allan Bloom celebrate and that Plato unfortunately tried to capture in a theory of human nature and of the liberal arts curriculum. But love is notoriously untheorizable. Such erotic relationships are occasions of growth, and their occurrence and their development are as unpredictable as growth itself. Yet nothing important happens in non-vocational higher education without them. Most of these relationships are with the dead teachers who wrote the books the students are assigned, but some will be with the live teachers who are giving the lectures. In either case, the sparks that leap back and forth between teacher and student, connecting them in a relationship that has little to do with socialization but much to do with self-creation, are the principal means by which the institutions of a liberal society get changed. Unless some such relationships are formed, the students will never realize what democratic institutions are good for: namely, making possible the invention of new forms of human freedom, taking liberties never taken before.

I shall end by returning to the conservative–radical contrast with which I began. I have been trying to separate both the conservative's insistence on community and the radical's insistence on individuality from philosophical theories about human nature and about the foundations of democratic society. Platonism and Nietzsche's inversion of Platonism seem to me equally unfruitful in thinking about education. As an alternative, I have offered Dewey's exaltation of democracy for its own sake and of growth for its own sake – an exaltation as fruitful as it is fuzzy.

This fuzziness annoys the conservatives because it does not provide enough sense of direction and enough constraints. The same fuzziness annoys the radicals because it provides neither enough fuel for resentment nor enough hope for sudden, revolutionary change. But the fuzziness that Dewey shared with Emerson is emblematic of what Wallace Stevens and Harold Bloom call 'the American Sublime'. That Sublime still lifts up the hearts of some fraction of each generation of college students.

8. The Humanistic Intellectual: Eleven Theses

(1989)

1. We should not try to define 'the humanities' by asking what the humanities departments share which distinguishes them from the rest of the university. The interesting dividing line is, instead, one that cuts across departments and disciplinary matrices. It divides people busy conforming to well-understood criteria for making contributions to knowledge from people trying to expand their own moral imaginations. These latter people read books in order to enlarge their sense of what is possible and important – either for themselves as individuals or for their society. Call these people the 'humanistic intellectuals'. One often finds more such people in the anthropology department than in the classics department, and sometimes more in the law school than in the philosophy department.

2. If one asks what good these people do, what social function they perform neither 'teaching' nor 'research' is a very good answer. Their idea of teaching – or at least of the sort of teaching they hope to do – is not exactly the communication of knowledge, but more like stirring the kids up. When they apply for a leave or a grant, they may have to fill out forms about the aims and methods of their so-called research projects, but all they really want to do is read a lot more books in the hope of becoming a different sort of person.

3. So the real social function of the humanistic intellectuals is to instil doubts in the students about the students' own self-images, and about the society to which they belong. These people are the teachers who help ensure that the moral consciousness of each new generation is slightly different from that of the previous generation.

4. But when it comes to the rhetoric of public support for higher education, we do not talk much about this social function. We cannot

tell boards of trustees, government commissions, and the like, that our function is to stir things up, to make our society feel guilty, to keep it off balance. We cannot say that the taxpayers employ us to make sure that their children will think differently than they do. Somewhere deep down, everybody – even the average taxpayer – knows that that is one of the things colleges and universities are for. But nobody can afford to make this fully explicit and public.

5. We humanistic intellectuals find ourselves in a position analogous to that of the 'social-gospel' or 'liberation theology' clergy, the priests and ministers who think of themselves as working to build the kingdom of God on earth. Their opponents describe their activity as leftist political action. The clergy, they say, are being paid to relay God's word, but are instead meddling in politics. We are accused of being paid to contribute to and communicate knowledge, while instead 'politicizing the humanities'. Yet we cannot take the idea of unpoliticized humanities any more seriously than our opposite numbers in the clergy can take seriously the idea of a depoliticized church.

6. We are still expected to make the ritual noises to which the trustees and the funding agencies are accustomed – noises about 'objective criteria of excellence', 'fundamental moral and spiritual values', 'the enduring questions posed by the human condition', and so on, just as the liberal clergy is supposed to mumble its way through creeds written in an earlier and simpler age. But those of us who have been impressed by the anti-Platonic, antiessentialist, historicizing, naturalizing writers of the last few centuries (people like Hegel, Darwin, Freud, Weber, Dewey and Foucault) must either become cynical or else put our own tortured private constructions on these ritual phrases.

7. This tension between public rhetoric and private sense of mission leaves the academy in general, and the humanistic intellectuals in particular, vulnerable to heresy hunters. Ambitious politicians like William Bennett – or cynical journalists like the young William Buckley (author of *God and Man at Yale*) or Charles Sykes (author of *Profscam*) – can always point out gaps between official rhetoric and actual practice. Usually, however, such heresy hunts peter out quickly in the face of faculty solidarity. The professors of physics and law, people whom

nobody wants to mess with, can be relied upon to rally around fellow members of the American Association of University Professors who teach anthropology or French, even if they neither know nor care what the latter do.

8. In the current flap about the humanities, however, the heresy hunters have a more vulnerable target than usual. This target is what Allan Bloom calls 'the Nietzscheanized left'. This left is an anomaly in America. In the past the American left has asked our country to be true to its ideals, to go still further along the path of expanding human freedom which our forefathers mapped: the path which led us from the abolition of slavery through women's suffrage, the Wagner Act and the Civil Rights Movement, to contemporary feminism and gay liberation. But the Nietzscheanized left tells the country it is rotten to the core – that it is a racist, sexist, imperialist society, one which can't be trusted an inch, one whose every utterance must be ruthlessly deconstructed.

9. Another reason this left is a vulnerable target is that it is extraordinarily self-obsessed and ingrown, as well as absurdly over-philosophized. It takes seriously Paul de Man's weird suggestion that 'one can approach the problems of ideology and by extension the problems of politics only on the basis of critical-linguistic analysis'. It seems to accept Hillis Miller's fantastic claim that 'the millennium [of universal peace and justice among men] would come if all men and women became good readers in de Man's sense'. When asked for a utopian sketch of our country's future, the new leftists reply along the lines of one of Foucault's most fatuous remarks. When asked why he never sketched a utopia, Foucault said, 'I think that to imagine another system is to extend our participation in the present system.' De Man and Foucault were (and Miller is) a lot better than these unfortunate remarks would suggest, but some of their followers are a lot worse. This over-philosophized and self-obsessed left is the mirror image of the over-philosophized and self-obsessed Straussians. The contempt of both groups for contemporary American society is so great that both have rendered themselves impotent when it comes to national, state or local politics. This means that they get to spend *all* their energy on academic politics.

10. The two groups are currently staging a sham battle about how to construct reading lists. The Straussians say that the criterion for what books to assign is intrinsic excellence, and the Nietzscheanized left says that it is fairness – e.g., fairness to females, blacks and Third Worlders. They are both wrong. Reading lists should be constructed so as to preserve a delicate balance between two needs. The first is the need of the students to have common reference points with people in previous generations and in other social classes – so that grandparents and grandchildren, people who went to the University of Wisconsin at Whitewater and people who went to Stanford, will have read a lot of the same books. The second is the need of the teachers to be able to teach the books which have moved them, excited them, changed their lives – rather than having to teach a syllabus handed down by a committee.

11. Philosophers of education, well-intended committees and governmental agencies have attempted to understand, define and manage the humanities. The point, however, is to keep the humanities changing fast enough so that they remain indefinable and unmanageable. All we need to keep them changing that fast is good old-fashioned academic freedom. Given freedom to shrug off the heresy hunters and their cries of 'politicization!', as well as freedom for each new batch of assistant professors to despise and repudiate the departmental Old Guard to whom they owe their jobs, the humanities will continue to be in good shape. If you don't like the ideological weather in the local English department these days, wait a generation. Watch what happens to the Nietzscheanized left when it tries to replace itself, around about the year 2010. I'm willing to bet that the brightest new Ph.D.s in English that year will be people who never want to hear the terms 'binary opposition' or 'hegemonic discourse' again as long as they live.

9. The Pragmatist's Progress: Umberto Eco on Interpretation

(1992)

When I read Umberto Eco's novel *Foucault's Pendulum*, I decided that Eco must be satirizing the way in which scientists, scholars, critics and philosophers think of themselves as cracking codes, peeling away accidents to reveal essence, stripping away veils of appearance to reveal reality. I read the novel as antiessentialist polemic, as a spoof of the metaphor of depth – of the notion that there are deep meanings hidden from the vulgar, meanings which only those lucky enough to have cracked a very difficult code can know. I took it as pointing up the similarities between Robert Fludd and Aristotle – or, more generally, between the books you find in the 'Occult' sections of bookstores and the ones you find in the 'Philosophy' sections.

More specifically, I interpreted the novel as a send-up of structuralism – of the very idea of structures which stand to texts or cultures as skeletons to bodies, programs to computers, or keys to locks. Having previously read Eco's *A Theory of Semiotics* – a book which sometimes reads like an attempt to crack the code of codes, to reveal the universal structure of structures – I concluded that *Foucault's Pendulum* stood to that earlier book as Wittgenstein's *Philosophical Investigations* to his *Tractatus Logico-Philosophicus*. I decided that Eco had managed to shrug off the diagrams and taxonomies of his earlier work, just as the older Wittgenstein shrugged off his youthful fantasies of ineffable objects and rigid connections.

I found my interpretation confirmed in the last 50 pages of the novel. At the beginning of those pages we find ourselves caught up in what purports to be an axial moment of history. This is the moment in which the hero, Casaubon, sees all the earth's seekers after the One True Meaning of Things assembled at what they believe to be the

World's Navel. The Cabbalists, the Templars, the Masons, the Pyramidologists, the Rosicrucians, the Voodooists, the emissaries from the Central Ohio Temple of the Black Pentacle – they are all there, whirling around Foucault's pendulum, a pendulum which is now weighted with the corpse of Casaubon's friend Belbo.

From this climax the novel slowly spirals down to a scene of Casaubon alone in a pastoral landscape, an Italian hillside. He is in a mood of wry abjuration, relishing small sensory pleasures, cherishing images of his infant child. A few paragraphs from the very end of the book, Casaubon meditates as follows:

> Along the Bricco's slopes are rows and rows of vines. I know them, I have seen similar rows in my day. No doctrine of numbers can say if they are in ascending or descending order. In the midst of the rows – but you have to walk barefoot, with your heels callused, from childhood – there are peach trees . . . When you eat the peach, the velvet of the skin makes shudders run from your tongue to your groin. Dinosaurs once grazed there. Then another surface covered theirs. And yet, like Belbo when he played the trumpet, when I bit into the peach I understood the Kingdom and was one with it. The rest is only cleverness. Invent; invent the Plan, Casaubon. That's what everyone has done, to explain the dinosaurs and the peaches.

I read this passage as describing a moment like that when Prospero breaks his staff, or when Faust listens to Ariel and abandons the quest of part I for the ironies of part II. It reminded me of the moment when Wittgenstein realized that the important thing is to be able to stop doing philosophy when one wants to, and of the moment when Heidegger concluded that he must overcome all overcoming and leave metaphysics to itself. By reading the passage in terms of these parallels, I was able to call up a vision of the great magus of Bologna renouncing structuralism and abjuring taxonomy. Eco, I decided, is telling us that he is now able to enjoy dinosaurs, peaches, babies, symbols and metaphors without needing to cut into their smooth flanks in search of hidden armatures. He is willing at last to abandon his long search for the Plan, for the code of codes.

By interpreting *Foucault's Pendulum* in this way I was doing the same sort of thing as is done by all those monomaniacal sectarian taxonomists who whirl round the pendulum. These people eagerly fit anything that comes along into the secret history of the Templars, or the ladder of Masonic enlightenment, or the plan of the Great Pyramid, or whatever their particular obsession happens to be. Shudders run from their cerebral cortices to their groins as they share the delights which Paracelsus and Fludd knew – as they discover the true significance of the fuzziness of peaches, seeing this microcosmic fact as corresponding to some macrocosmic principle. Such people take exquisite pleasure in finding that their key has opened yet another lock, that still another coded message has yielded to their insinuations and given up its secrets.

My own equivalent of the secret history of the Templars – the grid which I impose on any book I come across – is a semiautobiographical narrative of the Pragmatist's Progress. At the beginning of this particular quest romance, it dawns on the Seeker after Enlightenment that all the great dualisms of Western philosophy – reality and appearance, pure radiance and diffuse reflection, mind and body, intellectual rigour and sensual sloppiness, orderly semiotics and rambling semiosis – can be dispensed with. They are not to be synthesized into higher unities, not *aufgehoben*, but rather actively forgotten. An early stage of Enlightenment comes when one reads Nietzsche and begins thinking of all these dualisms as just so many metaphors for the contrast between an imagined state of total power, mastery and control and one's own present impotence. A further state is reached when, upon rereading *Thus Spake Zarathustra*, one comes down with the giggles. At that point, with a bit of help from Freud, one begins to hear talk about the Will to Power as just a high-falutin euphemism for the male's hope of bullying the females into submission, or the child's hope of getting back at Mummy and Daddy.

The final stage of the Pragmatist's Progress comes when one begins to see one's previous peripeties not as stages in the ascent toward Enlightenment, but simply as the contingent results of encounters with various books which happened to fall into one's hands. This stage is pretty hard to reach, for one is always being distracted by daydreams: daydreams in which the heroic pragmatist plays a Walter Mitty-like role in the immanent teleology of world history. But if the pragmatist can escape from such daydreams, he or she will eventually come to think of himself or herself as, like everything else, capable of as many descriptions as there are purposes to be served. There are as many descriptions as there are uses to which the pragmatist might be put, by his or her self or by others. This is the stage in which all descriptions (including one's self-description as a pragmatist) are evaluated according to their efficacy as instruments for purposes, rather than by their fidelity to the object described.

So much for the Pragmatist's Progress – a narrative I often use for purposes of self-dramatization, and one into which I was charmed to find myself being able to fit Professor Eco. Doing so enabled me to see both of us as having overcome our earlier ambitions to be code-crackers. This ambition led me to waste my 27th and 28th years trying to discover the secret of Charles Sanders Peirce's esoteric doctrine of 'the reality of Thirdness' and thus of his fantastically elaborate semiotico-metaphysical 'System'. I imagined that a similar urge must have led the young Eco to the study of that infuriating philosopher, and that a similar reaction must have enabled him to see Peirce as just one more whacked-out triadomaniac. In short, by using this narrative as a grid, I was able to think of Eco as a fellow pragmatist.

This agreeable sense of camaraderie began to evaporate, however, when I read Eco's article 'Intentio lectoris'.[1] For in that article, written at roughly the same time as *Foucault's Pendulum,* he insists upon a distinction between *interpreting* texts and *using* texts. This, of course, is a distinction we pragmatists do not wish to make. On our view, all anybody ever does with anything is use it.[2] Interpreting something, knowing it, penetrating to its essence, and so on, are all just various ways of describing some process of putting it to work. So I was abashed to realize that Eco would probably view my reading of his novel as a use rather than an interpretation, and that he did not think much of non-interpretative uses of texts. I was dismayed to find him insisting on a distinction similar to E. D. Hirsch's distinction between meaning and significance – a distinction between getting inside the text itself and relating the text to something else. This is exactly the sort of distinction antiessentialists like me deplore – a distinction between inside and outside, between the nonrelational and the relational features of something. For, on our view, there is no such thing as an intrinsic, nonrelational property.

So I shall focus on Eco's use–interpretation distinction, and do my best to minimize its importance. I begin with one of Eco's own polemical applications of this distinction – his account, in 'Intentio lectoris', of how Marie Bonaparte spoiled her own treatment of Poe. Eco says that when Bonaparte detected 'the same underlying fabula' in 'Morella', 'Ligeia' and 'Eleonora', she was 'revealing the *intentio operis*'. But, he continues, 'Unfortunately, such a beautiful textual analysis is interwoven with biographical remarks that connect textual evidence with aspects (known by extratextual sources) of Poe's private life.' When Bonaparte invokes the biographical fact that Poe was morbidly attracted by women with funereal features, then, Eco says, 'she is using and not interpreting texts'.

My first attempt to blur this distinction consists in noting that the boundary between one text and another is not so clear. Eco seems to think that it was all right for Bonaparte to read 'Morella' in the light of 'Ligeia'. But why? Merely because of the fact that they were written by the same man? Is that not being unfaithful to 'Morella', and running the danger of confusing the *intentio operis* with an *intentio auctoris* inferred from Poe's habit of writing a certain sort of text? Is it fair for me to read *Foucault's Pendulum* in the light of *A Theory of Semiotics* and *Semantics and the Philosophy of Language*? Or should I, if I want to interpret the first of these books, try to bracket my knowledge that it was written by the author of the other two?

If it is all right for me to invoke this knowledge about authorship, how about the next step? Is it all right for me to bring in my knowledge of what it is like to study Peirce – of what it is like to watch the hearty pragmatist of the 1870s transmogrify into the frenzied constructor of existential graphs of the 1890s? Can I fairly use my biographical knowledge of Eco, my knowledge that he spent a lot of time on Peirce, to help explain his having written a novel about occultist monomania?

These rhetorical questions are the initial softening-up moves I would make in order to begin to blur Eco's use–interpretation distinction. But the big push comes when I ask why he *wants* to make a great big distinction between the text and the reader, between *intentio operis* and *intentio lectoris*. What purpose is served by doing so? Presumably Eco's answer is that it helps you respect the distinction between what he calls 'internal textual coherence' and what he calls 'the uncontrollable drives of the reader'. He says that the latter 'controls' the former, and that the only way to check a conjecture against the *intentio operis* 'is to check it against the text as a coherent whole'. So presumably we erect the distinction as a barrier to our monomaniacal desire to subsume everything to our own needs.

One of those needs, however, is to convince other people that we are right. So we pragmatists can view the imperative to check your interpretation against the text as a coherent whole simply as a reminder that, if you want to make your interpretation of a book sound plausible, you cannot just gloss one or two lines or scenes. You have to say something about what most of the *other* lines or scenes are doing there. If I wanted to persuade you to accept my interpretation of *Foucault's Pendulum*, I should have to account for the 39 pages which intervene between the climactic *Walpurgisnacht* scene in Paris and the peaches and dinosaurs of Italy. I should have to offer a detailed account of the role of the recurrent flashbacks to partisan activities during the Nazi occupation. I should have to explain why, after the moment of abjuration, the last paragraphs of the book introduce a threatening note. For Casaubon ends his pastoral idyll by foreseeing his imminent death at the hands of the pursuing monomaniacs.

I do not know whether I could do all this. It is possible that, given three months of leisure and a modest foundation grant, I might produce a graph which connected all or most of these and other dots, a graph which still profiled Eco as a fellow pragmatist. It is also possible that I would fail, and would have to admit that Eco had other fish than mine to fry, that my own monomania was not flexible enough to accommodate his interests. Whatever the outcome, I agree with Eco that such a graph would be needed before you could decide whether my interpretation of *Foucault's Pendulum* was worth taking seriously.

But given this distinction between a first blush, brute force, unconvincing application of a particular reader's obsession to a text and the product of a three-month-long attempt to make that application subtle and convincing, do we need to describe it in terms of 'the text's intention'? Eco makes clear that he is not claiming that that intention can narrow interpretations down to a single correct one. He happily admits that we can 'show how Joyce [in *Ulysses*] acted in order to create many alternative figures in the carpet, without deciding how many they can be and which of them are the best ones'. So he thinks of the intention of the text rather as the production of a Model Reader, including 'a Model Reader entitled to try infinite conjectures'.

What I do not understand in Eco's account is his view of the relation between those latter conjectures and the intention of the text. If the text of *Ulysses* has succeeded in getting me to envisage a plurality of figures to be found in the carpet, has its internal coherence done all the controlling it can do? Or can it also control the responses of those who wonder whether some given figure is really in the carpet or not? Can it help them choose between competing suggestions – help separate the best interpretation from its competitors? Are its powers exhausted after it has rejected those competitors which are simply unable to connect enough dots – unable to answer enough questions about the function of various lines and scenes? Or does the text have powers in reserve which enable it to say things like 'that graph does, indeed, connect most of my points, but it nevertheless gets me all wrong'?

My disinclination to admit that any text can say such a thing is reinforced by the following passage in Eco's article. He says that 'the text is an object that the interpretation builds up in the course of the circular effort of validating itself on the basis of what it makes up as its result'. We pragmatists relish this way of blurring the distinction between finding an object and making it. We like Eco's redescription of what he calls 'the old and still valid hermeneutic circle'. But, given this picture of texts being made as they are interpreted, I do not see any way to preserve the metaphor of a text's *internal* coherence. I should think that a text just has whatever coherence it happened to acquire during the last roll of the hermeneutic wheel, just as a lump of clay only has whatever coherence it happened to pick up at the last turn of the potter's wheel.

So I should prefer to say that the coherence of the text is not something it has before it is described, any more than the dots had coherence before we connected them. Its coherence is no more than the fact that somebody has found something interesting to say about a group of marks or noises – some way of describing those marks and noises which relates them to some of the other things we are interested in talking about. (For example, we may describe a given set of marks as words of the English language, as very hard to read, as a Joyce manuscript, as worth a million dollars, as an early version of *Ulysses*, and so on.) This coherence is neither internal nor external to anything; it is just a function of what has been said so far about those marks. As we move from relatively uncontroversial philology and book chat into relatively controversial literary history and literary criticism, what we say must have some reasonably systematic inferential connections with what we or others have previously said – with previous descriptions of these same marks. But there is no point at which we can draw a line between what we are talking about and what we are saying about it, except by reference to some particular purposes, some particular *intentio* which *we* happen, at the moment, to have.

These, then, are the considerations I should bring to bear against Eco's use–interpretation distinction. Let me now turn to a more general difficulty I have with his work. When I read Eco or any other writer on language, I naturally do so in the light of my own favourite philosophy of language – Donald Davidson's radically naturalistic and holistic view. So my first question, on reading Eco's 1984 book *Semiotics and the Philosophy of Language* (immediately after reading *Foucault's Pendulum*) was: How close is Eco going to come to Davidsonian truth?

Davidson follows through on Quine's denial of an interesting philosophical distinction between language and fact, between signs and non-signs. I hoped that my interpretation of *Foucault's Pendulum* – my reading of it as what Daniel Dennett calls 'a cure for the common code' – might be confirmed, despite the disconfirmation I had found in 'Intentio lectoris'. For I hoped that Eco would show himself at least somewhat less attached to the notion of 'code' than he had been when, in the early 1970s, he wrote *A Theory of Semiotics*. My hopes were raised by some passages in *Semiotics and the Philosophy of Language* and cast down by others. On the one hand, Eco's suggestion that we think about semiotics in terms of labyrinthine inferential relations within an encyclopedia, rather than in terms of dictionary-like relations of equivalence between sign and thing signified, seemed to me to be pointing in the right holistic, Davidsonian direction. So did his Quinean remarks that a dictionary is just a disguised encyclopedia, and that 'any encyclopedia-like semantics must blur the distinction between analytic and synthetic properties'.[3]

On the other hand, I was troubled by Eco's quasi-Diltheyan insistence on distinguishing the 'semiotic' from the 'scientific', and on distinguishing philosophy from science[4] – an un-Quinean, un-Davidsonian thing to do. Further, Eco always seemed to be taking for granted that signs and texts were quite different from other objects – objects such as rocks and trees and quarks. At one point he writes:

> The universe of semiosis, that is, the universe of human culture, must be conceived as structured like a labyrinth of the third type: (a) it is structured according to a *network of interpretants*. (b) It is virtually *infinite* because it takes into account multiple interpretations realized by different cultures ... it is infinite because every discourse about the encyclopedia casts in doubt the previous structure of the encyclopedia itself. (c) It does not register only 'truths' but, rather, what has been said about the truth or what has been believed to be true ...[5]

This description of 'the universe of semiosis ... the universe of human culture' seems to be a good description of the universe *tout court*. As I see it, the rocks and the quarks are just more grist for the hermeneutic process of making objects by talking about them. Granted, one of the things we say when we talk about rocks and quarks is that they antedate us, but we often say that about marks on paper as well. So 'making' is not the right word either for rocks or for marks, any more than is 'finding'. We don't exactly make them, nor do we exactly find them. What we do is to react to stimuli by emitting sentences containing marks and noises such as 'rock', 'quark', 'mark', 'noise', 'sentence', 'text', 'metaphor' and so on.

We then infer other sentences from these, and others from those, and so on – building up a potentially infinite labyrinthine encyclopedia of assertions. These assertions are always at the mercy of being changed by fresh stimuli, but they are never capable of being *checked against* those stimuli, much less against the internal coherence of something outside the encyclopedia. The encyclopedia can get *changed* by things outside itself, but it can only be *checked* by having bits of itself compared with other bits. You cannot *check* a sentence against an object, although an object can *cause* you to stop asserting a sentence. You can only check a sentence against other sentences, sentences to which it is connected by various labyrinthine inferential relationships.

This refusal to draw a philosophically interesting line between nature and culture, language and fact, the universe of semiosis and some other universe, is where you wind up when, with Dewey and Davidson, you stop thinking of knowledge as accurate representation, of getting the signs lined up in the right relations to the non-signs. For you also stop thinking that you can separate the object from what you say about it, the signified from the sign, or the language from the metalanguage, except *ad hoc*, in aid of some particular purpose. What Eco says about the hermeneutic circle encourages me to think that he might be more sympathetic to this claim than his essentialist-sounding distinction between interpretation and use would at first suggest. These passages encourage me to think that Eco might someday be willing to join Stanley Fish and Jeffrey Stout in offering a *thoroughly* pragmatic account of interpretation, one which no longer contrasts interpretation with use.

Another aspect of Eco's thought which encourages me to think this is what he says about deconstructive literary criticism. For, many of the things which Eco says about this kind of criticism parallel what we Davidsonians and Fishians say about it. In the final paragraphs of 'Intentio lectoris' Eco says that 'many of the examples of deconstruction provided by Derrida' are 'pretextual readings, performed not in order to interpret the text but to show how much language can produce unlimited semiosis'. I think this is right, and that Eco is also right when he goes on to say:

> It so happened that a legitimate philosophical practice has been taken as a model for literary criticism and for a new trend in

textual interpretation . . . It is our theoretical duty to acknowledge that this happened and to show why it should not have
happened.[6]

Any explanation of why this unfortunate thing happened would bring
us back, sooner or later, to the work and influence of Paul de Man. I
agree with Professor Kermode that Derrida and de Man are the two
men who 'give genuine prestige to theory'. But I think it important to
emphasize that there is a crucial difference between the two men's
theoretical outlooks. Derrida, on my reading, never takes philosophy
as seriously as de Man does, nor does he wish to divide language, as
de Man did, into the kind called 'literary' and some other kind. In
particular, Derrida never takes the metaphysical distinction between
what Eco calls 'the universe of semiosis' and some other universe –
between culture and nature – as seriously as de Man did. De Man makes
heavy use of the standard Diltheyan distinction between 'intentional
objects' and 'natural objects'. He insists on contrasting language and
its imminent threat of incoherence, produced by 'universal semiosis',
with the putatively coherent and unthreatened rocks and quarks.[7]
Derrida, like Davidson, edges away from these distinctions, viewing
them as just more remnants of the Western metaphysical tradition.
De Man, on the other hand, makes them basic to his account of
reading.

We pragmatists wish that de Man had not sounded this Diltheyan
note, and that he had not suggested that there is an area of culture called
'philosophy' which can lay down guidelines for literary interpretation.
More particularly, we wish he had not encouraged the idea that you
could, by following these guidelines, find out what a text is 'really
about'. We wish that he had dropped the idea that there is a special
kind of language called 'literary language' which reveals what language
itself 'really is'. For the prevalence of such ideas seems to me largely
responsible for the unfortunate idea that reading Derrida on metaphysics will give you what Eco calls 'a model for literary criticism'. De
Man offered aid and comfort to the unfortunate idea that there is
something useful called the 'deconstructive method'.

For us pragmatists, the notion that there is something a given text is *really* about, something which rigorous application of a method will reveal, is as bad as the Aristotelian idea that there is something which a substance really, intrinsically, *is* as opposed to what it only apparently or accidentally or relationally is. The thought that a commentator has discovered what a text is really doing – for example, that it is *really* demystifying an ideological construct, or *really* deconstructing the hierarchical oppositions of Western metaphysics, rather than merely being capable of being *used* for these purposes – is, for us pragmatists, just more occultism. It is one more claim to have cracked the code, and thereby detected What Is *Really* Going On – one more instance of what I read Eco as satirizing in *Foucault's Pendulum*.

But opposition to the idea that texts are really about something in particular is also opposition to the idea that one particular interpretation might, presumably because of its respect for 'the internal coherence of the text', hit upon what that something is. More generally, it is opposition to the idea that the text can tell you something about what *it* wants, rather than simply providing stimuli which make it relatively hard or relatively easy to convince yourself or others of what you were initially inclined to say about it. So I am distressed to find Eco quoting Hillis Miller with approval when Miller says: 'the readings of deconstructive criticism are not the wilful imposition by a subjectivity of a theory on the texts, but are coerced by the texts themselves'.[8] To my ear, this is like saying that my use of a screwdriver to drive screws is 'coerced by the screwdriver itself', whereas my use of it to pry open cardboard packages is 'wilful imposition by subjectivity'. A deconstructor like Miller, I should have thought, is no more entitled to invoke this subjectivity–objectivity distinction than are pragmatists like Fish, Stout and myself. People who take the hermeneutic circle as seriously as Eco does should, it seems to me, also eschew it.

To enlarge on this point, let me drop the screwdriver and use a better example. The trouble with screwdrivers as an example is that nobody talks about 'finding out how they work', whereas both Eco and Miller talk this way about texts. So let me instead use the example of a computer program. If I use a particular word-processing program for writing essays, nobody will say that I am wilfully imposing my subjectivity. But the outraged author of that program might conceivably say this if she finds me using it to make out my income tax return, a purpose for which that particular program was never intended and for which it is ill-suited. The author might want to back her point up by enlarging on how her program works, going into detail about the various subroutines which make it up, their marvellous internal coherence and their utter unsuitability for purposes of tabulation and calculation. Still, it would be odd of the programmer to do this. To get her point, I do not need to know about the cleverness with which she designed the various subroutines, much less about how they look in BASIC or in some other compiler language. All she really needs to do is to point out that I can get the sort of tabulations and computations I need for the tax return out of her program only through an extraordinarily inelegant and tedious set of manoeuvres, manoeuvres I could avoid if I were only willing to use the right tool for the right purpose.

This example helps me to make the same criticism of Eco on the one hand and of Miller and de Man on the other. For the moral of the example is that you should not seek more precision or generality than you need for the particular purpose at hand. I see the idea that you can learn about 'how the text works' by using semiotics to analyse its operation as like spelling out certain word-processing subroutines in BASIC: you can do it if you want to, but it is not clear why, for most of the purposes which motivate literary critics, you should bother. I see the idea that what de Man calls 'literary language' has as its function the dissolution of the traditional metaphysical oppositions, and that *reading* as such has something to with hastening this dissolution, as analogous to the claim that a quantum-mechanical description of what goes on inside your computer will help you understand the nature of programs in general.

In other words, I distrust both the structuralist idea that knowing more about 'textual mechanisms' is essential for literary criticism and the post-structuralist idea that detecting the presence, or the subversion, of metaphysical hierarchies is essential. Knowing about mechanisms of textual production or about metaphysics can, to be sure, sometimes be useful. Having read Eco, or having read Derrida, will often give you something interesting to say about a text which you could not otherwise have said. But it brings you no closer to what is *really* going on in the text than having read Marx, Freud, Matthew Arnold or F. R. Leavis. Each of these supplementary readings simply gives you one more context in which you can place the text – one more grid you can place on top of it or one more paradigm to which to juxtapose it. Neither piece of knowledge tells you anything about the nature of texts or the nature of reading. For neither has a nature.

Reading texts is a matter of reading them in the light of other texts, people, obsessions, bits of information, or what have you, and then seeing what happens. What happens may be something too weird and idiosyncratic to bother with – as is probably the case with my reading of *Foucault's Pendulum*. Or it may be exciting and convincing, as when Derrida juxtaposes Freud and Heidegger, or when Kermode juxtaposes Empson and Heidegger. It may be *so* exciting and convincing that one has the illusion that one now sees what a certain text is *really* about. But what excites and convinces is a function of the needs and purposes of those who are being excited and convinced. So it seems to me simpler to scrap the distinction between using and interpreting, and just distinguish between uses by different people for different purposes.

I think that resistance to this suggestion (which has been made most persuasively by Fish) has two sources. One is the philosophical tradition, going back to Aristotle, which says that there is a big difference between practical deliberation about what to do and attempts to discover the *truth*. This tradition is invoked when Bernard Williams says, in criticism of Davidson and me: 'There is clearly such a thing as practical reasoning or deliberation, which is not the same as thinking about how things are. It is *obviously* not the same . . .'⁹ The second source is the set of intuitions which Kant marshalled when he distinguished between value and dignity. Things, Kant said, have value, but persons have dignity. Texts are, for this purpose, honorary persons. To merely use them – to treat them merely as means and not also as ends in themselves – is to act immorally. I have inveighed elsewhere against the Aristotelian practice–theory and the Kantian prudence–morality distinctions, and I shall try not to repeat myself here. Instead, I want briefly to say what can be salvaged from both distinctions. For there is, I think, a useful distinction which is vaguely shadowed forth by these two useless distinctions. This is between knowing what you want to get out of a person or thing or text in advance and hoping that the person or thing or text will help you want something different – that he or she or it will help you to change your purposes, and thus to change your life. This distinction, I think, helps us highlight the difference between methodical and inspired readings of texts.

Methodical readings are typically produced by those who lack what Kermode, following Valéry, calls 'an appetite for poetry'.[10] They are the sort of thing you get, for example, in an anthology of readings on Conrad's *Heart of Darkness* which I recently slogged through – one psychoanalytic reading, one reader-response reading, one feminist reading, one deconstructionist reading, and one new historicist reading. None of the readers had, as far as I could see, been enraptured or destabilized by *Heart of Darkness*. I got no sense that the book had made a big difference to them, that they cared much about Kurtz or Marlow or the woman 'with helmeted head and tawny cheeks' whom Marlow sees on the bank of the river. These people, and that book, had no more changed these readers' purposes than the specimen under the microscope changes the purpose of the histologist.

Unmethodical criticism of the sort which one occasionally wants to call 'inspired' is the result of an encounter with an author, character, plot, stanza, line or archaic torso which has made a difference to the critic's conception of who she is, what she is good for, what she wants to do with herself: an encounter which has rearranged her priorities and purposes. Such criticism uses the author or text not as a specimen reiterating a type but as an occasion for changing a previously accepted taxonomy, or for putting a new twist on a previously told story. Its respect for the author or the text is not a matter of respect for an *intentio* or for an internal structure. Indeed, 'respect' is the wrong word. 'Love' or 'hate' would be better. For a great love or a great loathing is the sort of thing that changes us by changing our purposes, changing the uses to which we shall put people and things and texts we encounter later. Love and loathing are both quite different from the jovial camaraderie which I imagined myself sharing with Eco when I treated *Foucault's Pendulum* as grist for my pragmatic mill – as a splendid specimen of a recognizable, greetable type.

146

It may seem that in saying all this I am taking the side of so-called 'traditional humanistic criticism' against the genre for which, as Professor Culler has said, the most convenient designation is the nickname 'theory'.[11] Although I think that this sort of criticism has been treated rather too harshly lately, this is not my intention. For in the first place, a lot of humanistic criticism was essentialist – it believed that there were deep permanent things embedded in human nature for literature to dig up and exhibit to us. This is not the sort of belief we pragmatists wish to encourage. In the second place, the genre we call 'theory' has done the English-speaking world a lot of good by providing an occasion for us to read a lot of first-rate books we might otherwise have missed – books by Heidegger and Derrida, for example. What 'theory' has not done, I think, is to provide a method for reading, or what Hillis Miller calls 'an ethic of reading'. We pragmatists think that nobody will ever succeed in doing either. We betray what Heidegger and Derrida were trying to tell us when we try to do either. We start succumbing to the old occultist urge to crack codes, to distinguish between reality and appearance, to make an invidious distinction between getting it right and making it useful.

*   *   *   *

NOTES

1 Umberto Eco, 'Intentio lectoris: the state of the art', *Differentia* (1988), vol. 2, pp. 147–68.
2. For a nice succinct statement of this pragmatist view of interpretation, see Jeffrey Stout, 'What is the meaning of a text?', *New Literary History* (1982), vol. 14, pp. 1–12.
3. Umberto Eco, *Semiotics and the Philosophy of Language* (1986), p. 73.
4. Eco, *Semiotics*, p. 10.
5. Eco, *Semiotics*, pp. 83–4.
6. Eco, 'Intentio lectoris', p. 166.
7. See Paul de Man, *Blindness and Insight* (2nd edition, 1983), p. 24, for de Man's straightforwardly Husserlian way of distinguishing between 'natural objects'

and 'intentional objects'. This is an opposition which Derrida would hardly wish to leave unquestioned. See also de Man, *The Resistance to Theory* (1986), p. 11, where de Man opposes 'language' to 'the Phenomenal world', as well as *Blindness*, p. 110, where he opposes 'scientific' texts to 'critical' texts.

8. J. Hillis Miller, 'Theory and practice', *Critical Inquiry* (1980), vol. 6, p. 611, quoted in Eco, 'Intentio lectoris', p. 163.

9. Bernard Williams, *Ethics and the Limits of Philosophy* (1985), p. 135.

10. See Frank Kermode, *An Appetite for Poetry* (1989), pp. 26–7.

11. See Jonathan Culler, *Framing the Sign: Criticism and Its Institutions* (1988), p. 15.

10. Religious Faith, Intellectual Responsibility and Romance

In thinking about William James, it helps to remember that James not only dedicated *Pragmatism* to John Stuart Mill, but reiterated some of Mill's most controversial claims. In 'The Moral Philosopher and the Moral Life', James says that 'The only possible reason there can be why any phenomenon ought to exist is that such a phenomenon actually is desired.'[1] This echo of the most ridiculed sentence in Mill's *Utilitarianism* is, I suspect, deliberate. One of James's most heartfelt convictions was that to know whether a claim should be met, we need *only* ask which other claims – 'claims actually made by some concrete person' – it runs athwart. We need not also ask whether it is a 'valid' claim. He deplored the fact that philosophers still followed Kant rather than Mill, still thought of validity as raining down upon a claim 'from some sublime dimension of being, which the moral law inhabits, much as upon the steel of the compass-needle the influence of the Pole rains down from out of the starry heavens'.[2]

The view that there is no source of obligation save the claims of individual sentient beings entails that we have no responsibility to anything other than such beings. Most of the relevant sentient individuals are our fellow humans. So talk about our responsibility to Truth, or to Reason, must be replaced by talk about our responsibility to our fellow human beings. James's account of truth and knowledge is a utilitarian ethics of belief, designed to facilitate such replacement. Its point of departure is Peirce's treatment of a belief as a habit of action, rather than as a representation. A utilitarian philosophy of religion must treat being religious as a habit of action. So its principal concern must be the extent to which the actions of religious believers frustrate the needs of other human beings, rather than the extent to which religion gets something right.

Our responsibility to Truth is not, for James, a responsibility to get things right. Rather, it is a responsibility to ourselves to make our beliefs cohere with one another, and to our fellow humans to make them cohere with theirs. As in Habermas's account of 'communicative rationality', our obligation to be rational is exhausted by our obligation to take account of other people's doubts and objections to our beliefs.[3] This view of rationality makes it natural to say, as James does, that the true is 'what would be better for us to believe'.[4]

But of course what is good for one person or group to believe will not be good for another person or group. James never was sure how to avoid the counterintuitive consequence that what is true for one person or group may not be true for another. He fluctuated between Peirce's identification of truth with what will be believed under ideal conditions, and Dewey's strategy of avoiding the topic of truth and talking instead about justification. But for my present purpose – evaluating James's argument in 'The Will to Believe' – it is not necessary to decide between these strategies.[5] For that purpose, I can duck questions about what pragmatists should say about truth. I need consider only the question of whether the religious believer has a right to her faith – whether this faith conflicts with her intellectual responsibilities.

It is a consequence of James's utilitarian view of the nature of obligation that *the obligation to justify one's beliefs arises only when one's habits of action interfere with the fulfilment of others' needs*. Insofar as one is engaged in a private project, that obligation lapses. The underlying strategy of James's utilitarian/pragmatist philosophy of religion is to *privatize* religion. This privatization allows him to construe the supposed tension between science and religion as the illusion of opposition between cooperative endeavours and private projects.[6]

On a pragmatist account, scientific inquiry is best viewed as the attempt to find a single, unified, coherent description of the world – the description which makes it easiest to predict the consequences of events and actions, and thus easiest to gratify certain human desires. When pragmatists say that 'creationist science' is *bad* science, their point is that it subordinates these desires to other, less widespread desires. But since religion has aims other than gratification of our need to predict and control, it is not clear that there need be a quarrel between religion and orthodox, atoms-and-void science, any more than between literature and science. Further, if a private relationship with God is not accompanied by a claim to knowledge of the Divine Will, there may be no conflict between religion and utilitarian ethics. A suitably privatized form of religious belief might dictate neither one's scientific beliefs nor anybody's moral choices save one's own. That form of belief might be able to gratify a need without threatening to thwart any needs of any others, and would thus meet the utilitarian test.

W. K. Clifford, James's chosen opponent in 'The Will to Believe', thinks that we have a duty to seek the truth, distinct from our duty to seek happiness. His way of describing this duty is not as a duty to get reality right, but rather as a duty not to believe without evidence. James quotes him as saying that 'if a belief has been accepted on insufficient evidence, the pleasure is a stolen one . . . It is sinful, because it is stolen in defiance of our duty to mankind . . . It is wrong always, everywhere, and for anyone to believe anything upon insufficient evidence.'[7]

Clifford asks us to be responsive to 'evidence', as well as to human needs. So the question between James and Clifford comes down to this: Is evidence something which floats free of human projects, or is the demand for evidence simply a demand from other human beings for cooperation on such projects?

The view that evidential relations have a kind of existence independent of human projects takes various forms, of which the most prominent are realism and foundationalism. Realist philosophers say that the only true source of evidence is the world as it is in itself.[8] The pragmatist objections to realism start from the claim that '. . . it is impossible to strip the human element from even our most abstract theorizing. All our mental categories without exception have been evolved because of their fruitfulness for life, and owe their being to historic circumstances, just as much as do the nouns and verbs and adjectives in which our languages clothe them.'[9] If pragmatists are right about this, the only question at issue between them and realists is whether the notion of 'the world as it is in itself' can be made fruitful for life. James's criticism of correspondence theories of truth boils down to the argument that a belief's purported 'fit' with the intrinsic nature of reality adds nothing which makes any practical difference to the fact that it is widely agreed to lead to successful action.

Foundationalism is an epistemological view which can be adopted by those who suspend judgement on the realist's claim that reality has an intrinsic nature. A foundationalist need only claim that every belief occupies a place in a natural, transcultural, transhistorical order of reasons – an order which eventually leads the inquirer back to one or another 'ultimate source of evidence'.[10] Different foundationalists offer different candidates for such sources: for example, Scripture, tradition, clear and distinct ideas, sense-experience, common sense. Pragmatists object to foundationalism for the same reasons as they object to realism. They think that the question of whether my inquiries trace a natural order of reasons or merely respond to the demands for justification prevalent in my culture is, like the question whether the physical world is found or made, one to which the answer can make no practical difference.

Clifford's demand for evidence can, however, be put in a minimalist form – one which avoids both realism and foundationalism, and which concedes to James that intellectual responsibility is simply responsibility to people with whom one has joined in a shared endeavour. In this minimalist form, this demand presupposes only that the meaning of statement consists in the inferential relations which it bears to other statements. To use the language in which the sentence is phrased commits one, on this view, to believing that a statement S is true if, and only if, one also believes that certain other statements which permit an inference to A, and still others which can be inferred from A, are true. The wrongness of believing without evidence is, therefore, the wrongness of pretending to participate in a common project while refusing to play by the rules.

This view of language was encapsulated in the positivist slogan that the meaning of a statement is its method of verification. The positivists argued that the sentences used to express religious belief are typically not hooked up to the rest of the language in the right inferential way, and hence can express only pseudobeliefs. The positivists, being empiricist foundationalists, thought the 'the right inferential way' meant 'making appeal, ultimately, to sense experience'. But a nonfoundationalist neopositivist can still put forward the following dilemma: If there are inferential connections, then there is a duty to argue; if there are not, then we are not dealing with a belief at all.

So even if we drop the foundationalist notion of 'evidence', Clifford's point can still be restated in terms of the responsibility to *argue*. A minimal Clifford-like view can be summed up in the claim that, although your emotions are your own business, your beliefs are everybody's business. There is no way in which the religious person can claim a right to believe as part of an overall right to privacy. For believing is inherently a public project: all us language-users are in it together. We all have a responsibility to each other not to believe anything which cannot be justified to the rest of us. To be rational is to submit one's beliefs – all one's beliefs – to the judgement of one's peers.

James resists this view. In 'The Will to Believe' he gave an argument for doing so. Most readers of that essay have thought it a failure, and that James there offers an unconvincing excuse for intellectual irresponsibility. James argues that there are live, momentous and forced options which cannot be decided by evidence – cannot, as James put it, 'be decided on intellectual grounds'. But people who side with Clifford typically rejoin that, where evidence and argument are unavailable, intellectual responsibility requires that options *cease* to be either live or forced. The responsible inquirer, they say, does not *let* herself be confronted by options of the sort James describes. When evidence and argument are unavailable, so, they think, is belief, or at least *responsible* belief. Desire, hope, and other noncognitive states can legitimately be had without evidence – can legitimately be turned over to what James calls 'our passional nature' – but *belief* cannot. In the realm of belief, which options are live and forced is not a private matter. The same options face us all; the same truth candidates are proposed to everyone. It is intellectually irresponsible either to disregard these options or to decide between these truth candidates in any other way than by argument from the sort of evidence which the very meanings of our words tell us is required for their support.

This nice sharp distinction between the cognitive and the noncognitive, between belief and desire, is, however just the sort of dualism which James wants to blur. On the traditional account, desire should play no role in the fixation of belief. On a pragmatist account, the only point of having beliefs in the first place is to gratify desires. James's claim that thinking is 'only there for behavior's sake'[11] is his improved version of Hume's claim that 'reason is, and ought to be, the slave of the passions'.

If one accepts that claim, one will have reason to be as dubious as James was of the purportedly necessary antagonism between science and religion. For, as I said earlier, these two areas of culture fulfil two different sets of desires. Science enables us to predict and control, whereas religion offers us a larger hope, and thereby something to live for. To ask, 'Which of their two accounts of the universe is true?' may be as pointless as asking, 'Is the carpenter's or the particle physicist's account of tables the true one?' For neither question needs to be answered if we can figure out a strategy for keeping the two accounts out of each other's way.[12]

Consider James's characterization of the 'religious hypothesis' as that (1) 'the best things are the more eternal things' and that (2) 'we are better even now if we believe [1]'.[13] Many people have said, when they reach this point in 'The Will to Believe', that if that hypothesis exhausts what James means by 'religion', then he is not talking about what they, or Clifford, are interested in. I shall return to this objection shortly. For now I merely remark that if you had asked James to specify the difference between accepting this hypothesis (a 'cognitive' state) and simply trusting the larger hope (a 'noncognitive' state) – or the difference between believing that the best things are the eternal things and relishing the thought that they are – he might well have replied that such differences do not make any difference.[14] What does it matter, one can imagine him asking, whether you call it a belief, a desire, or a hope, a mood, or some complex of these, so long as it has the same cash value in directing action? We know what religious faith is, we know what it does for people. People have a right to have such faith, just as they have a right to fall in love, to marry in haste, and to persist in love despite endless sorrow and disappointment. In all such cases, 'our passional nature' asserts its rights.

I suggested earlier that a utilitarian ethics of belief will reinterpret James's intellectual–passion distinction so as to make it coincide with a distinction between what needs justification to other human beings and what does not. A business proposal, for example needs such justification, but a marriage proposal (in our romantic and democratic culture) does not. Such an ethics will defend religious belief by saying, with Mill, that our right to happiness is limited only by others' rights not to have their own pursuits of happiness interfered with. This right to happiness includes the rights to faith, hope and love – intentional states which can rarely be justified, and typically should not have to be justified, to our peers. Our intellectual responsibilities are responsibilities to cooperate with others on common projects designed to promote the general welfare (projects such as constructing a unified science, or a uniform commercial code), and not to interfere with their private projects. For the latter – projects such as getting married or getting religion – the question of intellectual responsibility does not arise.

James's critics will hear this riposte as an admission that religion is not a cognitive matter, and that his 'right to believe' is a misnomer for 'the right to yearn' or 'the right to hope' or 'the right to take comfort in the thought that . . .' But James is not making, and should not make, such an admission. He is, rather, insisting that the impulse to draw a sharp line between the cognitive and noncognitive, and between beliefs and desires, even when this explanation is relevant to neither the explanation nor the justification of behaviour, is a residue of the false (because useless) belief that we should engage in two distinct quests – one for truth and the other for happiness. Only that belief could persuade us to say *amici socii, sed magis amica veritas.*

The philosophy of religion I have just sketched out is one which is shadowed forth in much of James's work, and is the one he *should* have invoked when replying to Clifford. Unfortunately, in 'The Will to Believe', he attempts a different strategy, and gets off on the wrong foot. Rather than fuzzing up the distinction between the cognitive and the noncognitive, as he should have, James here takes it for granted, and thus yields the crucial terrain to his opponent. The italicized thesis of 'The Will to Believe' reads: '*Our passional nature not only lawfully may, but must, decide an option between propositions, whenever it is a genuine option that cannot by its nature be decided on intellectual grounds*'.[15] Here, as in his highly unpragmatic claim that 'in our dealings with objective nature we obviously are recorders, not makers of the truth',[16] James accepts exactly what he should reject: the idea that the mind is divided neatly down the middle into intellect and passion, and the idea that possible topics of discussion are divided neatly into the cognitive and the noncognitive ones.

When philosophy goes antifoundationalist, the notion of 'source of evidence' gets replaced by that of 'consensus about what would count as evidence'. So objectivity as intersubjectivity replaces objectivity as fidelity to something nonhuman. The question, 'Is there any evidence for p?' gets replaced by the question, 'Is there any way of getting a consensus on what would count in favour of p?' The distinction between settling the question of p on intellectual grounds and turning it over to one's passional nature thus turns into the question, 'Am I going to be able to justify p to other people?' So James should have rephrased the issue between Clifford and himself as, 'What sort of belief, if any, can I have in good conscience, even after I realize that I cannot justify this belief to others?' The stark Cliffordian position says: No beliefs, only hopes, desires, yearnings and the like. The quasi-Jamesian position I want to defend says: Do not worry too much about whether what you have is a belief, a desire, or a mood. Just insofar as such states as hope, love and faith promote only such private projects, you need not worry about whether you have a right to have them.

Still, to suggest that the tension between science and religion can be resolved merely by saying that the two serve different ends may sound absurd. But it is no more nor less absurd than the attempt by liberal (mostly Protestant) theologians to demythologize Christianity, and more generally to immunize religious belief from criticism based on accounts of the universe which trace the origin of human beings, and of their intellectual faculties, to the unplanned movements of elementary particles.[17]

For some people, such as Alasdair MacIntyre, the effect of this latter attempt is to drain all the point out of religion. Theologies which require no *sacrificium intellectus* are, these people think, hardly worth discussing. MacIntyre disdainfully remarks of Tillich that his 'definition of God in terms of ultimate human concern in effect makes of God no more than an interest of human nature'.[18] A pragmatist, however, can reply that Tillich did nothing worse to God than pragmatist philosophy of science had already done to the elementary particles. Pragmatists think that those particles are not the very joints at which things as they are in themselves divide, but are objects which we should have had no reason to mention unless we had devoted ourself to one of the many interests of human nature – the interest in predicting and controlling our environment.

Pragmatists are not instrumentalists, in the sense of people who believe that quarks are 'mere heuristic fictions'. They think that quarks are as real as tables, but that quark talk and table talk need not get in each other's way, since they need not compete for the role of What is There Anyway, apart from human needs and interests. Similarly, pragmatist theists are not anthropocentrists, in the sense of believing that God is a 'mere posit'. They believe that God is as real as sense impressions, tables, quarks and human rights. But, they add, stories about our relations to God do not necessarily run athwart the stories of our relations to these other things.

Pragmatist theists, however, do have to get along without personal immortality, providential intervention, the efficacy of sacraments, the Virgin Birth, the Risen Christ, the Covenant with Abraham, the authority of the Koran, and a lot of other things which many theists are loath to do without. Or, if they want them, they will have to interpret them 'symbolically' in a way which MacIntyre will regard as disingenuous, for they must prevent them from providing premises for practical reasoning. But demythologizing is, pragmatist theists think, a small price to pay for insulating these doctrines from 'scientific' criticism. Demythologizing amounts to saying that, whatever theism is good for, it is not a device for predicting or controlling our environment.

From a utilitarian point of view, both MacIntyre and 'scientific realists' (philosophers who insist that, in Sellars's words, 'science is the measure of the things that are, that they are') are unfairly privileging some human interests, and therefore some areas of culture, over others.[19] To insist on the 'literal reality' of the Resurrection is of a piece with insisting, in the manner of David Lewis, that the only non-'gerrymandered' objects in the universe – the only objects that have not been shaped by human interests – are those of which particle physics speaks.[20] For utilitarians, it is not a sense of intellectual responsibility which makes us think that we must choose between religion and science, but rather an unwillingness to admit that both, equally, are what they are because human beings have the interests they do.

Scientific realism and religious fundamentalism are products of the same urge. The attempt to convince people that they have a duty to develop what Bernard Williams calls an 'absolute conception of reality' is, from a Tillichian or Jamesian point of view, of a piece with the attempt to live 'for God only', and to insist that others do so also. Both scientific realism and religious fundamentalism are private projects which have got out of hand. They are attempts to make one's own private way of giving meaning to one's own life – a way which romanticizes one's relation to something starkly and magnificently nonhuman, something Ultimately True and Real – obligatory for the general public.

I said earlier that many readers of 'The Will to Believe' feel let down when they discover that the only sort of religion James has been discussing is something as wimpy as the belief that 'perfection is eternal'. They have a point. For when Clifford raged against the intellectual irresponsibility of the thesis, what he really had in mind was the moral irresponsibility of fundamentalists – the people who burnt people at the stake, forbade divorce and dancing, and found various other ways of making their neighbours miserable for the greater glory of God.[21] Once 'the religious hypothesis' is disengaged from the opportunity to inflict humiliation and pain on people who do not profess the correct creed, it loses interest for many people. It loses interest for many more once it is disengaged from the promise that we shall see our loved ones after death. Similarly, once science is disengaged from the claim to know reality as it is in itself it loses its appeal for the sort of person who sees pragmatism as a frivolous, or treasonous, dereliction of our duty to Truth.

A pragmatist philosophy of religion must follow Tillich and others in distinguishing quite sharply between faith and belief. Liberal Protestants, to whom Tillich sounds plausible, are quite willing to talk about their faith in God, but demur at spelling out just what beliefs that faith includes. Fundamentalist Catholics, to whom Tillich sounds blasphemous, are happy to enumerate their beliefs by reciting the Creed, and to identify their faith with those beliefs. The reason the Tillichians think they can get along either without creeds, or with a blessedly vague symbolic interpretation of credal statements, is that they think the point of religion is not to produce any *specific* habit of action, but rather to make the sort of difference to a human life which is made by the presence or absence of love.

The best way to make Tillich and fuzziness look good, and to make creeds look bad, is to emphasize the similarity between having faith in God and being in love with another human being. People often say that they would not be able to go on if it were not for their love for their spouse or their children. This love is often not capable of being spelled out into beliefs about the character, or the actions, of these beloved people. Further, this love often seems inexplicable to people acquainted with those spouses and children – just as inexplicable as faith in God seems to those who contemplate the extent of seemingly unnecessary human misery. But we do not mock a mother who believes in her sociopathic child's essential goodness, even when that goodness is visible to no one else. James urges us not to mock those who accept what James calls 'the religious hypothesis' – the hypothesis that says 'the best things are the more eternal things'[22] – merely because we see no evidence for this hypothesis, and a lot of evidence against it.

The loving mother is not attempting to predict and control the behaviour of her child, and James's ascent to the religious hypothesis is not part of an attempt to predict and control anything at all. Concentration on the latter attempt, the attempt to which most of common sense and science is devoted, gives rise to the idea that all intentional states are either beliefs or desires: for the actions we take on the basis of prediction and in the hope of control are the results of practical syllogisms, and such syllogisms must include both a desire that a given state of affairs obtain and the belief that a certain action will help it do so. The same concentration gives rise to the idea that anything that counts as a belief – as a cognitive state – must be capable of being cashed out in terms of specific practical consequences, and to the related idea that we must be able to spell out the inferential relations between any belief and other beliefs in considerable, and quite specific, detail.

These two ideas have often led commentators to see a tension between James's pragmatism and his trust in his own religious experiences, and between the Dewey of *Reconstruction in Philosophy* and the Dewey of *A Common Faith*. The question of whether the tension seen in James's and Dewey's works is real or apparent boils down to the question: Can we disengage religious belief from inferential links with other beliefs by making them too vague to be caught in a creed – by fuzzing them up in Tillichian ways – and still be faithful to the familiar pragmatist doctrine that beliefs have content only by virtue of inferential relations to other beliefs?[23]

To give up this latter claim would be to abandon the heart of both classical and contemporary pragmatism, for it would be to abandon the holistic view of intentional content which permits pragmatists to substitute objectivity as intersubjectivity for objectivity as correspondence to the intrinsic nature of reality. But what becomes of intersubjectivity once we admit that there is no communal practice of justification – no shared language game – which gives religious statements their content? The question of whether James and Dewey are inconsistent now becomes the question: Is there some practice other than justification of beliefs by beliefs which can give content to utterances?

Yes, there is. Contemporary externalists in the philosophy of mind insist, as James and Dewey would heartily agree, that the only reason we attribute intentional states to human beings at all is that doing so enables us to explain what they are doing, and so helps us figure out what they might do next. When we encounter paradigmatic cases of unjustifiable beliefs – Kierkegaard's belief in the Incarnation, the mother's belief in the essential goodness of her sociopathic child – we can still use the attribution of such beliefs to explain what is going on:

why Kierkegaard, or the mother, are doing what they are doing. We can give content to an utterance like 'I love him' or 'I have faith in Him' by correlating such utterances with patterns of behaviour, even when we cannot do so by fixing the place of such utterances in a network of inferential relations.

The fact that Kierkegaard is not about to explain how Christ can be both mortal and immortal, nor the mother to say how a good person could have done what her child has done, is irrelevant to the utility of ascribing those beliefs to them. Just as we can often answer the question, 'Why did she do that?' by attributing a practical syllogism to the agent, so we can often answer it simply by saying, 'She loves him' or, 'She hopes against hope that he . . .' or, 'She has faith in him'. The 'him' here may be either her son, her lover, or her god. We thereby give an explanation of action which is not capable of being broken down into beliefs and desires – into individual sentential attitudes connected with other such attitudes by familiar inferential links – but which is none the less genuinely explanatory.

So far I have been content to accept James's own description of the religious hypothesis. But it is, I think, an unfortunate one. Just as I think James took the wrong tack, and partially betrayed his own pragmatism, in his reply to Clifford, so I think that he betrayed his own better instincts when he chose this definition of religion.[24] For that definition associates religion with the conviction that a power that is not ourselves will do unimaginably vast good, rather than with the hope that we ourselves will do such good. Such a definition of religion stays at the second of Dewey's three stages of the development of the religious consciousness – the one Dewey called 'the point now reached by religious theologians' – by retaining the notion of something non-human which is nevertheless on the side of human beings.[25]

The kind of religious faith which seems to me to lie behind the attractions of both utilitarianism and pragmatism is, instead, a faith in the future possibilities of moral humans, a faith which is hard to distinguish from love for, and hope for, the human community. I shall call this fuzzy overlap of faith, hope and love 'romance'. Romance, in this sense, may crystallize around a trade union as easily as around a congregation, around a novel as easily as around a sacrament, around a God as easily as around a child.

There is a passage in the work of the contemporary novelist Dorothy Allison which may help explain what I have in mind. Towards the beginning of a remarkable essay called 'Believing in Literature', Allison says that 'literature, and my own dream of writing, has shaped my own system of belief – a kind of atheist's religion . . . the backbone of my convictions has been a belief in the progress of human society as demonstrated in its fiction'.[26] She ends the essay as follows:

> There is a place where we are always alone with our own mortality, where we must simply have something greater than ourselves to hold onto – God or history or politics or literature or a belief in the healing power of love, or even righteous anger. Sometimes I think they are all the same. A reason to believe, a way to take the world by the throat and insist that there is more to this life than we have ever imagined.[27]

What I like best about this passage is Allison's suggestion that all these may be the same, that it does not greatly matter whether we state our reason to believe – our insistence that some or all finite, mortal humans can be far more than they have yet become – in religious, political, philosophical, literary, sexual or familial terms. What matters is the insistence itself – the romance, the ability to experience overpowering hope, or faith, or love (or, sometimes, rage).

What is distinctive about this state is that it carries us beyond argument, because beyond presently used language. It thereby carries us beyond the imagination of the present age of the world. I take this state to be the one described (in italics) by James as '*a positive content of experience which is literally and objectively true as far as it goes*': namely, '*the fact that the conscious person is continuous with a wider self through which saving experiences come*'.[28] The images and tropes which connect one with this wider self may be, as Allison suggests, political or familial, literary or credal. I think James would have liked Allison's pluralism, and would have thought that what she says in the above passage harmonizes with his own praise of polytheism in the final pages of *Varieties*, and with his insistence that, 'The divine can mean no single quality, it must mean a group of qualities, by being champions of which in alternation, different men may all find worthy missions'.[29]

In past ages of the world, things were so bad that 'a reason to believe, a way to take the world by the throat' was hard to get except by looking to a power not ourselves. In those days, there was little choice but to sacrifice the intellect in order to grasp hold of the premises of practical syllogisms – premises concerning the after-death consequences of baptism, pilgrimage or participation in holy wars. To be imaginative and to be religious, in those dark times, came to almost the same thing – for this world was too wretched to lift up the heart. But things are different now, because of human beings' gradual success in making their lives, and their world, less wretched. Nonreligious forms of romance have flourished – if only in those lucky parts of the world where wealth, leisure, literacy and democracy have worked together to prolong our lives and fill our libraries.[30] Now the things of this world are, for some lucky people, so welcome that they do not have to look beyond nature to the supernatural, and beyond life to an afterlife, but only beyond the human past to the human future.

James fluctuated between two states of mind, two ways of dealing with the panic which both he and his father had experienced, and the return of which he always dreaded.[31] In one of these, the Whitmanesque dream of plural, democratic vistas stretching far away into the future was enough.[32] Then he would respond to the possibility of panic by saying, as in the quotation from Fitzjames Stephen which ends 'The Will to Believe': 'Act for the best, hope for the best, and take what comes . . . If death ends all, we cannot meet death better'.[33] In those moods, James could find this bravura as appropriate for the death of the species as for that of an individual.

But in other moods James was unable to shrug off panic in the name of healthy mindedness, unable to rid himself of a panic-inducing picture of mankind as

> in a position similar to that of a set of people living on a frozen lake, surrounded by cliffs over which there is no escape, yet knowing that little by little the ice is melting, and the inevitable day drawing near when the last film of it will disappear, and

to be drowned ignominiously will be the human creature's portion.[34]

In such moods he is driven to adopt the 'religious hypothesis' that somewhere, somehow, perfection is eternal, and to identify 'the notion of God' with the 'guarantee' of 'an ideal order that shall be permanently perserved'.[35] In such moods he demanded, at a minimum, what Whitehead called 'objective immortality' – the memory of human achievements in the mind of a 'fellow-sufferer who understands'.[36] At the maximum, he hoped that in his own best moments he had made contact with that mind.

All of us, I think, fluctuate between such moods. We fluctuate between God as a perhaps obsolete name for a possible human future, and God as an external guarantor of some such future. Those who, like Dewey, would like to link their days each to each by transmuting their early religious belief into a belief in the human future, come to think of God as Friend rather than as Judge and Saviour. Those who, like me, were raised atheist and now find it merely confusing to talk about God, nevertheless fluctuate between moods in which we are content with utility and moods in which we hanker after validity as well. So we waver between what I have called 'romance' and needy, chastened humility. Sometimes it suffices to trust the human community, thought of as part of what Dewey called 'the community of causes and consequences in which we, together with those not born, are enmeshed ... the widest and deepest symbol of the mysterious totality of being the imagination calls the universe'.[37] Sometimes it does not.

James was not always content to identify the 'wider self through which saving experiences come' with Dewey's 'widest and deepest symbol' of the universe. In Whitmanesque moods he could identify this wider self with an Americanized humanity at the farthest reach of the democratic vistas. Then he could (to paraphrase the title of his father's book) think of democracy as the Redeemed Form of God. But in Wordsworthian moods he held what he called an 'over-belief' in something far more deeply interfused with nature than the transitory glory of democratic fellowship. Then he thought of the self from which saving experiences come as standing to even a utopian human community as the latter stands to the consciousness of our dogs and cats.[38]

We can, I think, learn two lessons from recapitulating what Henry Levinson calls 'the religious investigations of William James'. The first is that we latest heirs of time are lucky enough to have considerable discretion about which options will be live for us and which will not. Unlike our less fortunate ancestors, we are in the position to put aside the unromantic, foundationalist view that all the truth candidates, and thus all the momentous options, have always already been available, live, and forced – because they are built into a language always and inevitably spoken by common sense. We can, with James, relish the thought that our descendants may face live and forced options which we shall never imagine. The second lesson is that, since letting his liveliest option be the choice between Whitman and Wordsworth – between two Romantic poets rather than between an atheistic creed and a theistic one – was enough to satisfy James's own religious needs, it may be enough to satisfy ours.

*   *   *   *

NOTES

1 William James, 'The Will to Believe' in *The Will to Believe and Other Essays in Popular Philosophy* (Cambridge, Mass.: Harvard University Press, 1979).

2 James, 'The Will to Believe', p. 148.

3 But Habermas, unlike James and Dewey, still believes in a 'transcendent moment of universal validity'. I have argued against Habermas's retention of this Kantian doctrine in '*Sind Aussage Universelle Geltungsanspruche?*', *Deutsche Zeitschrift für Philosophie*, Spring 1995.

4 William James, *Pragmatism* (Cambridge, Mass.: Harvard University Press, 1975).

5 In fact I prefer a third strategy, that of Davidson, who cuts truth off from justification by making it a nonepistemic notion. I defend the counterintuitive implications of this strategy in 'Is Truth a Goal of Inquiry?: Donald Davidson vs. Crispin Wright' in my *Truth and Progress*.

6 Many people would agree with Stephen Carter's claim that this reduces religion to a 'hobby', and would accept his invidious contrast between a mere 'individual metaphysic' and a 'tradition of group worship'. (See his *The Culture of Disbelief: How American Law and Politics Trivialize Religious Devotion* (New York: Basic Books, 1993), especially chapter 2). I argue against Carter's views in the next chapter in this book, 'Religion as Conversation-stopper'.

7 James, 'The Will to Believe', p. 18.

8 See, for example, John McDowell's claim that without 'direct confrontation by a worldly state of affairs itself', thought's 'bearing on the world' will remain inexplicable (*Mind and World* (Cambridge, Mass.: Harvard University Press, 1994), pp. 142–3).

9 James, *Essays, Comments, and Reviews* (Cambridge, Mass.: Harvard University Press, 1987). Compare Nietzsche, *The Will to Power*, section 514.

10 See Michael Williams, *Unnatural Doubts* (Oxford: Blackwell, 1993), p. 116: '. . . we can characterize foundationalism as the view that our beliefs, simply in virtue of certain elements in their contents, stand in *natural epistemological relations* and thus fall into *natural epistemological kinds*'.

11 James, 'The Will to Believe', p. 92.

12 Although I have no proof text to cite, I am convinced that James's theory of truth as 'the good in the way of belief' originated in the need to reconcile his admiration for his father with his admiration for such scientific friends as Peirce and Chauncey Wright.

13 James, 'The Will to Believe', pp. 29 30. Note that for a pragmatist (2) is superfluous; '*p*' and 'we are better off even now if we believe *p*' comes pretty close, for pragmatists, to saying the same thing.

14 Pragmatists can, of course, make a distinction between hope and knowledge in cases where knowledge of causal mechanisms is available. The quack hopes, but the medical scientist knows, that the pills will cure. But in other cases, such as marriage, the distinction often cannot usefully be drawn. Does the groom know, or merely hope, that he is marrying the right person? Either description will explain his actions equally well.

15 James, 'The Will to Believe', p. 20.

16 James, 'The Will to Believe', p. 26. Here James buys in on a dualism between objective nature (The Way the World Is) and something else – a dualism which critics of the correspondence theory of truth, such as the future author of *Pragmatism*, must eventually abjure.

17 Paul Tillich claimed that his existentialist, symbolic theology was an expression of 'The Protestant Principle' – the impulse that led Luther to despise scholastic proofs of God's existence and to label Reason 'a whore'. James said that, 'as, to papal minds, protestantism has often seemed a mere mess of anarchy and confusion, such, no doubt will pragmatism often seem to ultra-rationalist minds in philosophy' (*Pragmatism*, p. 62); see also *Varieties of Religious Experience* (Cambridge, Mass.: Harvard University Press, 1985).

18 Alasdair MacIntyre and Paul Ricoeur, *The Religious Significance of Atheism* (New York: Columbia University Press, 1969), p. 53.

19 In his 'Atheism, Relativism, Enlightenment and Truth' (*Studies in Religion*, vol. 23, pp. 167–78), my fellow pragmatist Barry Allen remarks that Hume saw no need to proclaim himself an atheist. Holbach and Diderot, by contrast, did see a need, for, unlike Hume, they substituted a duty to Truth for a duty to God, a duty explained in terms of what Allen elsewhere (in his *Truth in Philosophy*) has called an 'onto-logical', specifically antipragmatic, account of truth. Holbach would, today, proclaim himself a scientific realist, and *therefore* an atheist. Hume would proclaim himself neither.

20 See David Lewis, 'Putnam's Paradox', *Australasian Journal of Philosophy*, 1983, pp. 226–8.

21 See, for example, Clifford's 'The Influence Upon Morality of a Decline in Religious Belief' in his *Lectures and Essays* (London: Macmillan, 1879), vol. II, pp. 244–52.

22 James, 'The Will to Believe', p. 29.

23 Davidson and other externalists have emphasized that this claim is compatible with saying that we can attribute content to intentional states only if we are able to correlate utterances with their extra-mental causes. They have, I think, thereby shown us how to be radically holistic and coherentist without running the danger of 'losing touch' with the world. Realist philosophers such as McDowell, however, have doubted whether Davidson's view allows 'cognitive' as opposed to merely 'causal' connections with the world. I attempt to reply to these doubts in 'The Very Idea of Answerability to the World' in my *Truth and Progress*.

24 Acceptance of the claim that 'perfection is eternal' was not, of course, James's only definition of religion. He had as many conflicting quasi-definatory things to say about religions as he did about truth.

25 See John Dewey, *A Common Faith* (New Haven: Yale University Press,

1934), p. 73. Dewey's own conception of the 'the human abode' is not of something nonhuman but friendly, but rather of a Wordsworthian community with nonhuman nature, with Spinoza's 'face of the whole universe'.

26 Dorothy Allison, *Skin: Talking about sex, class and literature* (Ithaca, N.Y.: Firebrand Books, 1994), p. 166.

27 Allison, p. 181.

28 James, *Varieties of Religious Experience*, p. 405.

29 James, *Varieties of Religious Experience*, p. 384.

30 James said that there is reason to think that 'the coarser religions, revivalistic, orgiastic, with blood and miracles and supernatural operations, may possibly never be displaced. Some constitutions need them too much' (*Varieties of Religious Experience*, p. 136). He could have added that people placed in certain circumstances (no wealth, no literacy, no luck) also need them too much.

31 'Not the conception or intellectual perception of evil, but the grisly blood-freezing heart-palsying sensation of it close upon one . . . How irrelevantly remote seem all our usual refined optimisms and intellectual and moral consolations in the presence of a need of help like this! Here is the real core of the religious problem: Help! help!' (*Varieties of Religious Experience*, p. 135).

32 See James's 'pluralistic way of interpreting' Whitman's 'To You' (*Pragmatism*, p. 133), and his account of the 'the great religious difference', the one 'between the men who insist that world *must and shall be*, and those who are contented with believing that the world *may be*, saved' (*Pragmatism*, p. 135).

33 James, 'The Will to Believe', p. 33.

34 James, *Varieties of Religious Experience*, p. 120.

35 James, *Pragmatism*, p. 55.

36 A. N. Whitehead, *Process and Reality* (New York: Macmillan, 1929), pp. 532–3.

37 Dewey, p. 85.

38 James, *Varieties of Religious Experience*, pp. 518–19.

11. Religion As Conversation-stopper

(1994)

These days intellectuals divide up into those who think that something new and important called 'the postmodern' is happening, and those who, like Habermas, think we are (or should be) still plugging away at the familiar tasks set for us by the Enlightenment. The ones who, like me, agree with Habermas typically see the secularization of public life as the Enlightenment's central achievement, and see our job as the same as our predecessors': getting our fellow citizens to rely less on tradition, and to be more willing to experiment with new customs and institutions.

Our scepticism about the postmodern may incline us to be sceptical also about the modern, and, more specifically, about Virginia Woolf's Foucault-like claim that human nature changed around 1910. But something crucially important to the progress of secularization did happen around then. To remind ourselves of what it was, it helps to reread *In Memoriam*. One of the striking things about the poem is the poet's need, and ability, to believe in the immortality of the soul. One of the striking things about the biographies of Tennyson is the biographers' agreement that Tennyson and Hallam never went to bed together. Two young men who loved each other that much would, nowadays, be quite likely to do so. But the same religious beliefs that let Tennyson hope so fervently to see his friend in heaven also kept him out of Hallam's arms.

The big change in the outlook of the intellectuals – as opposed to a change in human nature – that happened around 1910 was that they began to be confident that human beings had only bodies, and no souls. The resulting this-worldliness made them receptive to the idea that one's sexual behaviour did not have much to do with one's moral worth — an idea that the Enlightenment-minded author of 'Locksley Hall' still found impossible to accept. It is hard to disentangle the idea that we have an immortal soul from the belief that this soul can be stained by the commission of certain sexual acts. For sex is the first thing that comes to mind when we think about the human body as something located down there, underneath the human soul. So when we started thinking that we might have only complicated, accomplished, vulnerable bodies, and no souls, the word 'impurity' began to lose both sexual overtones and moral resonance.

For these reasons, the biggest gap between the typical intellectual and the typical nonintellectual is that the former does not use 'impurity' as a moral term, and does not find religion what James called a 'live, forced and momentous option'. She thinks of religion as, at its best, Whitehead's 'what we do with our solitude', rather than something people do together in churches. Such an intellectual is bound to be puzzled or annoyed by Stephen L. Carter's *The Culture of Disbelief: How American Law and Politics Trivialize Religious Devotion*. For Carter puts in question what, to atheists like me, seems the happy, Jeffersonian compromise that the Enlightenment reached with the religious. This compromise consists in privatizing religion – keeping it out of what Carter calls 'the public square', making it seem bad taste to bring religion into discussions of public policy. Whereas many religiously inclined intellectuals stick to what he calls an 'individual metaphysic', Carter, an Episcopalian, defines religion as 'a tradition of group worship'.

We atheists, doing our best to enforce Jefferson's compromise, think it bad enough that we cannot run for public office without being disingenuous about our disbelief in God; despite the compromise, no uncloseted atheist is likely to get elected anywhere in the country. We also resent the suggestion that you have to be religious to have a conscience – a suggestion implicit in the fact that only *religious* conscientious objectors to military service go unpunished. Such facts suggest to us that the claims of religion need, if anything, to be pushed back still further, and that religious believers have no business asking for more public respect than they now receive. Carter, however, thinks that privatizing religion trivializes it. He says that 'the legal culture that guards the public square still seems most comfortable thinking of religion as a hobby, something done in privacy, something that mature, public-spirited adults do not use as the basis for politics'.

Carter's inference from privatization to trivialization is invalid unless supplemented with the premise that the nonpolitical is always trivial. But this premise seems false. Our family or love lives are private, nonpolitical and nontrivial. The poems we atheists write, like the prayers our religious friends raise, are private, nonpolitical and non-trivial. Writing poems is, for many people, no mere hobby, even though they never show those poems to any save their intimates. The same goes for reading poems, and for lots of other private pursuits that both give meaning to individual human lives and are such that mature, public-spirited adults are quite right in not attempting to use them as a basis for politics. The search for private perfection, pursued by theists and atheists alike, is neither trivial nor, in a pluralistic democracy, relevant to public policy.

Carter criticizes

> the effort by the contemporary liberal philosophers to create a conversational space in which individuals of very different viewpoints can join dialogic battle, in accord with a set of dialogic conventions that all can accept. The philosophical idea is that even though all of us have differing personal backgrounds and biases, we nevertheless share certain moral premises in common.

Carter here gives a good description both of the least common denominator of the positions of Rawls and Habermas, the two most prominent social thinkers of the present day, and of the central secularizing message of the Enlightenment. He is quite right to say that 'all these efforts to limit the conversation to premises held in common would exclude religion from the mix'. But he thinks that such exclusion is unjust.

Such exclusion, however, is at the heart of the Jeffersonian compromise, and it is hard to see what more just arrangement Carter thinks might take the place of that compromise. Contemporary liberal philosophers think that we shall not be able to keep a democratic political community going unless the religious believers remain willing to trade privatization for a guarantee of religious liberty, and Carter gives us no reason to think they are wrong.

The main reason religion needs to be privatized is that, in political discussion with those outside the relevant religious community, it is a conversation-stopper. Carter is right when he says:

> One good way to end a conversation – or to start an argument – is to tell a group of well-educated professionals that you hold a political position (preferably a controversial one, such as being against abortion or pornography) because it is required by your understanding of God's will.

Saying this is far more likely to end a conversation than to start an argument. The same goes for telling the group, 'I would never have an abortion' or, 'Reading pornography is about the only pleasure I get out of life these days.' In these examples, as in Carter's, the ensuing silence masks the group's inclination to say, 'So what? We weren't discussing your private life; we were discussing public policy. Don't bother us with matters that are not our concern.'

This would be my own inclination in such a situation. Carter clearly thinks such a reaction inappropriate, but it is hard to figure out what he thinks *would* be an appropriate response by nonreligious interlocutors to the claim that abortion is required (or forbidden) by the will of God. He does not think it good enough to say: OK, but since I don't think there is such a thing as the will of God, and since I doubt that we'll get anywhere arguing theism vs. atheism, let's see if we have some shared premises on the basis of which to continue our argument about abortion. He thinks such a reply would be condescending and trivializing. But are we atheist interlocutors supposed to try to keep the conversation going by saying, 'Gee! I'm impressed. You must have a really deep, sincere faith'? Suppose we try that. What happens then? What can *either* party do for an encore?

Carter says that he wants 'a public square that does not restrict its access to citizens willing to speak in a purely secular language, but instead is equally open to religious and nonreligious argument'. This may mean simply that he wants us atheists to stop screaming 'keep religion out of politics!' when the clergy say that abortion is against

God's will while nodding approvingly when they say that gaybashing is. If so, I entirely agree with him. The best parts of his very thoughtful, and often persuasive, book are those in which he points up the inconsistency of our behaviour, and the hypocrisy involved in saying that believers somehow have no right to base their political views on their religious faith, whereas we atheists have every right to base ours on Enlightenment philosophy. The claim that in doing so we are appealing to reason, whereas the religious are being irrational, is hokum. Carter is quite right to debunk it.

Carter is also right to say that liberal theory has not shown that 'the will of any of the brilliant philosophers of the liberal tradition, or, for that matter, the will of the Supreme Court of the United States, is more relevant to moral decisions than the will of God'. But he is wrong in suggesting that it has to show this. All liberal theory has to show is that moral decisions that are to be enforced by a pluralist and democratic state's monopoly of violence are best made by public discussion in which voices claiming to be God's, or reason's, or science's, are put on a par with everybody else's.

It is one thing to say that religious beliefs, or the lack of them, will influence political convictions. Of course they will. It is another thing to say, as Carter says, that the public square should be open to 'religious argument', or that liberalism should 'develop a politics that accepts whatever form of dialogue a member of the public offers'. What is a specifically religious 'form of dialogue', except perhaps a dialogue in which some members cite religious sources for their beliefs? What could a specifically religious argument be, except an argument whose premises are accepted by some people because they believe that these premises express the will of God? I may accept those same premises for purely secular reasons – for example, reasons having to do with maximizing human happiness. Does that make my argument a non-religious one? Even if it is exactly the argument made by my religious fellow citizen? Surely the fact that one of us gets his premises in church and the other in the library is, and should be, of no interest to our audience in the public square. The arguments that take place there, political arguments, are best thought of as neither religious nor nonreligious.

Carter frequently speaks of religion as a 'source of moral knowledge' rather than as a 'source of moral beliefs'. Of course, if we knew that religion were a source of moral knowledge, we should be foolish to shove it to the outskirts of the square. But part of the moral of Rawls's and Habermas's work – and especially of Habermas's replacement of 'subject-centred' with 'communicative' reason – is that we should be suspicious of the very idea of a 'source of moral knowledge'. It is reasonable to call a physics textbook or teacher a source of knowledge. Knowledge is justified true belief. Since physics is a relatively noncontroversial area, what such teachers and textbooks say is usually both justified and (as far as anybody now knows) true. When it comes to morals rather than science, however, every textbook, Scripture and teacher is offset by a competing textbook, Scripture or teacher. That is why, in the public square of a pluralistic democracy, justification is always up for grabs, and why the term 'source of moral knowledge' will always be out of place.

I take the point of Rawls and Habermas, as of Dewey and Peirce, to be that the epistemology suitable for such a democracy is one in which the only test of a political proposal is its ability to gain assent from people who retain radically diverse ideas about the point and meaning of human life, about the path to private perfection. The more such consensus becomes the test of a belief, the less important is the belief's source. So when Carter complains that religious citizens are forced 'to restructure their arguments in purely secular terms before they can be presented', I should reply that 'restructuring the arguments in purely secular terms' just means 'dropping reference to the source of the premises of the arguments', and that this omission seems a reasonable price to pay for religious liberty.

Carter thinks that 'contemporary liberal philosophers ... make demands on [the religion's] moral conscience to reformulate that conscience – to destroy a vital aspect of the self – in order to gain the right to participate in the dialogue alongside other citizens'. But this requirement is no harsher, and no more a demand for self-destruction, than the requirement that we atheists, when we present our arguments, should claim no authority for our premises save the assent we hope they will gain from our audience. Carter seems to think that religious

174

believers' moral convictions are somehow more deeply interwoven with their self-identity than those of atheists with theirs. He seems unwilling to admit that the role of Enlightenment ideology in giving meaning to the lives of atheists is just as great as Christianity's role in giving meaning to his own life. Occasionally he suggests that we contemporary liberal ideologues suffer from the same spiritual shallowness that American law attributes to the nonreligious pacifist. Even if this were the case, however, Carter would still need to tell us why a speaker's depth of spirituality is more relevant to her participation in public debate than her hobby or her hair colour.

12. Thomas Kuhn, Rocks and the Laws of Physics

(1997)

The death in June 1996 of Thomas S. Kuhn, the most influential philosopher to write in English since the Second World War, produced many long, respectful obituaries. Most of these obituaries referred to him as a historian of science rather than as a philosopher. Kuhn would not have objected to that description, but it is a bit misleading.

If I had written an obituary, I should have made a point of calling Kuhn a great philosopher, for two reasons. First, I think that 'philosopher' is the most appropriate description for somebody who remaps culture – who suggests a new and promising way for us to think about the relation among various large areas of human activity. Kuhn's great contribution was to offer such a suggestion, one that has altered the self-images, and the rhetoric, of many different disciplines.

My second reason for calling Kuhn a great philosopher is resentment over the fact that Kuhn was constantly being treated, by my fellow professors of philosophy, as at best a second-rate citizen of the philosophical community. Sometimes he was even treated as an intruder who had no business attempting to contribute to a discipline in which he was untrained. I do not think too much should be made of the fuzzy philosopher–nonphilosopher distinction, and I should hate to try to sharpen it up. But I found it annoying that people who used 'real philosopher' as an honorific when speaking of themselves and their friends should feel entitled to withhold it from Kuhn.

Kuhn was one of my idols, because reading his *The Structure of Scientific Revolutions* (1962) had given me the sense of scales falling from my eyes. The fact that he came to philosophical issues sideways, so to speak – having taken a Ph.D. in physics and then becoming a self-taught historian of seventeenth-century science – seemed to me a very bad reason to try to exclude him from our ranks.

The main reason Kuhn was kept at arm's length by the philosophy professors in that anglophone philosophy is dominated by the so-called analytic tradition – a tradition that has prided itself in having made philosophy more like science and less like literature or politics. The last thing philosophers in this tradition want is to have the distinctiveness of science impugned – to be told, as Kuhn told them, that the successes of science are not due to the application of a special 'scientific method', and that the replacement of one scientific theory by another is not a matter of hard, cold logic, but comes about in the same way as does the replacement of one political institution by another.

Kuhn's major contribution to remapping culture was to help us see that the natural scientists do not have a special access to reality or to truth. He helped dismantle the traditional hierarchy of disciplines, a hierarchy that dates back to Plato's image of the divided line. That line stretched from the messy material world up into a near immaterial world. In the hierarchy Plato proposed mathematics (which uses pure logic, and no rhetoric at all) is up at the top and literary criticism and political persuasion (which use mostly rhetoric, and practically no logic at all) are down at the bottom.

Kuhn fuzzed up the distinction between logic and rhetoric by showing that revolutionary theory-change is not a matter of following our inferences, but of changing the terminology in which truth candidates were formulated, and thereby changing criteria of relevance. He helped break down the idea that there are 'canons of scientific reasoning' that Galileo had obeyed and Aristotle had not.

He thereby helped make the question, 'How can we set out our discipline on the secure path of a science?', obsolete. This was the question that Kant had posed about philosophy, and to which Husserl and Russell had offered competing answers. It was the question that B. F. Skinner answered by asking psychologists to confine themselves to a vocabulary dominated by notions like 'stimulus', 'response', 'conditioning' and 'reinforcement'. It was the question Northrop Frye answered by suggesting a taxonomy of myths, a set of pigeonholes that future literary critics could occupy themselves with filling up.

Kuhn could not, of course, have made this question obsolete all by himself. He was abetted by the self-criticisms of analytic philosophy offered by the later Wittgenstein, Quine, Sellars, Goodman and others – self-criticisms that were the main topics of discussion within analytic philosophy at the time *The Structure of Scientific Revolutions* first appeared.

All these self-critical analytic philosophers had, in their youths, bought in on Russell's suggestion that 'logic is the essence of philosophy' and on his vision of philosophy as a matter of analysing complexes into simples. But then they became sceptical both about the notion that there was something called 'logic' that would guide such analysis, and about the idea that there were any simples into which to analyse non-simples. Russell's candidates for such simples – sensory data, and clear and distinct ideas of such universals as the logical connectives – no longer seemed satisfactory. Goodman pointed out that simplicity itself is relative to a choice of description. Sellars, like Kuhn, pointed out that there is no non-*ad hoc* way to divide sensory experience up into what is 'given to the mind' and what is 'added by the mind'. Wittgenstein asked, 'Why did we think that logic was something sublime?' Quine and Goodman, taking a leaf from Skinner, pointed out that it might be better to view logic as a pattern of human behaviour rather than as an immaterial force shaping such behaviour.

Nobody suggested that these internal critics of what Quine called 'dogmas of empiricism' – doctrines that Russell and Carnap had taken as self-evident – were 'not really philosophers'. For they did not endanger the professional self-esteem, the habit of self-congratulation, that made even the most self-critical analytic philosophers rejoice in having been born at the right time – a time in which philosophy had become clear, rigorous and scientific. Kuhn did endanger this self-esteem, because reading his book made analytic philosophers wonder if the notion of 'scientific clarity and rigour' was as clear, rigorous and scientific as they had assumed.

I made myself somewhat unpopular among analytic philosophers by drawing, in various books and articles, some of the morals that seemed to me implicit in Kuhn's new map of culture. Drawing these morals was a way of overcoming my own earlier training. Carnap and others had persuaded me, in my early twenties, that philosophers should indeed try to become more 'scientific' and 'rigorous'. I was even briefly persuaded that learning symbolic logic was probably a good way of achieving this end. (Having been forced to learn the proofs of some of Goedel's results in order to pass my Ph.D. examinations, I became loftily condescending toward philosophers whose training left them unable to juggle logical symbols.) But by the time I had reached the age of 30 (just about the time of the publication of Kuhn's *Structure*), I had begun to doubt whether the creative analytic philosophers, as opposed to the hacks, were using anything like an 'analytic method'. I could not see how the idea of such a method could survive the various attacks that had been made on Russell's candidates for 'simples'. It seemed to me that Quine, Sellars and Wittgenstein were just being brilliant, in idiosyncratic and freewheeling ways.

I also had doubts about whether symbolic logic added more than a stylistic elegance to analytic philosophers' prose, and about whether the famous clarity and rigour on which my colleagues prided themselves (as I too had, for a time) amounted to more than a preference for answering certain sorts of questions and for ignoring others. As far as I could see, what made us 'analytic' had nothing to do with applying a method called 'conceptual analysis' or 'investigation of logical form'. All that united us was that we took certain doctrines advanced by Carnap and Russell seriously enough to want to refute them.

Kuhn's notion of the history of science as a history of what he called 'disciplinary matrices' was a great help to me in formulating this view of analytic philosophy. So was his notion of paradigm. After reading *Structure* I began to think of analytic philosophy as one way of doing philosophy among others, rather than as the discovery of how to set philosophy on the secure path of a science. This led to a certain edginess in my relations with my colleagues, most of whom thought that Kuhn had shown, at most, that Carnap's 'logic of confirmation' needed a few minor qualifications. These colleagues did not think that Kuhn's work had any metaphilosophical implications.

Carnap and Russell, I came to think, had suggested something new for philosophy to be, just as had, successively, Aristotle, Locke and Kant. Each of the latter had created a disciplinary matrix, and thereby a philosophical tradition – a tradition made up of the people who took the founders' terminology and arguments seriously. In the Kuhnian view, analytic philosophy was a matter of testing the utility of the new model that Carnap and Russell had suggested. The model might prove fruitful, or it might prove to be just one more way of rejuvenating tired old philosophical controversies by phrasing them in a new jargon. Only time could tell. But there was no a priori reason to think that either symbolic logic or the famous 'rigour and clarity' on which the analytic philosophers kept pluming themselves, would pay off. There was no reason to think of Carnap's and Russell's model for philosophy as 'more scientific' or even more rigorous than Hegel's, Husserl's or Heidegger's. About all that one could say was that their books were easier to understand.

This is not to say that Kuhn showed the notion of 'being scientific' to be empty. Like other vague and inspiring ideas, this one can be filled in, and made concrete, in various ways. One way is to ask whether a discipline can offer accurate predictions, and can therefore be helpful for engineering, or medicine, or other practical purposes. Galilean mechanics was good at this, Aristotelian physics not very good at all. Medicine before Harvey offered fewer confirmed predictions than after Harvey. But Kuhn helped us realize that it is pointless to try to explain greater predictive success, in these cases, by saying that Galileo and Harvey were 'more scientific' than Aristotle and Galen. Rather, by showing that we can predict more than we had thought we could, these two men helped change the meaning of 'science' in such a way that 'able to make useful predictions' became a more important criterion for 'being an able scientist' than it had been previously.

But, in any case, this way of firming up the notion of scientificity is of no use when it comes to philosophy. Philosophers have never predicted anything successfully, and do not try to do so. So, for metaphilosophical purposes, the criterion of scientificity has to be different. The obvious alternative is: ability to get agreement among informed inquirers. The main reason admirers of physics distrust literary critics is that no consensus ever seems to form about the right interpretation of a text: there is little convergence of opinion. At the opposite extreme, mathematicians are usually unanimous about whether or not a theorem has been proved. Physicists are closer to the mathematics end of the spectrum, and politicians and social scientists closer to the literary criticism end. Analytic philosophers claimed (not very plausibly, as things turned out) that analytic philosophers were more capable of consensus than non-analytic philosophers, and in that sense were more scientific.

The trouble is that intersubjective agreement about who has succeeded and who has failed is easy to get if you can lay down criteria of success in advance. If all you want is fast relief, your choice of analgesic is clear (though the winning drug may have unfortunate, belated side effects). If you know that all you want out of science is accurate prediction, you have a fast way to decide between competing theories (though this criterion by itself would, at one time, have led you to favour Ptolemaic over Copernican astronomy). If you know that all you want is rigorous demonstration, you can check out mathematicians' proofs of theorems and then award the prize to the one who has proved the most (although the award will then always go to a hack, whose theorems are of no interest). But intersubjective agreement is harder to get when the criteria of success begin to proliferate, and even harder when those criteria themselves are up for grabs. So you can always increase the amount of consensus among philosophers by making your philosophizing more scholastic and minute, and decrease it by making your philosophizing more ambitious.

Reading Kuhn led me, and many others, to think that instead of mapping culture on to a epistemico-ontological hierarchy topped by the logical, objective and scientific, and bottoming out in the rhetorical, subjective and unscientific, we should instead map culture on to a sociological spectrum ranging from the chaotic left, where criteria are constantly changing, to the smug right, where they are, at least for the moment, fixed.

Thinking in terms of such a spectrum makes it possible to see a single discipline moving leftward in revolutionary periods and rightward in stable, dull periods – the sort of periods where you get what Kuhn called 'normal science'. In the fifteenth century, when most philosophy was scholastic and almost all physics contentedly Aristotelian, both physics and philosophy were pretty far to the right. In the seventeenth, both were pretty far to the left, but literary criticism was much further to the right than it was to become after the Romantic movement. In the nineteenth, physics had settled down and moved right, and philosophy was desperately trying to do so as well. But in the twentieth century, philosophy has had to settle for splitting itself up into separate traditions ('analytic' and 'Continental'), each of which claimed to be 'doing *real* philosophy', and each of which have fairly clear internal criteria of professional success. In this respect – lack of international consensus about who is doing worthwhile work – it remains much more like contemporary literary criticism than like any of the contemporary natural sciences.

This new, Kuhnian sociological view of the relation of the disciplines to one another has made people in many disciples more relaxed about the question of whether they have a rigorous research method, or whether their work produces knowledge rather than mere opinion. Since sociologists began reading Kuhn, for example, it has become easier for them to grant that Weber and Durkheim were great sociologists, even though neither was familiar with the powerful methods of statistical analysis in which sociologists are now trained. This permits them to concede that contemporary sociologists who abstain from statistics (David Riesman and Richard Sennett, for example) might be perfectly respectable members of the profession. To take another example, since psychologists began reading Kuhn, the question of whether Freudian depth psychology is as 'scientifically reputable' as Skinner's work with pigeons has seemed less pressing. Adolf Grunbaum is one of the relatively few philosophers of science to care whether Freud produced testable generalizations.

All of the social sciences, and all of the learned professions, have by now gone through a process of Kuhnianization, marked by an increased willingness to admit that there is no single model for good work in an academic discipline, that the criteria for good work have changed throughout the course of history, and probably will continue to change. Though analytic philosophy has been something of a holdout, even there there has been an increased willingness to historicize: to grant that there is no point in dividing the history of philosophy into sense and nonsense, and to admit that even Hegel and Heidegger might have done useful philosophical work.

These post-Kuhnian attempts to substitute a spectrum ranging from the controversial to the noncontroversial for the traditional Platonic hierarchy are, however, still staunchly resisted by two sorts of people. One is the kind of analytic philosopher who prides himself on being a 'realist' and who sees what he calls 'relativism' as a clear and present danger to our culture. (John Searle, who has bracketed me with Kuhn and Derrida as one of the more dangerous relativists, is perhaps the most conspicuous example.)[1] The other is the natural scientist who enjoys his inherited position at the top of an epistemico-ontological hierarchy, and has no intention of being toppled. Such scientists will tell you that 'no real scientist' takes Kuhn seriously.

Scientists of this sort think that they know all they need to know about philosophy of science simply by *being* scientists. They see no need to reflect on the questions that philosophers of science debate, and about which 'realist' philosophers disagree with Davidson, Putnam and Kuhn-disciples like myself. They seem to think that philosophers of science should test their views about the nature of science simply by asking native informants – asking their physicist friends, for example, whether they have finally managed to get physics right.

Steven Weinberg, a Nobel laureate in physics, is a good example of this way of thinking. Weinberg spoils a recent judicious and sensible article in *The New York Review of Books*[2] about the 'Sokal hoax' (a spoof article offering a defence of so-called postmodernist views on the basis of recent developments in physics) by concluding it with the usual scientist's exorcism of Kuhn: None of us who are really at home in the field take Kuhn seriously.

Here is a sample of Weinberg doing philosophy of science:

> What I mean when I say that the laws of physics are real is that they are real in pretty much the same sense (whatever that is) as the rocks in the fields, and not in the same sense (as implied by [Stanley] Fish) as the rules of baseball. We did not create the laws of physics or the rocks in the field, and we sometimes

unhappily find that we have been wrong about them, as when we stub our toe on an unnoticed rock, or when we find we have made a mistake (as most physicists have) about some scientific law. But the languages in which we describe rocks or in which we state physical laws are certainly created socially, so I am making an implicit assumption (which in everyday life we all make about rocks) that the statements about the laws of physics are in a one-to-one correspondence with aspects of objective reality. To put it another way, if we ever discover intelligent creatures on some distant planet and translate their scientific works, we will find that we and they have discovered the same laws . . . The objective nature of scientific knowledge has been denied by Andrew Ross and Bruno Latour and (as I understand them) by the influential philosophers Richard Rorty and the late Thomas Kuhn, but it is taken for granted by most natural scientists.

I have come to think that the laws of physics are real because my experience with the laws of physics does not seem to me very different in any fundamental way with my experience with rocks. For those who have not lived with the laws of physics, I can offer the obvious argument that the laws of physics work, and there is no other known way of looking at nature that works in anything like the same sense.[3]

I imagine that Weinberg thinks he is being as sensible and judicious in this concluding portion of his article as in its earlier portions. But he is not. He is just blowing smoke. He is throwing around terms ('objectively real', 'one-to-one correspondence', etc.) that have been the subject of endless philosophical reflection and controversy as if he and the common reader knew perfectly well what they meant, and could afford to ignore the pseudo-sophistication of the people who have spent their lives trying to figure out what sense, if any, might be given to them.

Weinberg treats Kuhn as a mere paradox-mongerer. He feels entitled to do so for no better reason than that, as a physicist, he is the ultimate court of appeal for any philosophical claim about the epistemico-ontological status of physical laws. The possibility that Kuhn might have rendered the whole idea of epistemological and ontological status obsolete, and with it the distinction between objective reality and some other kind of reality, does not cross his mind.

Earlier in his article Weinberg sensibly remarks that some distinguished scientists draw absolutely fabulous philosophical consequences from what might seem rather limited empirical results. (He mentions Heisenberg and Prigogine; he might also have mentioned Piaget and Eccles.) He rightly rebukes such people for exceeding their briefs, without realizing that that is what he himself is doing. He is assuming that he does not have to learn anything about the context of the discussion to which he thinks he is contributing: he can just charge in and straighten everybody out. He thinks that a physicist, by virtue of being a physicist, knows all that is necessary about the relation of physics to the rest of culture, and therefore can adjudicate philosophical disputes about its relation to other human activities.

Compare Weinberg's testimony to his experience with the laws of physics with a good old-fashioned moral theologian's testimony to his experience with the Will of God. This Will, the theologian tells us, is much more like a great big rock than like the rules of baseball. We did not create the prohibitions against usury and sodomy, though of course we can misinterpret them – an experience that, he assures us, is much like stubbing one's toe against a rock. Having lived with the moral law for a long time, and dealt with it on intimate terms, he is prepared to assure us that there is the same sort of one-to-one correspondence with objective reality in morals as there is in geology. The paradox-mongering speculations of atheistic relativists, he explains, are not taken seriously by anybody who is really at home in the field.

Weinberg tells us that all of us, in everyday life, recognize that there is a 'one-to-one correspondence' between what we say about rocks and 'aspects of objective reality'. But ask yourself, common reader, in your capacity as everyday speaker about rocks, whether you recognize anything of the sort. If you do, we philosophers would be grateful for some details. Do both the subject and the predicate of your sentences about rocks ('This rock is hard to move', say) stand in such a relation of correspondence? Are you sure that hard-to-moveness is really an aspect of *objective* reality? It's not hard for some of your neighbours to move, after all. Doesn't that make it an aspect of only *subjective* reality?

Or is it that the whole sentence stands in one-to-one correspondence to a single aspect of objective reality? Which aspect is that? The rock? Or the rock in its context, as obstacle to your gardening endeavours? What is an 'aspect' anyway? The way something looks in a certain context? Aren't some contexts more objective than others? Maybe it is only the rock as viewed by the particle physicist that is an aspect of objective reality (a view favoured by many eminent 'realist' philosophers)? Maybe the rock under other descriptions than the physicists' gets increasingly non-objective as sentences about it get fancier? Or perhaps all descriptions of the rock are on an epistemico-ontological par (a view favoured by many of us 'relativist' philosophers).

And do, while you are at it, tell us more about *correspondence*, a notion which has given us philosophers a great deal of trouble. Is the relation of correspondence a matter of properly educated humans' ability to utter noncontroversial statements about rocks at a single glance? Is this desirable relation absent in the case of their ability to utter noncontroversial statements about the batter's hits and strikes? Or is the relevant sort of correspondence a causal, physical matter (as Saul Kripke has suggested)? Or is the notion of correspondence so hopeless that it, along with that of 'accurate representation of reality', should be discarded from philosophy altogether (as Donald Davidson has suggested)?

I can come up with conundrums like this for a long time, but I suspect that Weinberg would not see the point of my raising any of them. The difference between us is that I am in the philosophy business and he is not. I concoct and hash over conundrums like that for a living. So did Kuhn. If you don't wish to discuss such conundrums – if you don't want to reflect on what you mean by 'objective' and 'corresponds' and 'works' and 'not made by us', and if you imagine that you can explicate 'real' by saying 'you know, like rocks' – you had better not think that you understand the epistemico-ontological status of physical laws better than Kuhn did (even if you happen to have discovered a few of those laws yourself). Kuhn and I may be quite wrong to abandon the traditional Platonic hierarchy of disciplines, but you will not be in a position to know whether we are or not until you have engaged in this sort of reflection.

Weinberg's attachment to the traditional Platonic hierarchy is clearest in a passage where he says

> What Herbert Butterfield called the Whig interpretation of history is legitimate in the history of science in a way that it is not in the history of politics or culture, because science is cumulative, and permits definite judgements of success or failure.[4]

Does Weinberg really want to abstain from definite judgements of the success or failure of, say, the constitutional changes brought about by the Reconstruction Amendments and by the New Deal's use of the interstate commerce clause? Does he really want to disagree with those who think that poets and artists stand on the shoulders of their predecessors, and accumulate knowledge about how to write poems and paint pictures? Does he really think that when you write the history of parliamentary democracy or of the novel that you should *not*, Whiggishly, tell a story of cumulation? Can he suggest what a non-Whiggish, legitimate history of these areas of culture would look like?

I doubt that Weinberg has any clearer idea what he means by 'legitimate' and 'definite' and 'cumulative' than of what he means by 'one-to-one correspondence'. But his intent is clear: it is to keep natural science at the top of the cultural pecking order.

I hope it is clear that I do not want to assign science a *lower* position on this pecking order. What I want to do is urge that we stop using terms like 'real' and 'objective' to construct such an order. I want to substitute questions about the utility of disciplines for questions about their status. It seems to me as silly to try to establish a hierarchy among disciplines, or cultural activities, as to establish one among the tools in a toolbox, or among the flowers in a garden.

For my anti-hierarchical purposes, I find it helpful to say, with

Kuhn, that 'whether or not individual practitioners are aware of it, they are trained to and rewarded for solving intricate puzzles – be they instrumental, theoretical, logical, or mathematical – at the interface between their phenomenal world and their community's beliefs about it.'[5] I would interpret this remark of Kuhn's as applying to all practitioners of all disciplines: physics as much as jurisprudence, philosophy as much as medicine, psychology as much as architecture.

As I read him, Kuhn gave us a way of seeing the history of physics, of philosophy, of the novel, and of parliamentary government, in the same terms: human beings trying to improve on their ancestors' solution to old problems in such a way as to solve some new, recently arisen problems as well. Kuhn suggested that in all these areas we could drop the notion of 'getting closer to the way things really are' or 'more fully grasping the essence of . . .' or 'finding out how it really should be done'. For all these, we can substitute the notion of capitalizing on past successes while at the same time coping with present problems.

Kuhn aimed, he once said, to 'deny all meaning to claims that successive scientific beliefs become more and more probable or better and better approximations to the truth and simultaneously to suggest that the subject of truth claims cannot be a relation between beliefs and a putatively mind-independent or "external" world'.[6] This suggestion is, admittedly, a shock to common sense, not to mention to the self-esteem of those accustomed to being at the top of the hierarchy of disciplines. But it is the sort of healthy shock that all great philosophers have administered to the common sense of their times. Philosophy is not a field in which one achieves greatness by ratifying the community's previous intuitions.

So much for my protest against Weinberg's attempt to dismiss Kuhn as somebody who lacked sufficiently intimate contact with the laws of physics. But I should end by making an embarrassing admission: Kuhn would have been embarrassed by my defence of him.

Kuhn thought physicists were *wonderful*, and was dubious about philosophers like me (the only marginally 'analytical' kind – the kind with a lot of literary interests, a fondness for metaphor, and other symptoms of intellectual squishiness). Not only were many of his heroes Nobel laureates in physics, but the more 'clear and rigorous' a philosopher was (the more he sounded like Carnap, roughly speaking), the better Kuhn liked him. As one of his obituaries accurately noted, Kuhn usually preferred his critics to his fans.

In interviews Kuhn took pains to distance himself from 'Rorty's relativism', and from the writings of various other fans who had tried to weave Kuhnian doctrines into the fabric of philosophical positions that Kuhn found unattractive. But, even though we were colleagues for some 15 years, I never got straight why Kuhn thought I was more 'relativistic' than he was, or where exactly he thought I went off the rails. I always hoped that when he published the book on which he was working in the last decade of his life – a return to the controversies raised by *Structure* – I would be able to cite chapter and verse to show him that we had been preaching pretty much the same doctrine.

I tend to explain away the fact that Kuhn found my enthusiasm for his work embarrassing by the thought that he sometimes confused criticism of the purportedly exalted epistemico-ontological status of physics with criticism of its aesthetic and moral grandeur. I too acknowledge this grandeur. I am happy to agree with C. P. Snow that modern physics is one of the most beautiful achievements of the human mind. I am happy, but not surprised, to be told by Weinberg that his is still a field in which unknown young people are making the big contributions – a field in which the author of a single paper can acquire an instant international reputation, a reputation that has nothing to do with academic politics, but is simply the prompt and proper reward for sheer brilliance.

I think that Kuhn was so impressed by this moral and aesthetic grandeur that he thought that any attempt to dismantle the old Platonic hierarchy should be accompanied by appropriate gestures of respect toward natural science – traditional gestures that I sometimes did not bother to make. He may have had a point. But I would still insist that getting rid of the old quasi-Platonic pecking order, and thereby creating an intellectual environment in which eminent scientists will no longer be tempted to indulge in rocky rhetoric such as Weinberg's, is a very useful project. Kuhn was one of the most influential philosophers of our century because he did as much as anyone else – even Wittgenstein – to get this useful work done.

* * * *

NOTES

1 See my reply to Searle's 'Rationality and Realism: What is at Stake?', reprinted as 'John Searle on Realism and Relativism' in my *Truth and Progress*.
2 Steven Weinberg, 'Sokal's Hoax', *New York Review of Books* (August 1996), vol. VIII, pp. 11–15.
3 Weinberg, pp. 14–15.
4 Weinberg, p. 15.
5 Thomas Kuhn, 'Afterwords' in *World Change: Thomas Kuhn and the Nature of Science*, Paul Horwich, ed. (Cambridge, Mass.: MIT Press, 1993), p. 338.
6 Kuhn, p. 330.

13. On Heidegger's Nazism

(1990)

Heidegger's writings – both early and late – are full of polemics against the appearance–reality distinction. In the early work, this polemic centres upon a Dewey-like insistence on the priority of *Welt* to *Wirklich-keit*, of the *Zuhanden* to the *Vorhanden*, and of *Auslegung* to *Aussage*. If one reads paragraphs 31–3 of *Being and Time* as I should like to, and as Mark Okrent has in his book *Heidegger's Pragmatism*, Heidegger will be seen as making theory an instrument of practice, as construing assertions as tools for the accomplishment of some human project. Even in the later work, where Heidegger treats pragmatism as a banal variety of Nietzschean nihilism, he still insists over and over that the Greek appearance–reality distinction is symptomatic of the West's metaphysical way of speaking Being. Indeed, he sometimes traces the pragmatism of our time – its technological understanding of Being – back to that distinction.

Yet Heidegger himself, in his own rhetorical practice, clings to the very appearance–reality distinction that he repudiates in theory. In *Being and Time* he constantly describes himself as excavating down to conditions of possibility deeper than those discerned by his predecessors. In his later works he is always telling us that every contemporary understanding of our historical situation other than his own is shallow – that it is unable to penetrate to the essence of technology, and instead gets hung up on superficial questions like nuclear holocaust. In these writings, Heidegger refuses to think of himself as one more finite and contingent bit of *Dasein* assembling tools for the accomplishment of various finite projects. Rather, he wants to see himself as projectless, will-less, a mere open ear, a conduit for the voice of Being.

Those who, like myself, have taken more from the early pragmatist

Heidegger than from the later listener to the voice of Being, are very suspicious of this project of becoming projectless. It seems to us that as Heidegger grew older he drew back from the insistence on finitude that dominated *Being and Time*. We see this as regression. We have to admit that Heidegger became a more original and more interesting thinker as he grew older and more megalomaniacal, but we regard this is as one more example of passionate and idiosyncratic error being more instructive than sober and useful truth. So for us Heidegger's writings are not a conduit through which we can hear the voice of Being. Rather, they are a toolbox. They are the receptacle in which Heidegger deposited the tools that he invented at various times to accomplish one or another project.

These projects were varied, and sometimes got in each other's way. Early on, Heidegger wanted to revive Aristotle in order to follow through on the neo-Thomist criticism of Descartes. Later he wanted to go beyond Nietzsche by going back behind Aristotle. Sometimes he wanted to describe *Dasein* in general, and at other times to describe only twentieth-century *Dasein*. Once he wanted to be the heroic leader of a national movement, but later he wanted to be the wise old hermit who knew that 'only a God can save us'. His suggestion that he always followed a single star seems to me self-deceptive self-flattery. I see the toolbox we have inherited from him as containing a very varied assortment, constructed for various different purposes – an assortment in which only some items are still useful. I think that the best tribute we can pay to Heidegger's achievements is to be selective about what we take from him. For myself, I should like to keep the pragmatist and ignore the Nazi, keep the plot outline of Heidegger's history of metaphysics while rewriting its downbeat ending, keep selected items of Heidegger's imagery and jargon while shrugging off his world-historical pretensions.

Heidegger would have been exasperated with this way of appropriating him. But so are his most implacable critics. These critics claim that his Nazism was not just one facet of his thought, just one of his various projects, but rather a vital clue to the underlying essence of his thought. They insist that his thought is just as tightly unified as he believed it to have been. They think that there is an underlying reality beneath the diverse appearances, that he really was following a single star – a dark, evil star.

For these critics, Heidegger is not just a collection of projects, some good and some bad. For they have the same essentialist attitude toward Heidegger as Heidegger had toward the twentieth century. Heidegger needed to see everything in our century other than its technologism as mere transitory appearance. The critics I have in mind need to see everything in Heidegger other than his antiegalitarianism and devotion to the *Führerprinzip* as superficial. By contrast, we pragmatists see the twentieth century as a mixed bag of good news and bad news, and Heidegger's work as a toolbox containing some splendid things lying next to a lot of outdated junk.

For those of us who wish to continue to pick over the tools in Heidegger's box, the fact that the man who designed these remarkable tools was first a Nazi and later a cowardly hypocrite is just one of history's many ironies. We wish the fact were otherwise. We have the same wistfulness about other thinkers whom we admire. We wish that Carnap had listened to Sidney Hook's good advice and not stooged for Stalin by sponsoring the 1948 Waldorf Peace Conference. We wish that Sartre had not waited until 1956 to break with the party line. We wish that Yeats and Shaw had not enthused over Mussolini before finding out what was happening to his political prisoners. We wish that the New Left of the 1960s had not enthused over Castro and Mao before finding out what was happening to their political prisoners. But we regard the political initiatives of these premature enthusiasts as largely irrelevant to their intellectual legacies.

This claim of irrelevance is not acceptable to critics who would like Heidegger to remain a pariah. They see the rectorial address as a glimpse of the real, the essential Heidegger, whereas I do not believe that there is such a thing as the essential Heidegger. I think that these critics are right only to the following extent: Heidegger was antiegalitarian throughout his life, and never cared in the slightest for the liberal project of increasing the sum of human happiness. But I doubt that this antiegalitarianism would seem very important to his readers, would seem an index to the real, true, essential Heidegger, if it were not for Heidegger's silence about the massacre of the Jews.

For this silence is what makes Heidegger's case different from that of Carnap or Sartre. Carnap and Sartre were judging political events in Russia and central Europe at a distance. But Heidegger watched his Jewish colleagues being dismissed from their jobs, and then watched them disappear to a fate about which he could easily have learned if he had thought it worth the trouble. That silence is also what makes Heidegger different from the general run of antiegalitarians. Many eminent twentieth-century writers have mistrusted democracy, but he was the only one to have remained unmoved by the Holocaust.

I think that Habermas and Derrida are right in saying that any of us might, given Heidegger's background, have thought that Hitler was Germany's only hope in 1933. They are right in saying that the really unforgivable thing is the postwar silence. I agree that this silence was unforgivable, but I am unable to deduce this silence from the content of Heidegger's books, or even to see it as a sign of something that should make us suspicious of those books. This is because I take a person's moral character – his or her selective sensitivity to the sufferings of others – to be shaped by chance events in his or her life. Often, perhaps usually, this sensitivity varies independently of the projects of self-creation that the person undertakes in his or her work.

I can clarify what I mean by 'chance events' and 'independent variation' by sketching a slightly different possible world – a world in which Heidegger joins his fellow antiegalitarian, Thomas Mann, in preaching resistance to Hitler. To see how this possible world might have been actual, imagine that in the summer of 1930 Heidegger suddenly finds himself deeply in love with a beautiful, intense, adoring philosophy student named Sarah Mandelbaum. Sarah is Jewish, but Heidegger barely notices this, dizzy with passion as he is. After a painful divorce from Elfride – a process that costs him the friendship of, among other people, the Husserls – Heidegger marries Sarah in 1932. In January 1933 they have a son, Abraham.

Heidegger jokes that Sarah can think of Abraham as named after the patriarch, but that he will think of him as named after Abraham a Santa Clara, the only other Messkirch boy to make good. Sarah looks up Abraham a Santa Clara's anti-Semitic writings in the library stacks, and Heidegger's little joke becomes the occasion of the first serious quarrel between husband and wife. But by the end of 1933, Heidegger is no longer making such jokes. For Sarah makes him *notice* that the Jewish *Beamte*, including his father-in-law, have been cashiered. Heidegger reads things about himself in the student newspaper that make him realize that his day in the sun may be over. Gradually it dawns upon him that his love for Sarah has cost him much of his prestige, and will sooner or later cost him his job.

But he still loves her, and eventually he leaves his beloved Freiburg for her sake. In 1935 Heidegger is teaching in Berne, but only as a visitor. Switzerland has by now given away all its philosophy chairs. Suddenly a call comes from the Institute for Advanced Study in Princeton. There Heidegger spends two years slowly and painfully learning English, aching for the chance once again to spellbind seminar rooms full of worshipfully attentive students. He gets a chance to do so in 1937 when some of his fellow émigrés arrange a permanent job for him at the University of Chicago.

There he meets Elizabeth Mann Borgese, who introduces him to her father. Heidegger manages to overcome his initial suspicion of the Hanseatic darling of fortune, and Mann his initial suspicion of the Black Forest *Bauernkind*. They find they agree with each other, and with Adorno and Horkheimer; that America is a *reductio ad absurdum* of Enlightenment hopes, a land without culture. But their contempt for America does not prevent them from seeing Hitler as having ruined Germany and being about to ruin Europe. Heidegger's stirring anti-Nazi broadcasts enable him to gratify a need to strike a heroic attitude before large masses of people – a need that he might, under other circumstances, have gratified in a rectorial address.

By the end of the Second World War, Heidegger's marriage is on the rocks. Sarah Heidegger is a social democrat to the core, loves America, and is a passionate zionist. She has come to think of Heidegger as a great man with a cold and impervious heart, a heart which had once opened to her but remains closed to her social hopes. She has come to despise the egotist as much as she admires the philosopher and the anti-Nazi polemicist. In 1947 she separates from Heidegger and takes the 14-year-old Abraham with her to Palestine. She is wounded in the civil war but eventually, after the proclamation of independence, becomes a philosophy professor at Tel Aviv University.

Heidegger himself returns to Freiburg in triumph in 1948. There he gets his old friend Gadamer a job, even though he is acidly contemptuous of Gadamer's acquiescence in the Nazi takeover of the German universities. He eventually takes as his third wife a war widow, a woman who reminds all his old friends of Elfride. When he dies in 1976, his wife lays on his coffin the Presidential Medal of Freedom, the medal of the order *Pour le Mérite*, and the gold medal of the Nobel Prize for Literature. This last had been awarded him in the year after the publication of his brief but poignant elegy for Abraham, who had died on the Golan Heights in 1967.

What books did Heidegger write in this possible world? Almost exactly the same ones as he wrote in the actual one. In this world, however, the *Introduction to Metaphysics* contains a contemptuous identification of the National Socialist movement with the mindless nihilism of modern technology, as well as the remark that Hitler is dragging Germany down to the metaphysical level of Russia and America. The seminars on Nietzsche are much the same as those he gave in our world, except for a digression on Nietzsche's loathing for anti-Semites, a digression that contains uncanny parallels to Sartre's contemporaneous but independent *Portrait of the Anti-Semite*. In this world, Heidegger writes most of the same exegetical essays he wrote in our world, but he adds appreciations of Thoreau and of Jefferson, composed for lectures at Harvard and at the University of Virginia respectively. These two essays evince Heidegger's familiar sentimental agrarianism and suspicion of the urban proletariat. His books in this world are, in short, documents of the same struggle he carried on in the actual world – the struggle to move outside the philosophical tradition and there 'sing a new song'. This struggle, this private pursuit of purity, was the core of his life. It was incapable of being greatly influenced either by his love for particular persons or by the political events of his time.

In our world, Heidegger said nothing political after the war. In the possible world I am sketching he puts his prestige as an anti-Nazi to work in making the German political right respectable. He is adored by Franz Josef Strauss, who pays regular and worshipful visits to

Todtnauberg. Occasionally Heidegger appears with Strauss at political rallies. Social Democrats like Habermas regret Heidegger's being consistently on the wrong side in postwar German politics. Sometimes, in private, they voice the suspicion that, in slightly different circumstances, Heidegger would have made a pretty good Nazi. But they never dream of saying such a thing in public about the greatest European thinker of our time.

In our actual world Heidegger was a Nazi, a cowardly hypocrite, and the greatest European thinker of our time. In the possible world I have sketched he was pretty much the same man, but he happened to have his nose rubbed in the torment of the Jews until he finally *noticed* what was going on, until his sense of pity and his sense of shame were finally awakened. In that world he had the good luck to have been unable to have become a Nazi, and so to have had less occasion for cowardice or hypocrisy. In our actual world, he turned his face away, and eventually resorted to hysterical denial. This denial brought on his unforgivable silence. But that denial and that silence do not tell us much about the books he wrote, nor conversely. In both worlds, the only link between Heidegger's politics and his books is the contempt for democracy he shared with, for example, Eliot, Chesterton, Tate, Waugh and Paul Claudel – people whom, as Auden predicted, we have long since pardoned for writing well. We could as easily have pardoned Heidegger his attitude towards democracy, if that had been all. But in the world without Sarah, the world in which Heidegger had the bad luck to live, it was not all.

To sum up: I have been urging that we can find in the early Heidegger's pragmatic antiessentialism reasons for abandoning the attempt to see the man and the books in a single vision, and perhaps even the attempt to see the books as stages on a single *Denkweg*. If we take that antiessentialism more seriously than Heidegger himself proved able to take it, we shall not be tempted to dramatize Heidegger in the way in which he dramatized his favourite thinkers and poets. We shall not assign thinkers and poets places in a world-historical narrative. We shall see both them and their books as vector sums of contingent pressures. We shall see Heidegger as one more confused, torn, occasionally desperate, human being, someone much like our-

selves. We shall read Heidegger's books as he least wanted them read
– as occasions for exploitation, recent additions to our *Bestand an Waren*.
We shall stop yearning for depth, and stop trying either to worship
heroes or to hunt down criminals. Instead, we shall settle for useful
tools, and take them where we can find them.

IV

Politics

14. Failed Prophecies, Glorious Hopes

(1998)

Failed prophecies often make invaluable inspirational reading. Consider two examples: the New Testament and the Communist Manifesto. Both were intended by their authors as predictions of what was going to happen – predictions based on superior knowledge of the forces which determine human history. Both sets of predictions have, so far, been ludicrous flops. Both claims to knowledge have become objects of ridicule.

Christ did not return. Those who claim that He is about to do so, and that it would be prudent to become a member of a particular sect or denomination in order to prepare for this event, are rightly viewed with suspicion. To be sure, nobody can prove that the Second Coming will not occur, thus producing empirical evidence for the Incarnation. But we have been waiting a long time.

Analogously, nobody can prove that Marx and Engels were wrong when they proclaimed that 'the bourgeoisie has forged the weapons that bring death to itself'. It may be that the globalization of the labour market in the next century will reverse the progressive bourgeoisization of the European and North American proletariat, and that it will become true that 'the bourgeoisie is incapable of continuing to rule, since it is unable even to assure an existence to the slaves within their slavery'. Maybe the breakdown of capitalism, and the assumption of the political power by a virtuous and enlightened proletariat, will then come to pass. Maybe, in short, Marx and Engels just got the timing a century or two wrong. Still, capitalism has overcome many crises in the past, and we have been waiting a long time for the emergence of this proletariat.

Again, no scoffer can be sure that what evangelical Christians call 'becoming a New Being in Christ Jesus' is not a genuinely transformative, miraculous experience. But those who claim to have been reborn in this way do not seem to behave as differently from the way they behaved in the past as we had hoped. We have been waiting a long time for prosperous Christians to behave more decently than prosperous pagans.

Analogously, we cannot be sure but that some day we may catch sight of new ideals which will replace those that Marx and Engels dismissively called 'bourgeois individuality, bourgeois independence, and bourgeois freedom'. But we have waited patiently for regimes calling themselves 'Marxist' to explain to us exactly what these new ideals look like, and how they are to be realized in practice. So far, all such regimes have turned out to be throwbacks to pre-Enlightenment barbarism rather than the first glimmerings of a post-Enlightenment utopia.

There are, to be sure, still people who read the Christian Scriptures in order to figure out what is likely to happen a few years or decades down the road. Ronald Reagan did, for example. Up until quite recently, many intellectuals read the Communist Manifesto for the same purpose. Just as the Christians have counselled patience, and assured us that it is unfair to judge Christ by the mistakes of his sinful servants, so the Marxists have assured us that all the 'Marxist' regimes so far have been absurd perversions of Marx's intent. The few surviving Marxists now admit that the Communist parties of Lenin, Mao and Castro bore no resemblance to the empowered proletariat of Marx's dreams, but were merely the tools of autocrats and oligarchs. Nevertheless, they tell us, some day there will be a genuinely revolutionary, genuinely proletarian, party – a party whose triumph will bring us a freedom as unlike 'bourgeois freedom' as the Christian doctrine that love is the only law is unlike the arbitrary dictates of Leviticus.

Most of us can no longer take either Christian or Marxist postponements and reassurances seriously. But this does not, and should not, prevent us from finding inspiration and encouragement in the New Testament and the Manifesto. For both documents are expressions of the same hope: that some day we shall be willing and able to treat the needs of all human beings with the respect and consideration with which we treat the needs of those closest to us, those whom we love.

Both texts have gathered greater inspirational power as the years have passed. For each is the founding document of a movement which has done much for human freedom and human equality. By this time, thanks to the rise in population since 1848, both may have inspired equal numbers of brave and self-sacrificing men and women to risk their lives and fortunes in order to prevent future generations from enduring needless suffering. There may already have been as many socialist martyrs as Christian martyrs. If human hope can survive the anthrax-laden warheads, the suitcase-sized nuclear devices, the overpopulation, the globalized labour market, and the environmental disasters of the coming century, if we have descendants who, a century from now, still have a historical record to consult and are still able to seek inspiration from the past, perhaps they will think of Saint Agnes and Rosa Luxemburg, Saint Francis and Eugene Debs, Father Damien and Jean Jaurès, as members of a single movement.

Just as the New Testament is still read by millions of people who spend little time wondering whether Christ will some day return in glory, so the Communist Manifesto is still read even by those of us who hope and believe that full social justice can be attained without a revolution of the sort Marx predicted: that a classless society, a world in which 'the free development of each is the condition for the free development of all' can come about as a result of what Marx despised as 'bourgeois reformism'. Parents and teachers should encourage young people to read both books. The young will be morally better for having done so.

We should raise our children to find it intolerable that we who sit behind desks and punch keyboards are paid ten times as much as people who get their hands dirty cleaning our toilets, and a hundred times as much as those who fabricate our keyboards in the Third World. We should ensure that they worry about the fact that the countries which industrialized first have a hundred times the wealth of those which have not yet industrialized. Our children need to learn, early on, to see the inequalities between their own fortunes and those of other children as neither the Will of God nor the necessary price for economic efficiency, but as an evitable tragedy. They should start thinking, as early as possible, about how the world might be changed so as to ensure that no one goes hungry while others have a surfeit.

The children need to read Christ's message of human fraternity alongside Marx and Engel's account of how industrial capitalism and free markets – indispensable as they have turned out to be – make it very difficult to institute that fraternity. They need to see their lives as given meaning by efforts towards the realization of the moral potential inherent in our ability to communicate our needs and our hopes to one another. They should learn stories both about Christian congregations meeting in the catacombs and about workers' rallies in city squares. For both have played equally important roles in the long process of actualizing this potentiality.

The inspirational value of the New Testament and the Communist Manifesto is not diminished by the fact that many millions of people were enslaved, tortured or starved to death by sincere, morally earnest people who recited passages from one or the other text in order to justify their deeds. Memories of the dungeons of the Inquisition and the interrogation rooms of the KGB, of the ruthless greed and arrogance of the Christian clergy and of the Communist nomenklatura, should indeed make us reluctant to hand over power to people who claim to know what God, or History, wants. But there is a difference between knowledge and hope. Hope often takes the form of false prediction, as it did in both documents. But hope for social justice is nevertheless the only basis for a worthwhile human life.

Christianity and Marxism still have the power to do a great deal of harm, for both the New Testament and the Communist Manifesto can still be effectively quoted by moral hypocrites and egomaniacal gangsters. In the US, for example, an organization called the Christian Coalition holds the Republican Party (and thus Congress) in its thrall. The leaders of this movement have convinced millions of voters that taxing the suburbs to help the ghettos is an unChristian thing to do. In the name of 'Christian family values', the Coalition teaches that for the US government to give a helping hand to the children of unemployable and unwed teenage mothers would 'undermine indi-vidual responsibility'.

The Coalition's activities are less violent than those of the now-moribund Sendero Luminoso movement in Peru. But the results of its work are equally destructive. Sendero Luminoso, in its murderous heyday, was headed by a crazed philosophy teacher who thought of himself as the successor of Lenin and Mao, as an inspired contemporary interpreter of the writings of Marx. The Christian Coalition is headed by a sanctimonious televangelist: the Reverend Pat Robertson – a contemporary interpreter of the Gospels who will probably cause much more suffering in the United States than Abiel Guzman managed to cause in Peru.

To sum up: it is best, when reading both the Communist Manifesto and the New Testament, to ignore prophets who claim to be the authorized interpreters of one or the other text. When reading the texts themselves, we should skip lightly past the predictions, and concentrate on the expressions of hope. We should read both as inspirational documents, appeals to what Lincoln called 'the better angels of our nature', rather than as accurate accounts of human history or of human destiny.

If one treats the term 'Christianity' as the name of one such appeal, rather than as a claim to knowledge, then that word still names a powerful force working for human decency and human equality. 'Socialism', similarly considered, is the name of the same force – an updated, more precise name. 'Christian Socialism' is pleonastic: nowadays you cannot hope for the fraternity which the Gospels preach without hoping that democratic governments will redistribute money and opportunity in a way that the market never will. There is no way to take the New Testament seriously as a moral imperative, rather than as a prophecy, without taking the need for such redistribution equally seriously.

Dated as the Communist Manifesto is, it is still an admirable statement of the great lesson we learned from watching industrial capitalism in action; that the overthrow of authoritarian governments, and the achievement of constitutional democracy, is not enough to ensure human equality or human decency. It is as true as it was in 1848 that the rich will always try to get richer by making the poor poorer, that total commodification of labour will lead to the immizer- ation of the wage-earners, and that 'the executive of the modern state is but a committee for managing the common affairs of the whole bourgeoisie'.

The bourgeoisie–proletariat distinction may by now be as outdated as the pagan–Christian distinction, but if one substitutes 'the richest 20 per cent' for 'the bourgeoisie' and 'the other 80 per cent' for 'the proletariat', most of the sentences of the Manifesto will still ring true. (Admittedly, however, they ring slightly less true in fully developed welfare states like Germany and slightly more true in countries like the US, in which greed has retained the upper hand, and in which the welfare state has remained rudimentary.) To say that history is 'the history of class struggle' is still true, if it is interpreted to mean that in every culture, under every form of government, and in every imaginable situation (e.g., England when Henry VIII dissolved the monasteries, Indonesia after the Dutch went home, China after Mao's death, Britain and America under Thatcher and Reagan) the people who have already got their hands on money and power will lie, cheat and steal in order to make sure that they and their descendants monopolize both for ever.

Insofar as history presents a *moral* spectacle, it is the struggle to break such monopolies. The use of Christian doctrine to argue for the abolition of slavery (and to argue against the American equivalent of the Nuremberg Laws – the racial segregation statutes) shows Christianity at its best. The use of Marxist doctrine to raise the consciousness of workers – to make it clear to them how they are being cheated – shows Marxism at its best. When the two have coalesced, as they did in the 'Social Gospel' movement, in the theologies of Paul Tillich and Walter Rauschenbusch, and in the most socialistic of the papal encyclicals, they have enabled the struggle for social justice to transcend the controversies between theists and atheists. Those controversies *should* be transcended: we should read the New Testament as saying that how we treat each other on earth matters a great deal more than the outcome of debate concerning the existence or nature of another world.

The trade union movement, which Marx and Engels thought of as only a transition to the establishment of revolutionary political parties, has turned out to be the most inspiring embodiment of the Christian virtues of self-sacrifice and of fraternal *agape* in recorded history. The rise of the trade unions is, morally speaking, the most encouraging development of modern times. It witnessed the purest and most unselfish heroism. Though many trade unions have become corrupt, and many others have ossified, the moral stature of the unions towers above that of the churches and the corporations, the governments and the universities. For the unions were founded by men and women who had an enormous amount to lose – they risked losing the chance of work altogether, the chance to bring food home to their families. They took that risk for the sake of a better human future. We are all deeply in their debt. The organizations they founded are sanctified by their sacrifices.

The Manifesto inspired the founders of most of the great unions of modern times. By quoting its words, the founders of the unions were able to bring millions of people out on strike against degrading conditions and starvation wages. Those words buttressed the faith of the strikers that their sacrifice – their willingness to see their children go without sufficient food rather than to yield to the owners' demand for a higher return on investment – would not be in vain. A document which has accomplished that much will always remain among the treasures of our intellectual and spiritual heritage. For the Manifesto spelled out what the workers were gradually coming to realize: that 'instead of rising with the progress of industry', the worker was in danger of 'sinking deeper and deeper below the conditions of existence of his own class'. This danger was avoided, at least temporarily, in Europe and North America thanks to the courage of workers who had read the Manifesto and who, as a result, were emboldened to demand their share of political power. Had they waited for the Christian kindness and charity of their superiors, their children would still be illiterate and badly fed.

The words of the Gospels and of the Manifesto may have provided equal quantities of courage and inspiration. But there are many respects in which the Manifesto is a better book to give to the young than the New Testament. For the latter document is morally flawed by its otherworldliness, by its suggestion that we can separate the question of our individual relation to God – our individual chance for salvation – from our participation in cooperative efforts to end needless suffering. Many passages in the Gospels have suggested to slaveowners that they can keep right on lashing their slaves, and to rich people that they can keep right on starving the poor. For they are going to Heaven anyway, their sins having been forgiven as a result of having accepted Christ as Lord.

The New Testament, a document of the ancient world, accepts one of the central convictions of the Greek philosophers who urge that contemplation of universal truths is the ideal life for a human being. This conviction is based on the premise that the social conditions of human life will never change in any important respect: we shall always have the poor with us – and perhaps the slaves as well. This conviction leads the writers of the New Testament to turn their attention from the possibility of a better human future to the hope of pie in the sky when we die. The only utopia these writers can imagine is in another world altogether.

We moderns are superior to the ancients – both pagan and Christian – in our ability to imagine a utopia here on earth. The eighteenth and nineteenth centuries witnessed, in Europe and North America, a massive shift in the locus of human hope: a shift from eternity to future time, from speculation about how to win divine favour to planning for the happiness of future generations. This sense that the human future can be made different from the human past, unaided by non-human powers, is magnificently expressed in the Manifesto.

It would be best, of course, if we could find a new document to provide our children with inspiration and hope – one which was as free of the defects of the New Testament as of those of the Manifesto. It would be good to have a reformist text, one which lacked the apocalyptic character of both books – which did not say that all things must be made new, or that justice 'can be attained only by the forcible overthrow of all existing social conditions'. It would be well to have a document which spelled out the details of a this-worldly utopia without assuring us that this utopia will emerge full-blown, and quickly, as soon as some single decisive change has occurred – as soon as private property is abolished, or as soon as we have all taken Jesus into our hearts.

It would be best, in short, if we could get along without prophecy and claims to knowledge of the forces which determine history – if generous hope could sustain itself without such reassurances. Some day perhaps we shall have a new text to give to our children – one which abstains from prediction yet still expresses the same yearning for fraternity as does the New Testament, and is as filled with sharp-eyed descriptions of our most recent forms of inhumanity to each other as the Manifesto. But in the meantime we should be grateful for two texts which have helped make us better – have helped us overcome, to some degree, our brutish selfishness and our cultivated sadism.

15. A Spectre is Haunting the Intellectuals: Derrida on Marx

(1995)

Suppose that Nietzsche had been much more central to the rhetoric of Nazism than he actually was. Suppose also that the Third Reich, after having conquered Britain and Russia, had lasted quite a while, breaking up only in 1989. For 55 years, every European who wanted to get ahead in the world had to join the Nazi Party. Everybody who joined the Nazi Party had to take a lot of boring courses in philosophy – the philosophy of Nietzscheanism-Hitlerism – taught by bored, third-rate hacks. One imagines that, after the breakup of the Reich, these Europeans would have wanted to give Nietzsche a rest.

People in eastern and central Europe tend to feel this way about Marx. They have heard a lot about Marx for many decades, and would like, at least for a while, not to hear any more. Those among them who have read Kolakowski suspect that the last eight pages of his *Main Currents of Marxism* tell you pretty much all you will ever need to know about Marx and Marxism-Leninism. If one reminds Czech or Ukrainian intellectuals that Marx was a remarkably original thinker, that he conjoined an extraordinarily vivid imagination with a very sharp eye for who was doing what to whom, and that he may haunt European thought for centuries, they are likely to shrug their shoulders. They react just as people who had had to pass exams on Nietzscheanism-Hitlerism would react to equally plausible praise of Nietzsche.

You get similar shrugs at the mention of Marx from a lot of anglophones who never studied him very hard when they were young, and are not inclined to start now. I am one such. Until I was 40 or so, I still solemnly swore that some time (next summer, maybe) I would finally get around to finishing *Kapital*, Aquinas's *Summa Theologica*, and Richardson's *Pamela*. But as the usual middle-aged realization of the shortness of life came over me, I let the obligation to finish these books slide gently off my back. So in this respect I am not the best reviewer of Derrida's *Specters of Marx*.[1] There is a lot of Marx I have never read, and am no longer ambitious to read.

American leftists of my generation tend to think of Marx as having explained the injustices produced by nineteenth-century capitalism better than anyone else. But we regret that he mixed up sharp-eyed economic and political analysis with a lot of windy Hegelisms. We think it a pity that the best political economist of the nineteenth century happened to major in philosophy, and never quite got over it. Like Sidney Hook, we suspect that Dewey filtered out everything that was worth saving in Hegel, and that all Marx adds to Dewey, Weber and the other philosophers of social democracy are some pungent details about exactly how the rich manage to keep the poor impotent, and some helpful hints for debunking the hypocrisy of defenders of the status quo. So a typical anglophone reaction to Althusser's claim that Marx discovered a new science was stark incredulity. We anglophones had the same reaction to Sartre's claim that existentialism is just an enclave within Marxism.

One *Marxisant* response to the weariness of the Czechs and Ukrainians, and to the happy-go-lucky pragmatism of anglophones like myself, is to urge, as Derrida parodically puts it, that Marx 'doesn't belong to the communists, to the parties, he ought to figure within our great canon of Western political philosophy. Return to Marx, let's finally read him as a great philosopher.'[2] Derrida spurns this response, and urges that we 'avoid the neutralizing anaesthesia of a new theoreticism, and . . . prevent a philosophical-philological return to Marx from prevailing'.[3]

For Derrida, the neutralizing anaesthesia of a new theoreticism is what you will get if you read someone who has the ability to move us beyond the present limits of our imagination, or our will, as if he were merely giving new answers to old questions. Marx is, for him, too important to be made into a scientist, a solver of political or philosophical problems. Derrida associates himself with Blanchot's criticism of Althusser's reading of Marx, and with Blanchot's remark that 'neither science nor thinking emerges from Marx's work intact'.[4] He reads

Marx as a fellow romantic idealist, not as the discoverer of a set of true propositions. So he warns us against the danger of 'play[ing] Marx off against Marxism so as to neutralize, or at any rate muffle the political imperative in the untroubled exegesis of a classical text'.[5]

Derrida took Marx very seriously indeed when he was young, read lots and lots of him, and remembers him, as he remembers Shakespeare, with affection and gratitude. Derrida is famous not only for a fabulous memory but for a splendidly warm, deeply sentimental sense of loyalty.[6] If a person or a book once meant something to him, once made a contribution to his becoming what he is, he is not about to let that person or book down. His fierce loyalty to the memory of a close friend led him to write a long, tortured (and, to me at least, utterly baffling) essay ('Like the Sound of a Shell Deep Within a Shell: Paul de Man's War') in reaction to the denunciation of de Man's early anti-Semitic articles. His great indebtedness to Heidegger's books has led him to write about them over and over again, each time with increased sensitivity and delicacy. He has written almost nothing about Marx until now, but he more than makes up for this in *Specters of Marx*.

What is most important about Marx for Derrida is that he reminds us of the possibility of justice. 'Justice', in Derrida's writing, has a very special role. It is his name for the ultimate romantic hope, the Great Undeconstructable, the only thing we should not allow ourselves to be ironic about. The thought of justice, the thought of what Derrida sometimes calls 'the democracy that is to come', haunts Europe. That haunting is the best thing about Europe, the reason why Eurocentrism remains attractive. If, like Derrida, you take Marx as Europe's most notable exemplar of the longing for justice, it is plausible to say that

> It will always be a fault not to read and reread Marx . . . It will be more and more a fault, a failing of theoretical, philosophical and political responsibility . . . Not without Marx, no future without Marx, without the memory and the inheritance of Marx: in any case of a certain Marx, of his genius, of at least one of his spirits.[7]

The function of the phrases 'a *certain* Marx' and 'at least *one* of his spirits' is to permit Derrida to forget about anything he doesn't like in Marx – just as we forget, if we are wise, everything about our early lovers which might diminish the memories of our loves. By saying that there are many Marxes, and then leaving most of them aside, he can preserve 'Marx' as a quasi-synonym of 'justice', and thus can (almost) get away with saying 'this gesture of fidelity to a certain spirit of Marxism is a responsibility incumbent, to be sure, on anyone'.[8]

If the final cause of *Specters of Marx* is justice, its material cause is the intertwined uses of words like 'spirit', 'spook', 'ghost', 'spectre', 'genius', 'haunt' and the like. Early in the book Derrida says:

> If I am getting ready to speak at length about ghosts, inheritance, and generations, generations of ghosts, which is to say about certain *others* who are not present, nor presently living, either to us, in us, or outside us, it is in the name of *justice*. Of justice where it is not yet, not yet *there*, where it is no longer, let us understand where it is no longer *present*, and where it will never be, no more than the law, reducible to laws or rights.[9]

Justice, in other words, is what the metaphysics of presence keeps trying and failing to identify with some set of institutions or principles. Such identification is impossible, because every institution or principle will produce new, unexpected, injustices of its own. Every imaginable utopia will need a social protest movement. Justice is a ghost that can never be laid.

So, in the course of his attempt to remind us once again of what is best about Marx and Europe, Derrida takes us back and forth between the perturbed spirit of Hamlet's father (a *Spuk*, a ghost) and the word *Geist* ('spirit' – like *Geschlecht*, one of the words whose absence, according to Derrida, haunts the text of Heidegger); between the use of *Gespenst* ('spectre') in the opening sentence of the Communist Manifesto and the use of 'Ghost' in 'Holy Ghost'; between the German *spucken* ('to spit, to vomit') and the German for 'to haunt' (*spuken*). 'The semantics of *Gespenst*', Derrida says, 'haunt the semantics of *Geist*'.[10] In that remark, as in much of the rest of the book, we see Derrida doing one of the things he does best: revitalizing worn-out philosophical terms by mating them with sexier, less jaded partners.

Much as I admire Derrida's skill at arranging fruitful miscegenation of this sort, as well as the intensity of his hope for justice, I still am not sure why he thinks that Marx is a particularly notable example of this hope. I am not sure that his loyalty to Marx, and his insistence that everybody else join him in not forgetting Marx, testifies to more than the memory of a significant, but accidental, youthful encounter. Certainly the history of European socialism, over the course of 200 or so years, is the biggest and best example of the hope for justice working itself out in practice. But there is a difference between that history and Marx. I agree with Kolakowski when he says

> The apocalyptic belief in the consummation of history, the inevitability of socialism, and the natural sequence of 'social formations'; the 'dictatorship of the proletariat', the exaltation of violence, faith in the automatic effect of nationalizing industry, fantasies concerning a society without conflict and an economy without money – all these have nothing in common with the idea of democratic socialism. The latter's purpose is to create institutions which can gradually reduce the subordination of production to profit, do away with poverty, diminish inequality, remove social barriers to educational opportunities, and minimize the threat to democratic liberties from state bureaucracy and the seductions of totalitarianism.[11]

Like many of us anglophone social democrats, Kolakowski regards Marx not as an epitome of socialism, but as a distraction from it. This is not just because Marx was overimpressed by philosophy, nor because he had the misfortune of being used as a front man by a whole rogues' gallery of bloody tyrants, but because he does not tell us much about how to go about creating institutions which might do these various jobs. Just about the only constructive suggestion Marx made, the abolition of private property, has been tried. It did not work. So now it is hard to find what Derrida calls a 'political imperative' in Marx – an imperative more specific or more novel than the old, old injunction to prevent the rich from continuing to steal from the poor.

Suppose Derrida had written 'it will always be a mistake not to keep thinking about the possibilities of building institutions which will foster the aims of democratic socialism, and not to bear in mind the ruthlessness, deviousness and hypocrisy of the opponents of those aims' instead of writing 'it will always be a mistake not to read and reread Marx'. Then it would have been very easy to agree with him. He would have got the same ready assent if he had written 'Not without socialism' instead of 'Not without Marx', provided that he had joined Kolakowski in distinguishing between socialism as the nationalization of industry and socialism as the building of institutions which will achieve the aims he and Kolakowski share. Kolakowski could, I think, easily agree with Derrida that the current gloating over the end of socialism in the first sense should not distract us from trying to build socialism in the second sense. But, like me, he might be puzzled by Derrida's claim that, 'In order to analyze these wars and the logic of these antagonisms [those created by protectionism, GATT, overproduction, foreign debt, etc.] a problematics coming from the Marxist tradition will be indispensable for a long time yet.'[12]

Derrida does not do much to back up this latter claim. He alternates between treating Marx as the thinker who reminded us of Justice, of The Democracy To Come (a function one might think fulfilled equally well by Jaurès, or by Debs), and Marx as somebody who formulated a 'problematics' which we don't get from anybody else. But he doesn't specify what it is about Marx's sense of injustice that makes his formulations of politico-economic problems especially useful, nor just what this utility consists in. He does offer (at pp. 81–4) a helpful list of ten current dangers which threaten to render vain all of Europe's hopes: rising unemployment, the exclusion of homeless citizens from political participation, ruthless economic warfare between nations, the globalization of the labour market, foreign debt, the arms industry, nuclear proliferation, inter-ethnic wars, the mafia and the drug cartels, and the impotence of international law. But he doesn't tie his discussion of these dangers in with anything characteristically Marxist.

Why, one can reasonably ask, isn't Keynes at least as good as Marx, and maybe better, when it comes to analysing the antagonisms created by GATT, NAFTA, and the globalization of the labour and capital markets? Admirable recent discussions of these antagonisms, such as Fitoussi's *Le Débat Interdit* and Luttwak's *The Endangered American Dream*, seem to get along nicely without ever invoking anything specifically

Marxist. It is hard to see that what Luttwak calls *Bandenkriege* (between, for example, the Cali and Medellin cartels, or between a cut-throat Azeri general and a bloodstained Armenian colonel) become more intelligible when placed within 'a problematics coming from the Marxist tradition'.

One of the few places in *Specters of Marx* at which the theme of spectrality hitches up with some fairly concrete discussion of economic matters is a section in which Derrida discusses Marx's notions of commodification and of use-value (roughly, pp. 150–70). Here is a typical excerpt:

> How do you recognize a ghost? By the fact that it does not recognize itself in a mirror. Now this is what happens with the *commerce* of the commodities *among themselves*. These ghosts that are commodities transform human producers into ghosts . . . The 'mysteriousness' of the commodity-form as presumed reflection of the social form is the incredible manner in which this mirror sends back the image (*zurueck-spiegelt*) when one thinks it is reflecting for men the image of 'the social characteristics of men's own labour': such an image objectivizes by naturalizing . . . The specular becomes the spectral at the threshold of this objectifying naturalization: 'it also reflects the social relation of the producers to the sum total of labour as a social relation between objects, a relation which exists apart from and outside the producers. Through this substitution [*quid pro quo*], the products of labour become commodities, sensuous things which are at the same time supersensible or social.'[13]

But *is* there anything mysterious, or spectral about commodities? One will find a mystery here only if one has a pretty primitive idea of value, or if one finds it weird that a thing should have the property it does by virtue of its relations to other things. There are, I suppose, some hick logocentrists who still think that some things or properties (the 'natural' and 'real' ones as opposed to the 'cultural' and 'artificial' ones) are what they are apart from any such relations. Such simple souls may still be impressed, or indignant, when the line between the natural and the social, the substantial and the relational, or the essential and the accidental, is blurred. But only such naïfs are still susceptible to the line of patter which we antiessentialist philosophers have developed. ('Ha! Fooled you! You thought it was *real*, but now you see that it's only a *social construct*! You thought it was just a familiar object of sense-perception, but look! It has a supersensible, spectral, spiritual, backside!')

There is not, in fact, much naïvety left these days. Tell a sophomore at an American college that something is only a social construct, and she is likely to reply, 'Yeah, I know. So are you, Mac.' It's not really news that everything is what it is because of its difference from everything else. So it is hard to know who is going to be intrigued by the following deconstruction of Marx's distinction between use-value and commodity-value:

> Marx wants to know and make known *where, at just what precise moment*, at what *instant* the ghost comes on stage . . . We are suggesting on the contrary that, before the *coup de théâtre* of this instant, before the 'as soon as it comes on stage as commodity, it changes into a sensuous supersensible thing' the ghost had made its apparition, without appearing in person, of course and by definition, but having already hollowed out in use-value, in the hardheaded wood of the headstrong table, the repetition (therefore substitution, exchangeability, iterability, the loss of singularity as the experience of singularity itself, the possibility of capital) without which a use could never even be determined.[14]

In other words, the table was no more or less relational, and therefore spectral, after it got commodified than in the good old days when it was just used, and not traded. Spectrality goes all the way back, and all the way down.

The hollowness of the hardheaded wood will be familiar to people who, in Derrida's words, 'understand Greek and philosophy'.[15] We who have read Aristotle's *Metaphysics* and Jonson's *Timber* are on good terms with *hyle* (a Greek word for 'wood' which Aristotle uses to mean 'matter'). We get the point, and the joke. We can happily agree with Derrida, that '[Marx's] genealogy, which transforms the ligneous into the non-ligneous . . . also gives a tableau of the becoming-immaterial of matter'.[16] That sort of sophistication is our very *lignum vitae*.

But who needs polylingual sophisticates like us? Well, we certainly need each other. People like me need people like Derrida – writers who can take the books both of us have read and make them seem wonderful and new. We need heroes and exemplars like him – people who can create themselves by rereading and redescribing everything from the postcard to the Parmenidean One, and thereby help us create ourselves. But does democratic socialism need him, or us? Or is the sort of thing Derrida does in this book useful (to use a distinction of which I am fond and Derrida is not) only for private, rather than public, purposes?

This question restates the one I raised earlier: whether it is really 'a fault not to read and reread Marx'. Maybe that is a fault for, at most, those of us who understand Greek and philosophy? Maybe Marx is now just an incubus for everybody else?

To compare putatively great things with small ones, consider the question of whether it would be a fault not to read and reread Alexandre Kojève. Derrida asks, 'Who can deny that the neo-Marxist and para-Heideggerian reading of the *Phenomenology of Spirit* by Kojève is interesting?'[17] I can. Kojève's book on Hegel is, as Derrida charmingly admits, written 'in that profoundly offhand, nutty and pataphysician manner which is, to be sure, his genius but which is also his entire responsibility, "the Snobbism in the pure state" of the cultural formalism of Japanese society'.[18] Redblooded Americans like myself of course resent Kojève's claim that 'the final stage of communism in the postwar United States does indeed, as it must, reduce man to animality'.[19] But even apart from his snobby preference for samurai over salespeople, and for Stalin over Eisenhower, Kojève's offhand nuttiness gets tiresome pretty quickly.

It is not enough to reply to the rhetorical question quoted above by saying: 'It [Kojève's Hegel book] played a formative and not negligible role, from many standpoints, for a certain generation of French intellectuals, just before or just after the war.'[20] So what? *Lots* of brilliant, nutty writers played a formative and not negligible role for one or another generation of intellectuals, somewhere, sometime. Henry George played such a role for a generation of American intellectuals around 1900. But this is no reason for anybody nowadays to find him interesting.

Might Marx be more like George and Kojève than like Aristotle and Kant? This question is one which, I think, Kolakowski would take seriously. It is one which I should very much like to answer, but I am too ignorant to do so. My main complaint about *Specters of Marx* is that I did not get nearly as much help in dealing with this question as I had hoped for. Derrida pretty much takes Marx's importance for granted (in the same bland way as Straussians take Kojève's for granted), and then makes things easy for himself by sticking to 'a certain Marx' without bothering to tell us just which *other* Marxes we can now dispense with, and why.

The most striking and unexpected tribute which Derrida pays to Marx in this book is the following:

> Such a deconstruction [a deconstruction of logocentrism, of the metaphysics of presence] would have been impossible and unthinkable in a pre-Marxist space. Deconstruction has never had any sense or interest, in my view at least, except as a radicalization, which is to say also *in the tradition* of a certain Marxism, in a certain *spirit of Marxism*.[21]

I reacted to this passage with considerable scepticism. I was tempted to respond 'Oh, come on, Derrida. You say that about *all* your grandfathers.'

Sure, I can pick out a strand in Marx of which Derrida's antilogo-centrism is a radicalization. But I could also find such a strand in Hegel, in Freud, in Plato, in Heidegger, and in Rousseau. I could spin antilogocentrism out of any of these. On the other hand, I could see it as having a lot of sense and interest in the absence of any one of them (though not of all of them). A commentator on Derrida who picked any of these other thinkers as founding *the* tradition which Derrida writes in order to impurify, and thereby radicalize, could produce as plausible an interpretation of his work as could a commentator who, using the passage I have just quoted as his jump-off point, placed him in the Marxist tradition.[22]

That passage about deconstruction as a continuation of Marxism by other means is, I suspect, a deliberate echo of the celebrated passage about existentialism as an enclave within Marxism, in Sartre's *Critique de la Raison Dialectique*, to which I referred earlier. It seems to me to play the same role for Derrida that the echoed passage did in Sartre: both are rather desperate protests to the effect that all that knowledge of Greek and philosophy, all that acquaintance with *hyle*, really *does*, appearances to the contrary, serve a vital public purpose. We sophisticates really *are* useful to democratic socialism. We are in its service – not just as citizens, but in our professional capacities.

There is, of course, a sense in which all us up-to-date antilogocentrists, whether Deweyans, Davidsonians or Derrideans, are faithful to Thesis Eleven. We are no longer trying to understand the world, in the sense in which both Aristotle and Hegel understood 'understand'. It is not that we think the world unintelligible, but rather that we view redescription of it as a tool for social or individual change, rather than as an attempt to grasp intrinsic features of the real. But now our choice is between trying to change the world or change ourselves. Sticking to changing ourselves, as Kierkegaard, Nietzsche and Proust did, seems selfish, unhealthy and decadent. So, when we notice that we have been devoting a lot of effort to this private project, we grow abashed. If we happen to have been born into recent generations of French intellectuals, we are likely to write passages about enclaves within Marxism, or about radicalizing a certain spirit in Marx. If we are American pragmatists, we start explaining how the inculcation of antilogocentrism in the young will contribute to the strength of democratic societies – how it will help to realize John Dewey's dreams.[23]

Such passages and such explanations are not (I sincerely, desperately, hope) merely self-deceptive. But they should be read, to quote Derrida, *dans un certain rire* and *dans un certain pas de la danse*.[24] They should be conjoined with constant reminders that Blanchot and Popper were right, and Althusser wrong: the sort of thing we philosophers know, and the sort of changes we can help make in the way people think, may eventually do some social good, but only in the very long run, and in a very indirect way. There is no science of history, nor any big discovery (by Marx or anybody else) of the one right, proper, adequate context in which to place unemployment, mafias, merchants of death, globalized labour markets and the rest.

Contexts provided by theories are tools for effecting change. The theories which provide new contexts are to be evaluated by their efficiency in effecting changes, not (as the logocentrists believed) by their adequacy to an object. Any tool is replaceable as soon as a handier, less clumsy, more easily portable tool is invented. The sheer clumsiness of attempts to use 'a problematic coming from the Marxist tradition' when dealing with contemporary problems is the most persuasive reason for doubting Derrida's claim that we must read and reread Marx.

*　*　*　*

NOTES

1 Jacques Derrida, *Specters of Marx: The State of the Debt, the Work of Mourning, and the Law of the New International*, Peggy Kamuf, trans. (London: Routledge, 1994).

2 Derrida, p. 32.

3 Derrida, p. 32.

4 Derrida, p. 34.

5 Derrida, p. 31.

6 Only a sentimental and loyal reader would have bothered to include (at p. 93) an affectionate tribute to one of the best-loved animals in world literature: the fretful porpentine of *Hamlet*, I, v, 1.20.

7 Derrida, p. 13.

8 Derrida, p. 90.

9 Derrida, p. xix.

10 Derrida, p. 707.

11 Kolakowski, *Main Currents of Marxism*, vol. III, pp. 528–9.

12 Derrida, pp. 63–4.

13 Derrida, p. 156; the final quotation is from Marx.

14 Derrida, p. 161.

15 Derrida, p. 152.

16 Derrida, p. 152.

17 Derrida, p. 72.

18 Derrida, p. 71.

19 Derrida, p. 71.

20 Derrida, p. 72. For details about the role Kojève played, see V. Descombes, *Le même et l'autre: quarante-cinq ans de la philosophie* (Paris: Minuit, 1979). Translated as *Modern French Philosophy* (Cambridge: Cambridge University Press).

21 Derrida, p. 92.

22 I find Derrida's own characterization (in the *Post Card*, self-quoted in a footnote to this book) of Freud and Heidegger as 'the two surviving grand-fathers' is significant. Like *Being and Nothingness*, many of Derrida's books were written by a man deeply impressed by both Heidegger and Freud, and badly needing to introduce the one to the other. I say something about Derrida's relation to these two in 'Derrida and the Philosophical Tradition' in my *Truth and Progress* (Cambridge: Cambridge University Press, 1998).

23 For a sample, see my reply to John Searle in *Truth and Progress*.

24 Jacques Derrida, '*Différance*', in *Marges de la Philosophie* (Paris: Minuit, 1972).

16. Love And Money

(1992)

Howards End asks whether it is sufficient to 'connect', whether love is enough. 'Only connect' has been taken as E. M. Forster's last word, but at various points in the novel he notes that connection is possible only when there is enough money. The heroine, Margaret Schlegel, wonders whether 'the very soul of the world is economic . . . [whether] the lowest abyss is not the absence of love, but the absence of coin'. Speaking in his own voice – a voice that mingles pity with self-disgust – Forster says, 'We are not concerned with the very poor. They are unthinkable, and only to be approached by the statistician or the poet. This story deals with gentlefolk, or with those who are obliged to pretend that they are gentlefolk.' At the novel's end, one of the people who has been obliged so to pretend, Leonard Bast, dies as a result of being caught up in the struggle between the Schlegels, the people who are good at loving, and the Wilcoxes, the people who know how to make money. But even if he had not died, he would have become unthinkable – because he had been reduced from pseudo-gentility to grinding poverty.

As long as Bast had enough money to keep up the pretension to gentility, he was conversable; Margaret and the others could make connections with him. But when he lost his job and had no money left he became unconversable. This was not because of the snobbery of the gentlefolk but because Bast himself, obsessed with the need to feed himself and his wife, could think and talk of nothing else. No money, no conversability and no connectability. No money, no chance for love. The very poor, those in the lowest abyss, the people whom Brecht called 'the ones who live in darkness', can afford neither love nor conversability. 'Only connect' has no relevance to them, for they cannot afford any disinterested actions. The light shed by novels does not reach them.

In *Aspects of the Novel*, Forster distinguishes 'the development of the novel', which is the same as 'the development of humanity', from the 'great tedious onrush known as history'. The latter includes 'trifles' which 'belong to history not to art'; Forster's examples of such trifles are the taming of the atom, landing on the moon and abolishing warfare. The former is 'a shy crablike sideways movement' towards tenderness, the tenderness which connection makes possible. Of tenderness Forster says:

> Far more mysterious than the call of sex to sex is the tenderness that we throw into that call; far wider is the gulf between us and the farmyard than that between the farmyard and the garbage that nourishes it. We are evolving, in ways that Science cannot measure, to ends that Theology dares not contemplate. 'Men did produce one jewel,' the gods will say, and saying, will give us immortality.

Forster sometimes seems on the brink of saying that the very poor, the people who cannot afford love or friendship because every moment of every day is filled with anxiety for the next bit of food, are more like the farmyard than like gentlefolk, more like garbage than like us. Wells and Shaw sometimes did say things like that. But Forster was too decent to agree with them. Instead, he hopes, as all us liberal gentlefolk hope, that eventually the Wilcoxes will produce so much money that, when shared out as it should be, there will be nobody left who is very poor. He knows that the very soul of the 'great tedious onrush known as history' *is* economic. He knows that tenderness only appears, that the shy crabwise movement only continues, when there is enough money to produce a little leisure, a little time in which to love. His decency consists in his confidence that tenderness *will*, in fact, appear when there is money enough. But he shares enough of Wells's and Shaw's realism to admit that money is the independent, and tenderness the dependent, variable.

Forster's hope that eventually there will be enough money to go around, enough so that its redistribution will make connection and tenderness ubiquitous, runs through liberal thought from the French Revolution to our own time. Every top-down liberal initiative, from the abolition of slavery through the extension of the franchise to the establishment of the International Monetary Fund and the World Bank, has been driven by the hope that someday we shall no longer need to distinguish us gentlefolk from those others, the people who live like animals. The cash value of the Christian ideal of universal brotherhood has, for the last two centuries, been the conviction that once science and technology have produced enough wealth – and enlightened, unselfish political initiatives have redistributed it – there will be no one left who is incapable of tenderness. All human beings will live in the light; all of them will be possible characters in novels.

Seen from this Forsterian vantage point, the distinction between Marxism and liberalism was largely a disagreement about whether you can get as much, or more, wealth to redistribute by politicizing the marketplace and replacing the greedy Wilcoxes with government planners. It turned out that you cannot. Liberals of Forster's time knew as well as the Marxists that the soul of history – if not of the novel or of humanity – is economic, but they thought that history had to be guided from the top down, by the gentlefolk. The Marxists hoped that once those on the bottom seized control, once the revolution turned things upside down, everything would automatically get better. Here again, alas, the Marxists were wrong. So now Marxism is no longer of much interest, and we are back with the question of what top-down initiatives we gentlefolk might best pursue.

This question looks manageable as long as we confine our attention to the northern hemisphere. If that part of the planet (suitably gerry-mandered so as, for example, to include Australia and exclude China) were all we had to worry about, it would be plausible to suggest that there is, or soon will be, enough money to go around – that our problems are simply those of redistribution. All we need to do is to formulate effective Schlegelian appeals to the tenderness of the gentlefolk who make up the electorates of the rich nations, appeals which will overcome Wilcoxian greed. There seems to be enough money sloshing around the northern hemisphere to make it practicable, eventually, to raise the east European standard of living to that of western Europe, that of Yorkshire to that of Surrey, and that of Bedford-Stuyvesant to that of Bensonhurst. There are relatively plausible scenarios for the working out of top-down initiatives, scenarios which end with the life chances of the Northerners roughly levelled out. Liberal hope, the hope for a decent world, a world in which Christianity's promises are fulfilled, nourishes itself on such scenarios.

The fear that is beginning to gnaw at the hearts of all us liberal gentlefolk in the North is that there are no initiatives which will save the southern hemisphere, that there will never be enough money in the world to redeem the South. We are beginning to be at a loss for scenarios which cross the north–south border, largely because of the scary population growth statistics for countries such as Indonesia, India and Haiti. This part of the planet is becoming increasingly unthinkable. We are more and more tempted to turn it over to the statisticians, and to the sort of poet whom we call 'the ethnologist'.

This temptation was brought home to me when, during my first trip to India, I met a fellow philosophy professor who is also a politician. Starting as a young MP in the sixties, anxious to bring Western thought and technology to bear on India's problems, and especially on the Indian birth rate, he had risen, in the course of 30 years, to various high offices, including that of Minister of Health. He was in a very good position to dream up concrete and optimistic scenarios, but had none to offer. After 30 years' work on the part of people like himself, he said, it was still the case that the only rational thing for parents in an Indian village to do was to try as hard as they could to have eight children. It had to be eight because two would die in childhood, three of the remainder would be girls and thus require dowries, and one of the remaining boys would run off to Bombay and never be heard of again. Two male children working desperately hard, all their lives, with no time off for tenderness, would be required to ensure that their sisters' dowries were paid, and their mother and father kept from starvation in their old age.

In the course of this trip, I found myself, like most Northerners in the South, not thinking about the beggars in the hot streets once I was back in my pleasantly air-conditioned hotel. My Indian acquaintances – fellow academics, fellow gentlefolk, honorary Northerners –

gave the same small percentage of what they had in their pockets to the beggars as I did, and then, like me, forgot about the individual beggars when they got home. As individuals, beggars were, just as Forster says, unthinkable. Instead, both of us thought about liberal initiatives which might eliminate the beggars as a class. But neither of us came up with any initiatives which inspired any confidence. The country, and perhaps the world, did not seem to have enough money to keep the number of Southerners who will be alive in the middle of the twenty-first century from despair, much less to open up to them the possibility of joining in the slow crabwise movement which has been taking place in the North.

Of course, there might be enough money, because science and technology might once again come to the rescue. There are a few scientific possibilities – e.g., a breakthrough in plasma physics which makes fusion energy, and thus (for example) desalination and irrigation on a gigantic scale, possible and cheap. But the hope is pretty faint. As things stand, nobody who reads the statistics about the unthinkably poor of the South can generate any optimism.

I should like to produce a bracing conclusion to end these pessimistic reflections, but all I can offer is the suggestion that we Northern gentlefolk at least keep ourselves honest. We should remind ourselves, as Forster reminded us, that love is *not* enough – that the Marxists were absolutely right about one thing: the soul of history *is* economic. All the talk in the world about the need to abandon 'technological rationality' and to stop 'commodifying', about the need for 'new values' or for 'non-Western ways of thinking', is not going to bring more money to the Indian villages. As long as the villagers have enough Weberian means–end rationality to see that they need eight children, such talk is not to any point. All the love in the world, all the attempts to abandon 'Eurocentrism', or 'liberal individualism', all the 'politics of diversity', all the talk about cuddling up to the natural environment, will not help.

The only things we know of which might help are top-down techno-bureaucratic initiatives like the cruel Chinese only-one-child-per-family policy (or, literalizing the top-down metaphor and pushing things one monstrous step further, spraying villages from the air with sterilizing chemicals). If there is a happy solution to the dilemma created by the need of very poor Brazilians to find work and the need of the rest of us for the oxygen produced by the Amazonian rain forest, it is going to be the result of some as yet unimagined bureaucratic-technological initiative, not of a revolution in 'values'. The slow crabwise movement is not going to speed up thanks to a change in philosophical outlook. Money remains the independent variable.

I think that the sudden popularity of anti-technological talk among us Northern liberals, our turn over the last 20 years from planning to dreaming, and from science to philosophy, has been a nervous, self-deceptive reaction to the realization that technology may not work. Maybe the problems our predecessors assumed it could solve are, in fact, too tough. Maybe technology and centralized planning will not work. But they are all we have got. We should not try to pull the blanket over our heads by saying that technology was a big mistake, and that planning, top-down initiatives, and 'Western ways of thinking' must be abandoned. That is just another, much less honest, way of saying what Forster said: that the very poor are unthinkable.

17. Globalization, the Politics of Identity and Social Hope

(1996)

The Brazilian philosopher Luiz Eduardo Soares has said that 'agreement on the possibility and desirability of mutual understanding and the building of peace through communication' has been 'shaken by recent dramatic developments: the revival of long-repressed hatreds and hostilities embedded in ethnic, religious and nationalist identities, the growing prestige of postmodern scepticism and the fragility of universalistic conceptions'. I think it might be useful for me to begin by saying how my own sense of the current intellectual situation differs from Soares'.

I do not think that 'the revival of long-repressed hatreds embedded in ethnic, religious and national identities' is a particularly striking or surprising phenomenon. It seems a natural sequel to the breakup of tyrannous empires. I cannot see that Quebecquois, Chechen and Serbian irredentism are symptoms of a world-historical abandonment of cosmopolitan ideals. Nor do I find it easy to associate the group identities invoked in such separatist movements with the identities invoked in such movements as feminism and gay liberation. As I shall be saying in more detail later on, I do not see that terms like 'politics of identity' point to anything interestingly new and different that has recently emerged on to the political scene.

Nor do I think that postmodern scepticism and the fragility of universalistic conceptions play much of a role on that scene. For these are merely *philosophical* matters, and I cannot believe that the degree of utopian hope manifested by the public, or even that manifested among the intellectuals, is greatly influenced by changes in opinion among philosophy professors. I think of the causal influence as going the other way: philosophy is responsive to changes in amount of political hope, rather than conversely.

Insofar as there has been a loss of faith in cosmopolitan and universalist notions, this seems to me a result of the increasing inability to believe that things could ever get much better than they are now. Specifically, the last few decades have witnessed the increasing inability to believe that some day we shall ever have a classless global society: one in which there are no vast differences between the opportunities open to children in one nation and in another, or between those open to children in one section of a city and those in another section of the same city.

In the days when this vision seemed capable of realization, there was less interest in the survival of minority and marginal cultures. This was not, I think, a result of contempt for these cultures. Rather, it was the thought that if the kind of global monoculture which seemed to be in prospect – a culture most of whose roots were in the European Enlightenment – could be attained, the loss of other cultural inheritances would not greatly matter. The utopia which filled people's imagination at the end of the Second World War did not involve everybody speaking only English and drinking only Coca-Cola, but even if it had this might well have seemed a cheap price to pay – as would a world in which everybody spoke only Chinese and drank only tea, for that matter.

Hopes for constructing such a classless society have been embodied, in our century, in two scenarios. The first is the familiar Marxist scenario of proletarian revolution, followed by the abolition of private entrepreneurship. The second is the scenario which was dominant in most Western intellectuals' minds at the end of the Second World War. These intellectuals thought that peace and technological progress would make possible hitherto undreamt-of economic prosperity within the framework of the free market. They believed that such prosperity would bring about successive political reforms, leading eventually to truly democratic institutions in every part of the world. Prosperity would make it possible to establish welfare states of the Scandinavian sort in all democratic countries. The institutions of such welfare states would ensure equality of opportunity among future generations. Equality of opportunity among the children of a city or of a country would become the rule rather than the exception.

It was not only intellectuals in North America and northern Europe who believed something like this second scenario. Most of the Western statesmen who signed the Charter of the United Nations also had something like this utopian scenario in mind – a scenario which led to pretty much the same utopia as that envisaged by Marxists, but did so without the need for violent revolution, and without the abolition of private property.

The intellectuals and statesmen of today have little faith in either of these two scenarios. The Marxist attempt to find a satisfactory replacement for the marketplace is an experiment which is almost universally judged to have failed. But the non-Marxist scenario seems as implausible as the Marxist. As Professor Soares has remarked in a recent paper, Brazil is a remarkable example of successful economic development, but is an equally remarkable example of inequality of opportunity.

In my country, the United States, social critics are warning that we are in danger of what they call 'Brazilianization' – that is, the emergence of an 'overclass' consisting of the top 20 per cent of the population, and the steady immiseration of everybody else. By now there is little difference between the favelas of Rio and the ghettos of Chicago, and little difference in lifestyle between the Chicago suburbs and that in the affluent sections of Rio. The middle class of Brazil and the US have far more in common with each other than with the poor of their own countries.

It seems to me that loss of faith in both of the alternative scenarios that were supposed to culminate in an egalitarian utopia plays a much greater role in our concern about globalization than do either the movements grouped together under 'identity politics', or any specifically philosophical developments.

The appropriate intellectual background to political deliberation is historical narrative rather than philosophical or quasi-philosophical theory. More specifically, it is the kind of historical narrative which segues into a utopian scenario about how we can get from the present to a better future. Social and political philosophy usually has been, and always ought to be, parasitic on such narratives. Hobbes's and Locke's accounts of the state were parasitic on different accounts of recent English history. Marx's philosophy was parasitic on his narrative of the rise of the bourgeoisie and his forecast of a successful proletarian revolution. Dewey's social theory was, and Rawls's political theory is, parasitic on different accounts of the recent history of the United States. All these philosophers formulated their taxonomies of social phenomena, and designed the conceptual tools they used to criticize existing institutions, by reference to a story about what had happened and what we might reasonably hope could happen in the future.

Nowadays, however, we are getting a lot of political and social philosophy which takes its starting point not from a historical narrative but rather from philosophy of language, or from psychoanalysis, or from discussion of such traditional philosophical *topoi* as 'identity' and 'difference', 'self' and 'subject', 'truth' and 'reason'. This seems to me the result of a loss of hope – or, more specifically, of an inability to construct a plausible narrative of progress. A turn away from narration and utopian dreams toward philosophy seems to me a gesture of despair. This impression is confirmed by the prevalence in recent political philosophy (particularly in the works of my friends Chantal Mouffe and Ernesto Laclau) of the word 'impossibility'.

I think this turn towards philosophy is likely to be politically sterile. When it comes to political deliberation, philosophy is a good servant but a bad master. If one knows what one wants and has some hope of getting it, philosophy can be useful in formulating redescriptions of social phenomena. The appropriation of these redescriptions, and of the jargon in which they are formulated, may speed up the pace of social change. But I think we are now in a situation in which resentment and frustration have taken the place of hope among politically concerned intellectuals, and that the replacement of narrative by philosophy is a symptom of this unhappy situation.

I shall come back to the topic of the role of philosophy later. But now let me now try to say something about globalization.

As I see it, the Marxists were right about at least one thing: the central political questions are those about the relations between rich and poor. For non-Marxists, the central political questions have been: how can the working class in a democratic society use the power of the ballot to prevent the capitalists from immiserating the proletariat, while still encouraging business enterprise? How can the state be a countervailing power, one which will prevent all the wealth winding up in the hands of an economic oligarchy, without creating bureaucratic stagnation? How can the political order take precedence over the economic while still leaving room for economic growth?

So the central fact of globalization is that the economic situation of the citizens of a nation state has passed beyond the control of the laws of that state. It used to be the case that a nation's laws could control, to an important and socially useful extent, the movement of that nation's money. But now that the financing of business enterprise is a matter of drawing upon a global pool of capital, so that enterprises in Belo Horizonte or in Chicago are financed by money held in the Cayman Islands by Serbian warlords, Hong Kong gangsters and the kleptocrat presidents of African republics, there is no way in which the laws of Brazil or the US can dictate that money earned in the country will be spent in the country, or money saved in the country invested in the country.

We now have a global overclass which makes all the major economic decisions, and makes them in entire independence of the legislatures, and *a fortiori* of the will of the voters, of any given country. The money accumulated by this overclass is as easily used for illegal purposes, such as supplying land mines to the latest entrepreneurial warlord or financing gangster takeovers of trade unions, as it is for legal ones. The absence of a global polity means that the super-rich can operate without any thought of any interests save their own. We are in danger of winding up with only two genuinely global, genuinely international, social groups: the super-rich and the intellectuals, that is, the people who attend international conferences devoted to measuring the harm being done by their super-rich fellow cosmopolitans.

How can such cosmopolitan, jetsetting intellectuals help increase the chances of a global egalitarian utopia? I suspect that the most socially useful thing we can do is to continually draw the attention of the educated publics of our respective countries to the need for a global polity, which can develop some sort of countervailing power to that of the super-rich. We should probably be doing more than we are to dramatize the changes in the world economy which globalization is bringing about, and to remind our fellow citizens that only global political institutions can offset the power of all that marvellously liquid and mobile capital.

I admit that the chance of revitalizing the United Nations, either for purposes of dealing with the warlords or for those of dealing with the conscienceless super-rich, is slim. But I suspect that it is the only chance for anything like a just global society. My own country is too poor and too nervous to serve as a global policeman, but the need for such a policeman is going to become ever greater as more and more warlords gain access to nuclear arms. No country can ask its own plutocrats to defend its interests, for any hard-nosed plutocrat will see economic nationalism as economically inefficient.

So much for my views on globalization. They are not views I hold in my capacity as a professor of philosophy, but simply the views of a concerned citizen of a country in decline. My native country has world-historical importance only because it cast itself in the role of vanguard of a global egalitarian utopia. It no longer casts itself in that role, and is therefore in danger of losing its soul. The spirit which animated the writing of Whitman and Dewey is no longer present.

In what follows, however, I am going to revert to my role as a philosophy professor, and, more specifically, as a follower of John Dewey. Although I think that historical narrative and utopian speculation are the best sort of background for political deliberation, I have no special expertise at constructing such narratives and speculations. So, in order to employ what expertise I have, I shall say something about the situation in contemporary philosophy.

First, I shall explain briefly why I do not think that 'identity' and 'difference' are concepts which can be made relevant to political deliberation. Then I shall say, at somewhat more length, why I think that tinkering with the notions of 'rationality' and 'truth' might, in the very long run, and in a very indirect way, have a certain amount of political utility.

The terms 'identity' and 'difference' have come into prominence in recent philosophy for two distinct, unrelated reasons. First, the

Nietzsche–Heidegger–Derrida criticism of the Greek metaphysical tradition has insisted that sameness and difference are relative to choice of description – that there is no such thing as the 'intrinsic' nature or the 'essential' attributes of anything. There is nothing which is vital to the self-identity of a being, independent of the descriptions we give of it. This insistence is found also in the work of philosophers like Wittgenstein, Quine and Davidson, and I am happy to join in the resulting chorus.

The second reason you hear a lot about identity and difference these days is that 'preservation of cultural identity' and 'identification with the oppressed group of which one is a member' have become political watchwords. Attempts to help native tributes threatened by economic development are run together with attempts to raise the consciousness of migrants or racial or sexual minorities. Out of this situation, the terms 'politics of identity' or 'politics of difference' have emerged, as descriptions of movements which are distinct from the familiar struggle of the poor against the rich.

I have, heaven knows, nothing against such movements. But I do not see that we need think of them as practising a new sort of politics, nor as requiring philosophical sophistication for their description or evaluation. As I see it, the emergence of feminism, gay liberation, various sorts of ethnic separatism, aboriginal rights, and the like, simply add further concreteness to sketches of the good old egalitarian utopia. The effect of these new movements is to say such things as: In a just global society, not only would all children have roughly equal chances, but the girls would have the same sort of chances as the boys. In that society, nobody would care about which sex you fall in love with, any more than about the lightness or darkness of your skin. In that society, people who wanted to think of themselves as Basque first, or black first, or women first, and citizens of their countries or of a global cooperative commonwealth second, would have little trouble doing so. For the institutions of that commonwealth would be regulated by John Stuart Mill's dictum that everybody gets to do what they like as long as it doesn't interfere with other people's doing the same.

As far as I can see, nothing theoretical that we have learned since Mill's time, and in particular nothing we have learned by deconstructing the metaphysics of presence, or from Freud or Lacan, give us reason to *revise*, as opposed to supplement, our previous descriptions of utopia. But we have learned things that cause us to expand those descriptions. For we in the West have become aware of forms of suffering and humiliation of which Mill was less aware. Since we invented cultural anthropology, we have become more aware of humiliations caused by colonialist arrogance. Since Freud, we have become better able to take homosexuality in our stride, and more willing to see homosexuals as an oppressed minority rather than a corrupting and subversive influence on society. By contrast, I am not sure that we at the end of the twentieth century know more about the humiliation of women by men than Mary Wollstonecraft and Harriet Taylor knew. Yet it is certainly true that nowadays lots of the male intellectuals, and not just most of the female ones, know at least a little of what those two ur-feminists knew.

The only interesting way to hook up the Nietzschean–Wittgensteinian relativization of identity to description with these new understandings of various humiliations inflicted on the weak by the strong is Foucault's. Foucault helped us see, or at least reminded us, that our own description of ourselves, and thus our own self-knowledge, is dependent on the linguistic resources available in our environment. He thereby helped us see why oppressed groups needed to develop new ways of talking, in order to produce a new kind of self-knowledge. Foucault was hardly the first to see these things, but his work certainly helped.

Still, neither Foucault, Derrida, Nietzsche nor Lacan can make obsolete the old-fashioned utopian scenario, the one that leads to a global society of freedom and equal opportunity. All they can do is supplement it. They cannot reveal the philosophical weaknesses of the bourgeois liberalism common to Mill and Dewey; they can only reveal its blind spots, its failure to perceive forms of suffering which it should have perceived. There were many such blind spots, but they were not a result of some wholesale failure to understand the nature of the subject, or of desire, or of language, or of society, or of history, or of anything else of similar magnitude. They were the sorts of blind spots which we all have – correctable not by increasing philosophical sophistication, but simply by having our attention called to the harm we have been doing without noticing that we are doing it.

Perhaps I have now said enough to explain why I think that there is less to be said about identity and difference than such writers as William Connelly and Iris Marion Young believe there to be. Connelly sees 'liberal individualism' as made blind to various forms of suffering by virtue of its failure to realize that individuality is one more social construction. I do not think this is so; Foucault had many precursors – George Herbert Mead among them. Seeing identity as a social construction is, to be sure, made easier once one has absorbed the nominalism common to Wittgenstein and Derrida, but it is hardly news.

Young sees the liberal tradition, the tradition of Mill and Dewey, as devoted to a project of 'homogenization' of difference. This seems wrong to me. I should have thought that both Mill and Dewey were dedicated to pluralism – to the maximization of opportunities for individual variation, and group variation insofar as the latter facilitates the ability of individuals to recreate themselves. It seems to me that the only homogenization which the liberal tradition requires is an agreement among groups to cooperate with one another in support of institutions which are dedicated to providing room for as much pluralism as possible. I do not see the politics of difference as differing in any interesting way from the ordinary interest-group politics which has been familiar throughout the history of parliamentary democracies.

Willingness to accept the liberal goal of maximal room for individual variation, however, is facilitated by a consensus that there is no source of authority other than the free agreement of human beings. This consensus, in turn, is facilitated by the adoption of philosophical views about reason and truth of the sort which are nowdays thought of as symptoms of 'postmodern scepticism' but which I think of as just good old American pragmatism.

The core of Dewey's thought was an insistence that nothing – not the Will of God, not the Intrinsic Nature of Reality, not the Moral Law – can take precedence over the result of agreement freely reached by members of a democratic community. The pragmatist claim that truth is not correspondence to the intrinsic nature of something that exists independently of our choice of linguistic descriptions is another expression of this insistence. The same insistence is found also in Habermas's attempt to substitute what he calls 'communicative' dialogical reason for 'subject-centred' monological reason. Both Dewey and Habermas are concerned to get rid of the idea that human beings are responsible to something nonhuman. They both deny that they have a duty to something which can supersede their duty to cooperate with one another in reaching free consensus.

Habermas's idea that assertions are universal validity claims, and more generally his idea that inquiry is somehow bound to converge to a single point, separate his view from Dewey's and from the French writers whom he criticizes in *The Philosophical Discourse of Modernity*. But I do not think that this residual theoretical universalism is very important. The much-discussed opposition between Derrida and Habermas seems to me a bit factitious. As I see the situation, Dewey, Derrida and Habermas are three antiauthoritarian philosophers of human freedom and social justice. The difference between these three men on the one hand and Foucault and Lacan on the other is that the former are still devoted to the utopian social hope which animated the two scenarios which I discussed at the beginning of my remarks, and the latter are not.

I think that the denial that anything has an intrinsic nature independent of our choice of description, the pragmatist claim that truth is not a matter of corresponding to any such intrinsic nature, the Habermasian claim that reason should be viewed dialogically, and the so-called 'death of the subject' are all parts of the same anti-authoritarian philosophical movement. That movement is well suited to a utopia in which the moral identity of every human being is constituted in large part, though obviously not exclusively, by his or her sense of participation in a democratic society.

The reason this kind of philosophy is relevant to politics is simply that it encourages people to have a self-image in which their real or imagined citizenship in a democratic republic is central. This kind of anti-authoritarian philosophy helps people set aside religious and ethnic identities in favour of an image of themselves as part of a great human adventure, one carried out on a global scale. This kind of philosophy, so to speak, clears philosophy out of the way in order to let the imagination play upon the possibilities of a utopian future.

V

Contemporary America

18. Looking Backwards from the Year 2096

(1996)

This essay attempts to look back at twentieth-century America from a vantagepoint at the end of the twenty-first century. It is written in the form of an excerpt from the article on 'Fraternity' in the seventh edition of *A Companion to American Thought*, published in 2095 and edited by Cynthia Rodriguez, S J and Youzheng Patel.

Our long, hesitant, painful recovery, over the last five decades, from the breakdown of democratic institutions during the Dark Years (2014–2044) has changed our political vocabulary, as well as our sense of the relation between the moral order and the economic order. Just as twentieth-century Americans had trouble imagining how their pre-Civil War ancestors could have stomached slavery, so we at the end of the twenty-first century have trouble imagining how our great-grandparents could have legally permitted a CEO to get 20 times more than her lowest paid employees. We cannot understand how Americans a hundred years ago could have tolerated the horrific contrast between a childhood spent in the suburbs and one spent in the ghettos. Such inequalities seem to us evident moral abominations, but the vast majority of our ancestors took them to be regrettable necessities.

As long as their political discourse was dominated by the notion of 'rights' – whether 'individual' or 'civil' – it was hard for Americans to think of the results of unequal distribution of wealth and income as immoral. Such rights talk, common among late-twentieth-century liberals, gave conservative opponents of redistributionist policies a tremendous advantage: 'the right to a job' (or 'to a decent wage') had none of the resonance of 'the right to sit in the front of the bus' or

'the right to vote' or even 'the right to equal pay for equal work'.
Rights in the liberal tradition were, after all, powers and privileges to
be wrested from the state, not from the economy.

Of course socialists had, since the mid-nineteenth century, urged
that the economy and the state be merged to guarantee economic
rights. But it had become clear by the middle of the twentieth century
that such merging was disastrous. The history of the pre-1989 'socialist'
countries – bloody dictatorships that paid only lip service to the
fraternity for which the socialist revolutionaries had yearned – made
it plausible for conservatives to argue that extending the notion of
rights to the economic order would be a step down the road to serfdom.
By the end of the twentieth century, even left-leaning American
intellectuals agreed that 'socialism, no wave of the future, now
looks (at best) like a temporary historical stage through which various
nations passed before reaching the great transition to capitalist
democracy'.[1]

The realization by those on the left that a viable economy requires
free markets did not stop them from insisting that capitalism would
be compatible with American ideas of human brotherhood only if the
state were able to redistribute wealth. Yet this view was still being
criticized as 'un-American' and 'socialist' at the beginning of the
present century, even as, under the pressures of a globalized world
economy, the gap between most Americans' incomes and those of the
lucky one-third at the top widened. Looking back, we think how easy
it would have been for our great-grandfathers to have forestalled the
social collapse that resulted from these economic pressures. They
could have insisted that all classes had to confront the new global
economy together. In the name of our common citizenship, they could
have asked everybody, not just the bottom two-thirds, to tighten their
belts and make do with less. They might have brought the country
together by bringing back its old pride in fraternal ideals.

But as it happened, decades of despair and horror were required
to impress Americans with lessons that now seem blindingly obvious.

The apparent incompatibility of capitalism and democracy is, of
course, an old theme in American political and intellectual life. It

began to be sounded more than two centuries ago. Historians divide our history into the 100 years before the coming of industrial capitalism and the more than 200 years since. During the first period, the open frontier made it possible for Americans to live in ways that became impossible for their descendants. If you were white in nineteenth-century America, you always had a second chance: something was always opening up out West.

So the first fault line in American politics was not between the rich and the poor. Instead, it was between those who saw ˚chattel slavery as incompatible with American fraternity and those who did not. (Abolitionist posters showed a kneeling slave asking, 'Am I not a man, and a brother?') But only 40 years after the Civil War, reformers were already saying that the problem of chattel slavery had been replaced by that of wage slavery.

The urgency of that problem dominates Herbert Croly's progressivist manifesto of 1909, 'The Promise of American Life'. Croly argued that the Constitution, and a tradition of tolerant individualism, had kept America hopeful and filled with what he called 'genuine good-fellowship' during its first 100 years. But beginning with the first wave of industrialization in the 1870s and 1880s, things began to change. Wage slavery – a life of misery and toil, without a sense of participation in the national life, and without any trace of the frontiersman's proud independence – became the fate of more and more Americans. Alexis de Tocqueville had rejoiced that an opulent merchant and his shoe-maker, when they met on the streets of Philadelphia in 1840, would exchange political opinions. 'These two citizens,' he wrote, 'are concerned with affairs of state, and they do not part without shaking hands.' Croly feared that this kind of unforced fraternity was becoming impossible.

From Croly to John Kenneth Galbraith and Arthur Schlesinger in the 1960s, reformers urged that we needed some form of redistribution to bring back Tocquevillian comity. They battled with conservatives who claimed that redistributive measures would kill economic prosperity. The reformers insisted that what Theodore Roosevelt had called 'the money power' and Dwight Eisenhower 'the military–industrial complex' was the true enemy of American ideals. The conservatives rejoined that the only enemy of democracy was the state and that the economy must be shielded from do-gooders.

This debate simmered through the first two decades following the Second World War. During that relatively halcyon period, most Americans could get fairly secure, fairly well-paying jobs and could count on their children having a better life than theirs. White America seemed to be making slow but steady progress towards a classless society. Only the growth of the increasingly miserable black underclass reminded white Americans that the promise of American life was still far from being fulfilled.

The sense that this promise was still alive was made possible, in part, by what the first edition of this 'Companion' called the 'rights revolution'. Most of the moral progress that took place in the second half of the twentieth century was brought about by the Supreme Court's invocation of constitutional rights, in such decisions as *Brown* v. *Board of Education* (1954) and *Romer* v. *Evans* (1996), the first Supreme Court decision favourable to homosexuals. But this progress was confined almost entirely to improvements in the situation of groups identified by race, ethnicity or sexuality. The situation of women and of homosexuals changed radically in this period. Indeed, it is now clear that those changes, which spread from America around the world, were the most lasting and significant moral achievements of the twentieth century.

But though such groups could use the rhetoric of rights to good effect, the trade unions, the unemployed and those employed at the ludicrously low minimum wage ($174 an hour, in 2095 dollars, compared with the present minimum of $400) could not. Perhaps no difference between present-day American political discourse and that of 100 years ago is greater than our assumption that the first duty of the state is to prevent gross economic and social inequality, as opposed to our ancestors' assumption that the government's only *moral* duty was to ensure 'equal protection of the laws' – laws that, in their majestic impartiality, allowed the rich and the poor to receive the same hospital bills.

The Supreme Court, invoking this idea of equal protection, began the great moral revival we know at the Civil Rights Movement. The *Brown* decision initiated both an explosion of violence and an upsurge of fraternal feeling. Some white Americans burned crosses and black churches. Many more had their eyes opened to the humiliations being inflicted on their fellow citizens: if they did not join civil rights marches, they at least felt relieved of guilt when the Court threw out miscegenation laws and when Congress began to protect black voting rights. For a decade or so there was an uplifting sense of moral improvement. For the first time, white and black Americans started to think of each other as fellow citizens.

By the beginning of the 1980s, however, this sense of fraternity was only a faint memory. A burst of selfishness had produced tax revolts in the 1970s, stopping in its tracks the fairly steady progress toward a fully fledged welfare state that had been under way since the New Deal. The focus of racial hate was transferred from the rural South to the big cities, where a criminal culture of unemployed (and, in the second generation, virtually unemployable) black youths grew up – a culture of near constant violence, made possible by the then-famous American 'right to bear arms'. All the old racial prejudices were revived by white suburbanites' claims that their tax money was being used to coddle criminals. Politicians gained votes by promising to spend what little money could be squeezed from their constituents on prisons rather than on day care.

Tensions between the comfortable middle-class suburbs and the rest of the country grew steadily in the closing decades of the twentieth century, as the gap between the educated and well paid and the uneducated and ill paid steadily widened. Class division came into existence between those who made 'professional' salaries and those whose hourly wage kept sinking towards the minimum. But the politicians pretended to be unaware of this steady breakdown of fraternity.

Our nation's leaders, in the last decade of the old century and the first of the new, seemed never to have thought that it might be dangerous to make automatic weapons freely and cheaply available to desperate men and women – people without hope – living next to the centres of transportation and communication. Those weapons burst into the streets in 2014, in the revolution that, leaving the cities in ruins and dislocating American economic life, plunged the country into the Second Great Depression.

The insurgency in the ghettos, coming at a time when all but the wealthiest Americans felt desperately insecure, led to the collapse of trust in government. The collapse of the economy produced a war of all against all, as gasoline and food became harder and harder to buy, and as even the suburbanites began to brandish guns at their neighbours. As the generals never stopped saying throughout the Dark Years, only the military saved the country from utter chaos.

Here, in the late twenty-first century, as talk of fraternity and unselfishness has replaced talk of rights, American political discourse has come to be dominated by quotations from Scripture and literature, rather than from political theorists or social scientists. Fraternity, like friendship, was not a concept that either philosophers or lawyers knew how to handle. They could formulate principles of justice, equality and liberty, and invoke these principles when weighing hard moral or legal issues. But how to formulate a 'principle of fraternity'? Fraternity is an inclination of the heart, one that produces a sense of shame at having much when others have little. It is not the sort of thing that anybody can have a theory about or that people can be argued into having.

Perhaps the most vivid description of the American concept of fraternity is found in a passage from John Steinbeck's 1939 novel *The Grapes of Wrath*. Steinbeck describes a desperately impoverished family, dispossessed tenant farmers from Oklahoma, camped out at the edge of Highway 66, sharing their food with an even more desperate migrant family. Steinbeck writes: ' "I have a little food" plus "I have none." If from this problem the sum is "We have a little food," the movement has direction.' As long as people in trouble can sacrifice to help people who are in still worse trouble, Steinbeck insisted, there is fraternity, and therefore social hope.

The movement Steinbeck had in mind was the revolutionary social-ism that he, like many other leftists of the 1930s, thought would be required to bring the First Great Depression to an end. 'The quality of owning,' he wrote, 'freezes you forever into the "I," and cuts you off forever from the "we." ' Late twentieth-century liberals no longer believed in getting rid of private ownership, but they agreed that the promise of American life could be redeemed only as long as Americans were willing to sacrifice for the sake of fellow Americans – only as long as they could see the government not as stealing their tax money but as needing it to prevent unnecessary suffering.

The Democratic Vistas Party, the coalition of trade unions and churches that toppled the military dictatorship in 2044, has retained control of Congress by successfully convincing the voters that its opponents constitute 'the parties of selfishness'. The traditional use of 'brother' and 'sister' in union locals and religious congregations is the principal reason why 'fraternity' (or, among purists, 'siblinghood') is now the name of our most cherished ideal.

In the first two centuries of American history Jefferson's use of rights had set the tone for political discourse, but now political argument is not about who has the right to what but about what can best prevent the re-emergence of hereditary castes – either racial or economic. The old union slogan 'An injury to one is an injury to all' is now the catch phrase of American politics. 'Solidarity is Forever' and 'This Land is Your Land' are sung at least as often as 'The Star-Spangled Banner'.

Until the last 50 years, moral instruction in America had inculcated personal responsibility, and most sermons had focused on individual salvation. Today morality is thought of neither as a matter of applying the moral law nor as the acquisition of virtues but as fellow feeling, the ability to sympathize with the plight of others.

In the churches, the 'social gospel' theology of the early twentieth century has been rediscovered. Walter Rauschenbusch's 'Prayer against the servants of Mammon' ('Behold the servants of Mammon, who defy thee and drain their fellow men for gain . . . who have made us ashamed of our dear country by their defilements and have turned our holy freedom into a hollow name . . .') is familiar to most church-goers. In the schools, students learn about our country's history from social novels describing our past failures to hang together when we needed to, the novels of Steinbeck, Upton Sinclair, Theodore Dreiser,

Richard Wright and, of course, Russell Banks's samizdat novel, *Trampling the Vineyards* (2021).

Historians unite in calling the twentieth the 'American' century. Certainly it was in the twentieth century that the United States was richest, most powerful, most influential and most self-confident. Our ancestors 100 years ago still thought of the country as destined to police, inform and inspire the world. Compared with the Americans of 100 years ago, we are citizens of an isolationist, unambitious, middle-grade nation.

Our products are only now becoming competitive again in international markets, and Democratic Vistas politicians continue to urge that our consistently low productivity is a small price to pay for union control of the workplace and worker ownership of the majority of firms. We continue to lag behind the European Community, which was able to withstand the pressures of a globalized labour market by having a fully fledged welfare state already in place, and which (except for Austria and Great Britain) was able to resist the temptation to impoverish the most vulnerable in order to keep its suburbanites affluent. Spared the equivalent of our own Dark Years, Europe, still, despite all that China can do, holds the position we lost in 2014: it still dominates both the world's economy and its culture.

For two centuries Americans believed that they were as far ahead of Europe, in both virtue and promise, as Europe was ahead of the rest of the world. But American exceptionalism did not survive the Dark Years: we no longer think of ourselves as singled out by divine favour. We are now, once again, a constitutional democracy, but we have proved as vulnerable as Germany, Russia and India to dictatorial takeovers. We have a sense of fragility, of susceptibility to the vicissitudes of time and chance, which Walt Whitman and John Dewey may never have known.

Perhaps no American writer will ever again begin a book, as Croly did, by saying, 'The faith of Americans in their own country is religious, if not in its intensity, at any rate in its almost absolute and universal authority.' But our chastened mood, our lately learned humility, may have made us better able to realize that everything depends on keeping our fragile sense of American fraternity intact.

* * * *

NOTES

1 From the article 'Socialism', by the labour historian Sean Wilentz, in the first edition of *A Companion to American Thought*, Richard Fox and James Kloppenberg, eds. (London and New York: Blackwell, 1995).

19. The Unpatriotic Academy

Most of us, despite the outrage we may feel about governmental cowardice or corruption, and despite our despair over what is being done to the weakest and poorest among us, still identify with our country. We take pride in being citizens of a self-invented, self-reforming, enduring constitutional democracy. We think of the United States as having glorious – if tarnished – national traditions.

Many of the exceptions to this rule are found in colleges and universities, in the academic departments that have become sanctuaries for left-wing political views. I am glad there are such sanctuaries, even though I wish we had a left more broadly based, less self-involved and less jargon-ridden than our present one. But any left is better than none, and this one is doing a great deal of good for people who have a raw deal in our society: women, African-Americans, gay men and lesbians. This focus on marginalized groups will, in the long run, help to make our country much more decent, more tolerant and more civilized.

But there is a problem with this left: it is unpatriotic. In the name of 'the politics of difference', it refuses to rejoice in the country it inhabits. It repudiates the idea of a national identity, and the emotion of national pride. This repudiation is the difference between traditional American pluralism and the new movement called multiculturalism. Pluralism is the attempt to make America what the philosopher John Rawls call 'a social union of social unions', a community of communities, a nation with far more room for difference that most. Multiculturalism is turning into the attempt to keep these communities at odds with one another.

Academic leftists who are enthusiastic about multiculturalism distrust the proposal made by Sheldon Hackney, chairman of the National Endowment of the Humanities, to hold televised town meetings to 'explore the meaning of American identity'. Criticizing Mr Hackney in the *New York Times* on 30 January 1994, Richard Sennett, a distinguished social critic, wrote that the idea of such an identity is just 'the gentlemanly face of nationalism', and speaks of 'the evil of a shared national identity'.

It is too early to say now [February 1994] whether the conversations Mr Hackney proposes will be fruitful. But whether they are or not, it is important to insist that a sense of shared national identity is not an evil. It is an absolutely essential component of citizenship, of any attempt to take our country and its problems seriously. There is no incompatibility between respect for cultural differences and American patriotism.

Like every other country, ours has a lot to be proud of and a lot to be ashamed of. But a nation cannot reform itself unless it takes pride in itself – unless it has an identity, rejoices in it, reflects upon it and tries to live up to it. Such pride sometimes takes the form of arrogant, bellicose nationalism. But it often takes the form of a yearning to live up to the nation's professed ideals.

That is the desire to which the Revd Dr Martin Luther King, Jr appealed, and he is somebody every American can be proud of. It is just as appropriate for white Americans to take pride in Dr King and in his (limited) success as for black Americans to take pride in Ralph Waldo Emerson and John Dewey and their (limited) successes. Cornel West wrote a book – *The American Evasion of Philosophy* – about the connections between Emerson, Dewey, W. E. B. Du Bois and his own preaching in African-American churches. The late Irving Howe, whose 'World of Our Fathers' did much to make us aware that we are a nation of immigrants, also tried to persuade us (in 'The American Newness: Culture and Politics in the Age of Emerson') to cherish a distinctively American, distinctively Emersonian, hope.

Mr Howe was able to rejoice in a country that had only in his lifetime started to allow Jews to be fully fledged members of society.

Cornel West can still identify with a country that, by denying them decent schools and jobs, keeps so many black Americans humiliated and wretched.

There is no contradiction between such identification and shame at the greed, the intolerance and the indifference to suffering that is widespread in the United States. On the contrary, you can feel shame over your country's behaviour only to the extent to which you feel it is your country. If we fail in such identification, we fail in national hope. If we fail in national hope, we shall no longer even try to change our ways. If American leftists cease to be proud of being the heirs of Emerson, Lincoln and King, Irving Howe's prophecy that 'the "newness" will come again' – that we shall once again experience the joyous self-confidence which fills Emerson's 'American Scholar' – is unlikely to come true.

If in the interests of ideological purity, or out of the need to stay as angry as possible, the academic left insists on a 'politics of difference', it will become increasingly isolated and ineffective. An unpatriotic left has never achieved anything. A left that refuses to take pride in its country will have no impact on that country's politics, and will eventually become an object of contempt.

20. Back to Class Politics

If you go to Britain and attend a Labour Party rally, you will probably hear the audience sing 'The Red Flag'. That song begins, 'The people's flag is deepest red. It's shrouded oft our martyred dead. But ere their limbs grew stiff and cold, Their hearts' blood dyed its every fold.'

You may find this song maudlin and melodramatic. But it will remind you of something that many people have forgotten: that the history of the labour unions, in Britain, America, and everywhere else in the world, is a blood-drenched history of violent struggle. Like the civil rights movement, the labour movement owed its successes to repeated and deliberate criminal acts – acts that we now think of as heroic civil disobedience, but which were brutally punished. To obstruct scabs from entering a workplace into which they are invited by the owners of that workplace is a criminal act, just as it is a criminal act to sit in at a lunch counter after the proprietor asks you to leave. The police who brutalized the strikers thought of themselves as preventing criminal acts from taking place, and they were right. But, of course, the strikers were also right when they replied that the police were acting as the agents of employers who refused to give their workers a decent share of the value those workers produced. To persuade the American people to see strikes, and violence against strikers, in this alternative way took a very long time. Only after an enormous amount of suffering, and very gradually, did it become politically impossible for mayors, governors and sheriffs to send in their men to break strikers' skulls. Only in recent years has this strategy once again become politically possible.

We are accustomed to seeing labour leaders photographed with presidents, and officials of General Motors and the United Auto

Workers jumping up and shaking hands at the end of a successful bargaining session. So we think of labour unions as fine old American institutions, built into the fabric of the country. We think of strikes as an accepted, and perfectly reasonable, method of bringing about a slightly fairer distribution of profits. But we should remember that the early history of labour unions in America, as in the rest of the world, is a history of the skulls of strikers being broken by truncheons, decade after decade. We should also realize that those truncheons have recently reappeared: as John Sweeney reminds us in his book, during the last few years they have been used on striking janitors in Los Angeles and striking coal miners in Virginia.

We should also remember that the history of the labour movement is one of heroic self-deprivation. Only after a great many striking mothers had seen their children go hungry were the unions able to accumulate enough money to set up strike funds, and to provide a little help. Only because millions of workers refused to become scabs by taking jobs that would have meant food for their families did the strikes eventually succeed. You would never guess from William Bennett's and Robert Bork's speeches about the need to overcome liberal individualism, that the labour unions provide by far the best examples in America's history of the virtues that these writers claim we must recapture. The history of the unions provides the best examples of comradeship, loyalty, and self-sacrifice.

Sometimes American unions have become corrupt, and have been taken over by greedy and cynical crooks. In this respect, their record is no better or worse than that of American churches, American law firms, American business firms, and even American academic departments. But at their best, the labour unions are America at its best. Like the civil rights movement, the union movement is a model of Americans getting together on their own and changing society from the bottom up – forcing it to become more decent, more democratic and more humane. The strikers who braved the wrath of the police and the National Guard created a moral atmosphere in which no one was willing to be seen crossing a picket line, or be caught wearing clothes that did not bear a union label, or be known to have scabbed. This unwillingness was an expression of the sort of human solidarity that made the events of 1989 possible in eastern Europe, and which made the Founding Fathers willing to risk their lives, their fortunes and their sacred honour. The fact that people are now once again willing to cross picket lines, and are unwilling to ask themselves who makes their clothes or who picks their vegetables, is a symptom of moral decline.

Most American schoolchildren learn something about the martyrs of the civil rights movement. They at least know how Martin Luther King, Jr died. Perhaps they have also heard of Medgar Evers or of Andrew Goodman, James Chaney and Michael Schwerner. But these schoolchildren usually have no idea of how it came about that most American workers have an eight-hour day and a five-day working week. They are unlikely to be taught about the conditions in the sweatshops and factories in which their great-grandparents worked, nor about how the unions made those conditions a little better for their grandparents and parents. They know nothing of the blood that had to be spilled, and the hunger that had to be endured, in order that unions could be transformed from criminal conspiracies into fine old American institutions.

We should help our students understand that social justice in America has owed much more to civil disobedience than to the use of the ballot. The students need to know that the deepest and most enduring injustices, like the unending humiliation of African-Americans and the miserable wages paid to unorganized workers, are always downplayed by the political parties, and by most of the press. They need to remember that the same argument now used against raising the minimum wage – that doing so will discourage economic efficiency and productivity – was once used against the eight-hour day. They need to be able to spot the resemblances between what the politicians were indirectly and gently bribed to ignore at the beginning of this century and what they are being indirectly and gently bribed to ignore now. They need to realize that the last 100 years of our country's history has witnessed a brutal struggle between the corporations and the workers, that this struggle is still going on, and that the corporations are winning. They need to know that the deepest social problems usually go unmentioned by candidates for political office, because it is not in the interest of the rich to have those problems discussed in public.

Today our country, like the other industrialized democracies, faces a problem that few politicians, except for scurrilous demagogues like Pat Buchanan and, in France, Jean-Marie Le Pen, seem willing to talk about: the wages of European and American workers are ridiculously high by world standards. There is less and less need to employ any of these workers, since the same work can be done elsewhere for a fifth of the cost. Furthermore, the globalization of the markets in capital and labour means that no nation's economy is sufficiently self-contained to permit long-term social planning by a national government. So the American economy is passing out of the control of the American government, and thus out of the control of the American voters.

This new situation is fine with the 1 percent of Americans who own 40 per cent of their country's wealth. Their dividends typically increase when jobs are exported from Ohio to south China, and from North Carolina to Thailand. The strength of the dollar does not matter to them, because their investment advisers can flip their money into other currencies at the touch of a button. They have less and less at stake in America's future, and more and more invested in an efficient and productive global economy – an economy made ever more efficient and productive by the constant expansion of the global labour market into poorer and poorer countries. There is little reason to believe that what is good for General Motors or Microsoft is good for America. The economic royalists whom Franklin Roosevelt denounced still had a lot invested in America's future. For today's super-rich, such an investment would be imprudent.

There is much too little public discussion of the changes that this globalized labour market will inevitably bring to America in the coming decades. Bill Bradley is one of the few prominent politicians to have insisted that we must prevent our country from breaking up into hereditary economic castes. Writers like Michael Lind and Edward Luttwak are sketching very plausible scenarios of an America in which the top fifth of the country, the well-educated professionals, carry out the orders of the international super-rich. These people will get paid between $75,000 and $500,000 a year to do so. The remaining four-fifths of the country, the four-fifths that now has a median family income of $30,000, will get a little less in every successive year, and will keep on doing all the dirty work. America, the country that was to have witnessed a new birth of freedom, will gradually be divided by class differences of a sort that would have been utterly inconceivable to Jefferson or to Lincoln or to Walt Whitman.

Unless the politicians begin to talk about long-term social planning, Lind and Luttwak argue, economic inequality, and the formation of hereditary economic castes, will continue unchecked. Maybe these authors are too pessimistic, but we shall never know unless the questions they pose are taken up by candidates for public office. The most important single reason for hoping that American labour unions will become much bigger and more powerful than they are now is that they are the only organizations who want to get these questions on the table – to force politicians to talk about what is going to happen to wages, and how we are going to avoid increasing economic injustice. If a revived union movement could get out the vote in the old mill towns, in the rural slums, and in the inner cities, instead of letting the suburban vote set the national political agenda, those questions *would* be on the table.

The whole point of America was that it was going to be the world's first classless society. It was going to be a place where janitors, executives, professors, nurses, and sales clerks would look each other in the eye and respect each other as fellow citizens. It was going to be a place where their kids all went to the same schools, and where they got the same treatment from the police and the courts. From the days of Franklin Roosevelt to those of Lyndon Johnson, we made enormous progress towards the creation of such a society. In the twenty years between the Second World War and Vietnam the newly respectable labour unions made their presence felt on the national scene, and accomplished a great deal. Those were the years in which academics like Daniel Bell, Arthur Schlesinger and John Kenneth Galbraith worked side by side with labour leaders like Walter Reuther and A. Philip Randolph.

The Vietnam War saw the end of the traditional alliance between the academics and the unions – an alliance that had nudged the Democratic Party steadily to the left during the previous 20 years. We are still living with the consequences of the anti-Vietnam War movement, and in particular with those of the rage of the increasingly manic student protesters of the late 1960s. These protesters were absolutely right that Vietnam was an unjust war, a massacre of which our country should always be ashamed. But when the students began to burn flags, they did deeper and more long-lasting damage to the American left than they could ever have imagined. When they began to spell 'America' with a 'k', they lost the respect and the sympathy of the union members. Until George McGovern's defeat in 1972, the New Left did not realize that it had unthinkingly destroyed an alliance that had been central to American leftist politics.

Since those days, leftists in the colleges and universities have concentrated their energies on academic politics rather than on national politics. As Todd Gitlin put it, we academics marched on the English department while the Republicans took over the White House. While we had our backs turned, the labour unions were being steadily ground down by the shift to a service economy, and by the machinations of the Reagan and Bush administrations. The best thing that could happen to the American left would be for the academics to get back into the class struggle, and for the labour union members to forgive and forget the stupid and self-defeating anti-American rhetoric that filled the universities of the late sixties.

This is not to say that those 25 years of inward-looking academic politics were in vain. American campuses are very much better places – *morally* better places – than they were in 1970. Thanks to all those marches on the English department, and various other departments, the situation of women, gays and lesbians, African-Americans and Hispanics has been enormously improved. Their new role in the academy is helping improve their situation in the rest of American society.

Nevertheless, leftist academic politics has run its course. It is time to revive the kind of leftist politics that pervaded American campuses from the Great Depression through to the early sixties – a politics that centres on the struggle to prevent the rich from ripping off the rest of the country. If the unions will help us revive this kind of politics, maybe the academy and the labour movement can get together again. Maybe together we can help bring our country closer to the goal that matters most: the classless society. That is the cause for which the American Federation of Labor and Congress of Industrial Organizations organizers are now fighting, and for which some of their predecessors died.

Afterword: Pragmatism, Pluralism and Postmodernism

(1998)

The word 'postmodernism' has been rendered almost meaningless by being used to mean so many different things. If you read a random dozen out of the thousands of books whose titles contain the word 'postmodern', you will encounter at least half a dozen widely differing definitions of that adjective. I have often urged that we would be better off without it – that the word is simply too fuzzy to convey anything.[1] For the purposes of this essay, however, I shall take a different tack. Even if the word 'postmodern' is too equivocal for profitable use, its popularity among intellectuals could do with an explanation. So I shall offer a suggestion about why so many intelligent and reflective people seem to think that everything has recently become quite different.

Various as the definitions of 'postmodern' are, most of them have something to do with a perceived loss of unity. My hunch is that this sense of loss results from the confluence of a philosophical movement which is now about a century old with the realization that the institutions of liberal democracy may not endure. The sense that everything has recently fallen to pieces results from combining a renunciation of the traditional theologicometaphysical belief that Reality and Truth are One – that there is One True Account of How Things Really Are – with the inability to believe that things are going to get better: that history will someday culminate in the universal adoption of egalitarian, democratic customs and institutions. The renunciation began, I shall argue, with Darwin's explanation of where we came from. The inability to believe has increased steadily during the last few decades, as it has become clear that Europe is no longer in command of the planet, and that the sociopolitical future of humanity has become utterly unforeseeable.

Freud famously said that Copernicus, Darwin and he himself had been responsible for successive cataclysmic decentrings – of the planet earth, of the human species, and of the conscious mind respectively. Carrying through this metaphor, we may say that the nineteenth century was willing to give up the conviction that the created universe exists for the sake of our species in exchange for the belief that the human race has finally taken control of its own destiny. But that view was bound up with the belief that Europe was the centre of the world, a belief which the late twentieth century is no longer able to hold. Whereas intellectuals of the nineteenth century undertook to replace metaphysical comfort with historical hope, intellectuals at the end of this century, feeling let down by history, are experiencing self-indulgent, pathetic hopelessness.

My account of these changes will divide into two parts: the first emphasizes the importance of Darwin for the development of utilitarianism, pragmatism and twentieth-century social hope; the second takes its point of departure from the account of our present historical situation offered by Clifford Geertz in his recent book *A World in Pieces*.[2]

Plato, and orthodox Christian theology, told us that human beings have an animal part and a divine part. The divine part is an extra added ingredient. Its presence within us is testimony to the existence of another, higher, immaterial, and invisible world: a world which offers us salvation from time and chance.

This dualistic account is plausible and powerful. We are indeed very different from the animals, and the difference seems one which mere complexity cannot explain. Lucretius and Hobbes tried to tell us that complexity is in fact sufficient – that we, like everything else in the universe, are best understood as accidentally produced assemblages of particles. But before Darwin this explanation never gained any substantial following. It was easy for Platonists and Christians to argue that materialist philosophies were merely perverse attempts to regress to the condition of animals.

Darwin, however, made materialism respectable. His account of the difference between us and the brutes became the common sense of the educated public. This happened for two reasons. The first was that Darwin had come up with the first detailed and plausible explanation of how both life and intelligence might have emerged from a meaningless swirl of corpuscles. (Lucretius and Hobbes had had no concrete evolutionary narrative to offer, only an abstract, theoretical possibility.) But Darwin's narrative, once its details had been filled in by Mendelian genetics and by an explosion in palaeontological research, was so convincing as to threaten the entire Western theological and philosophical tradition. It was the first drama to challenge seriously Plato's Myth of the Cave and Dante's *Divine Comedy*. An imaginative achievement on a level with these great works, this narrative offered the same combination of quest romance and theoretical synthesis.

Yet Darwin's theory might never have become the common sense of European intellectuals if the ground had not already been prepared by the democratic revolutions of the late eighteenth century and by the Industrial Revolution. These revolutions, taken together, testify to the power of human beings to change the conditions of human life; they made nineteenth-century Europeans able to feel confident in humanity's ability to take charge of its own affairs. Unlike their ancestors, these Europeans felt that they could go it alone – that they could achieve human perfection without reliance on a nonhuman power.

In previous ages, only the presence of such a power seemed to account for the fact that we did not, or at least should not, live as the animals did. Intellectuals took for granted that we were linked to the gods either by special divine favour, or by a connaturality with the divine made evident in our possession of the extra added ingredient which the animals lack, the soul or mind. If there was no such ingredient and no such linkage, Plato argued, the life of Socrates would make no sense. For there would be no reason not to regress to the bestiality of men like Cleon and Callicles.

Both before and after Plato, religious thinkers thought that commands from, and providential interventions by, a personal deity or deities were necessary if men were to live together in peace and concord. In Plato and the secularist philosophical tradition which he helped found, the divine was depersonalized, deprived of will and emotion. But, theists and secularists agreed, we humans can do more than just struggle to survive and breed only because we share something precious with each other which animals do not have. This precious extra gives us the ability to cooperate. We do so because we are commanded to do so, either by God or by something like Kant's pure, nonempirical faculty of practical reason.

But in nineteenth-century Europe and America, large numbers of intellectuals began to wonder if their predecessors might not have made too much of the idea of morality as obedience – as conformity to something like the Ten Commandments, or Plato's idea of the good, or Kant's categorical imperative. When Blake wrote that 'one law for the lion and the ox is oppression' and Shelley that poets were the unacknowledged legislators of the world, they anticipated Nietzsche's thought that self-creation could take the place once occupied by obedience.

The Romantics were inspired by the successes of antimonarchist and anticlericalist revolutions to think that the desire for something to obey is a symptom of immaturity. These successes made it possible to envisage building a new Jerusalem without divine assistance, thereby creating a society in which men and women would lead the perfected lives which had previously seemed possible only in an invisible, immaterial, post-mortem paradise. The image of progress toward such a society – horizontal progress, so to speak – began to take the place of Platonic or Dantean images of vertical ascent. History began to replace God, Reason and Nature as the source of human hope. When Darwin came along, his story of prehuman history encouraged this replacement. For it became possible to see deliberate self-creation, a conscious overcoming of the past, as a continuation of the biological story of animal species perpetually, albeit unconsciously, surpassing one another.

This new outburst of human self-confidence is part of a familiar story, as is the suggestion that Darwin's animalization of man could not have found credence in earlier times. Many historians of ideas have noted that we would not have been able to accept our fully fledged animality if we had still felt as much in need of nonhuman authority as had our ancestors. But I now want to make a slightly less familiar point, namely that these developments also made it possible to believe that there are many different, but equally valuable, sorts of human life. They made the idea of convergence to unity less compelling. Vertical ascent from the Many to the One entails such convergence, but horizontal progress can be thought of as ever-increasing proliferation.

From Plato to Hegel, it was natural to think of the various ways of leading a human life as hierarchically ordered. The priests took precedence over the warriors, the wise over the vulgar, the patriarchs over their wives, the nobles over the common people, the *Geisteswissenschaftler* over the *Naturwissenschaftler*. Such hierarchies were constructed by calculating the relative contribution of animality and of the extra added ingredient which makes us truly human. Women were said to have less of this ingredient than men, barbarians than Greeks, slaves than free men, true believers than heathens, blacks than whites, and so on. The standard way of justifying both subordination and conformity was by reference to such an ingredient, and such a hierarchy. Ever since Plato wrote the first vertical quest romance, it has been natural to ask such questions as 'Where does this fall in the Great Chain of Being?' or, 'What step does it occupy on "the world's great altar-stairs, that lead from nature up to God"³?'

After Darwin, however, it became possible to believe that nature is not leading up to anything – that nature has nothing in mind. This idea, in turn, suggested that the difference between animals and humans is not evidence for the existence of an immaterial deity. It suggested further that humans have to dream up the point of human life, and cannot appeal to a nonhuman standard to determine whether they have chosen wisely. The latter suggestion made radical pluralism intellectually viable. For it became possible to think that the meaning of one human life may have little to do with the meaning of any other human life, while being none the worse for that. This latter thought enabled thinkers to disassociate the need for social cooperation (and the consequent need to agree on what, for public purposes, should be done) from the Greek question: What is the Good Life for Man?

Such developments made it possible to see the aim of social organization as freedom rather than virtue, and to see the virtues in Meno's way rather than Socrates': as a collection of unrelated sorts of excellence. It became possible to substitute a Rabelaisian sense of the value of sheer human variety for a Platonic search for unity. In particular, these developments helped people to see sex as no more bestial, no 'lower', than any other source of human delight (for example, religious devotion, philosophical reflection, or artistic creation). In the twentieth century, the thought that we are free citizens of democratically ruled republics has gone hand in hand with the thought that our neighbours' sources of private pleasure are none of our business.

This latter thought is at the core of Mill's *On Liberty*, a treatise which begins with an epigraph (from Wilhelm von Humboldt) which states that the point of social organization is to encourage the widest possible human diversity. Mill had learned from the Romantics that there may be no point in grading either poems or people according to a single, pre-established scale; what counts is originality and authenticity, rather than conformity to an antecedent standard.

So for Mill and other romantic utilitarians, it became possible both to think that the only plausible answer to the question 'What is intrinsically good?' is 'human happiness', and to admit that this answer provides no guidance for choices between alternative human lives. Mill knew that his and Harriet Taylor's lives were better than those of most of their fellow citizens, just as he knew that Socrates' life was better than that of a pig. But he was willing to admit that he could not prove this to the satisfaction of those fellow citizens, and to conclude that democratic citizenship does not require agreement on the relative value of these sorts of lives.

The culminating moment of this line of thought comes with pragmatism's renunciation of the idea that truth consists in correspondence with reality. For this renunciation has as a corollary that the search for truth is not distinct from the search for human happiness. It also implies that there is no need to make all true propositions cohere into one unified vision of how things are.

A French philosopher named René Berthelot entitled his 1912 book *Romantic Utilitarianism: a study of the pragmatist movement*. That title was, I think, exactly right. So was Berthelot's suggestion that Nietzsche and

James were concerned with the same questions, namely: Given a Darwinian account of how we got here, can we still think of our inquiries as aiming at the One True Account of How Things Really Are? Should we not substitute the idea of a plurality of different aims of inquiry – aims which may require mutual adjustment but do not require synthesis? May we not think of true beliefs as reliable guides to human action, rather than as accurate representations of something nonhuman.

The utilitarian claim that we have no goal save human happiness, and that no divine command or philosophical principle has any moral authority unless it contributes to the achievement of this goal, has as a corollary the pragmatist claim that our desire for truth cannot take precedence over our desire for happiness. In a sense, the critics of utilitarianism and pragmatism are right in saying that these doctrines animalize human beings. For both drop the idea of the extra added ingredient. They substitute the idea that human beings have, thanks to having invented language, a much larger behavioural repertoire than the beasts, and thus much more diverse and interesting ways of finding joy.

I shall use the term 'philosophical pluralism' to mean the doctrine that there is a potential infinity of equally valuable ways to lead a human life, and that these ways cannot be ranked in terms of degrees of excellence, but only in terms of their contribution to the happiness of the persons who lead them and of the communities to which these persons belong. That form of pluralism is woven into the founding documents of both utilitarianism and pragmatism.

William James, who viewed himself as following in Mill's footsteps – doing to our concept of truth what Mill had done to our concept of right action – spent half his philosophical life crusading against the idealist doctrine that the universe and Truth must both somehow be One. In particular, he urged that science and religion could coexist comfortably as soon as it became clear that these two areas of culture serve different purposes, and that different purposes require different tools. Religious tools are needed to make possible certain kinds of human life, but not others. Scientific tools are of no use for many human projects, and of great use for many others.

Nietzsche, described as 'a German pragmatist' by Berthelot, agreed with James about truth. He spent much of his time campaigning against the idea that what we call 'knowledge' is anything more than a set of gimmicks for keeping a certain species alive and healthy. Displaying both ignorance and ingratitude, Nietzsche mocked both Mill and Darwin, yet he had no hesitation in appropriating their best ideas. Had he lived to read James, he would probably not have recognized a fellow disciple of Emerson, but would have mocked him as an ignoble, calculating Yankee merchant. But Nietzsche would nevertheless have echoed James's and Dewey's Emersonian appeals to the future to produce an ever-expanding profusion of new sorts of human lives, new kinds of human beings.

I think it is important for an understanding of post-Darwinian intellectual life to grasp the importance of the pragmatists' refusal to accept the correspondence account of truth: the theory that true beliefs are accurate representations of a pre-existent reality. This goes along with their refusal to believe that nonhuman reality has an intrinsic character, a character which human beings ought to respect. For notions like 'Reality' or 'Nature', Nietzsche and James substituted the biologistic notion of the environment. The environment in which we human beings live poses problems to us but, unlike a capitalized Reason or a capitalized Nature, we owe it neither respect nor obedience. Our task is to master it, or to adapt ourselves to it, rather than to represent it or correspond to it. The idea that we have a moral duty to correspond to reality is, for Nietzsche and James, as stultifying as the idea that the whole duty of man is to please God.

The link between Darwinism and pragmatism is clearest if one asks oneself the following question: At what point in biological evolution did organisms stop just coping with reality and start representing it? To pose the riddle is to suggest the answer: Maybe they never *did* start representing it. Maybe the whole idea of mental representation was just an uncashable and unfruitful metaphor. Maybe this metaphor was inspired by the same need to get in touch with a powerful nonhuman authority which made the priests think themselves more truly human than the warriors. Maybe, now that the French and Industrial Revolutions have given human beings a new self-confidence, they can drop the idea of representing reality and substitute the idea of using it.

Abandoning the correspondence theory of truth means no longer insisting that truth, like reality, is one and seamless. If a true belief is simply the sort of belief which surpasses the competition as a rule for successful future action, then there may be no need to reconcile all one's beliefs with all one's other beliefs – no need to attempt to see reality steadily and as a whole. Perhaps, James famously suggested, our beliefs can be compartmentalized, so that there is no need, for example, to reconcile one's regular attendance at Mass with one's work as an evolutionary biologist. Conflict between beliefs adopted for diverse purposes will only arise when we engage in projects of social cooperation, when we need to agree about what is to be done. So the pursuit of a political utopia becomes disjoined from both religion and science. It has no religious or scientific or philosophical foundations, but only utilitarian and pragmatic ones. A liberal democratic utopia, on the pragmatists' view, is no truer to human nature or the demands of an ahistorical moral law than is a fascist tyranny. But it is much more likely to produce greater human happiness. A perfected society will not live up to a pre-existent standard, but will be an artistic achievement, produced by the same long and difficult process of trial and error as is required by any other creative effort.

So far I have been trying to show how Darwinism, utilitarianism and pragmatism conspired to exalt plurality over unity – how the dissolution of the traditional theologicometaphysical world picture helped the European intellectuals drop the idea of the One True Account of How Things Really Are. The new social hopes which filled the nineteenth century helped them accomplish this transvaluation of traditional philosophical values, and the resulting philosophical pluralism reinforced the sense that a perfected society would make possible ever-proliferating human diversity. At the end of that century, it seemed entirely plausible that the human race, having broken through age-old barriers, was now about to create a global, cosmopolitan, social democratic, pluralist community. The institutions of this perfected society would not only eliminate traditional inequalities but would leave plenty of room for its members to pursue their individual visions of human perfection.

I turn now to some questions which have begun to burden intellectuals in recent decades, and which are often referred to as 'the problems of postmodernity'. These questions are raised by the fact that, as Clifford Geertz puts it, the liberalism, the aspiration towards such a perfected society, is itself 'a culturally specific phenomenon, born in the West and perfected there'. The very universalism to which liberalism is committed and which it promotes, Geertz continues,

> has brought it into open conflict both with other universalisms with similar intent, most notably with that set forth by a revenant Islam, and with a large number of alternative versions of the good, the right, and the indubitable, Japanese, Indian, African, Singaporean, to which it looks like just one more attempt to impose Western values on the rest of the world – the continuation of colonialism by other means.[4]

What Geertz says of liberalism is true also of its philosophical partners, utilitarianism and pragmatism. Most of those attracted by those two philosophical doctrines are people who had previously decided that their favourite utopia is the liberal one described in *On Liberty*: a world in which nothing remains sacred save the freedom to lead your life by your own lights, and nothing is forbidden which does not interfere with the freedom of others. If you lose faith in this utopia, you may begin to have doubts about philosophical pluralism.

Although this partnership relation is real and important, it should be clear that neither utilitarianism nor pragmatism *entails* a commitment to liberalism. That is why Nietzsche can be as good a pragmatist as James, and why Dostoevsky's Grand Inquisitor can be as good a utilitarian as Mill. On the other hand, liberalism comes close to entailing them. For although romantic utilitarians do not necessarily want to disenchant the world, they certainly want to disenchant the past. So they need to melt much that had seemed solid into air. The redefinitions of 'right' and 'true' offered by Mill and James respectively are indispensable to this melting process. For any non-utilitarian definition of 'right' and any non-pragmatist definition of 'true' will lend aid and comfort to the idea that there is an authority – for example, the eternal moral law, or the intrinsic structure of reality – which takes precedence over agreement between free human beings about what to do or what to believe.

Geertz says that the partisans of liberalism

> must reconceive it as a view not from nowhere but from the special somewhere of (a certain sort of) Western political experi- ence, a statement . . . about what we who are the heirs of that experience think we have learned about how people with differences can live together amongst one another with some degree of comity.[5]

That is exactly how Dewey wanted us to conceive of pragmatism: not as the result of a deeper understanding of the intrinsic nature of truth or knowledge, but as the view of truth and knowledge one will be likely to adopt if, as a result of one's own experience with various sociopolitical alternatives, one's highest hope is the creation of the liberal utopia sketched by Mill. Pragmatists are entirely at home with the idea that political theory should view itself as suggestions for future action emerging out of recent historical experience, rather than attempting to legitimate the outcome of that experience by reference to something ahistorical.

But the sceptics Geertz cites, the people who suspect that liberalism is an attempt to impose the outcome of a specifically European experi- ence on people who have had no share in this experience, are likely to suggest that European confidence in liberalism and its philosophical corollaries is simply confidence in the success of Europe to make the rest of the world submit to its will. How can you Europeans tell, such sceptics ask, whether your devotion to liberalism is a result of its intrinsic merits or simply a result of the success of liberal societies in taking control of most of the resources, and most of the population, of the world?

Perhaps, these sceptics suggest, yesterday's unbounded faith in liberalism and its philosophical corollaries was a result of a tacit conviction of the inevitability of liberalism's triumph. From the beginning of the colonialist period until the recent past, it seemed obvious to most Europeans, and plausible to many non-Europeans, that nothing could withstand the force of Europe's intellectual example any more than it could the force of Europe's commercial and military power. But perhaps the transvaluation of traditional philosophical values to which I have referred – the shift from unity to plurality – was simply an attempt by philosophers to climb on an economic and military bandwagon? Perhaps philosophy was simply following the flag?

A Deweyan response to such a postcolonial sceptic would go something like this: Sure, pragmatism and utilitarianism might never have gotten off the ground without a boost from colonialist and imperialist triumphalism. But so what? The question is not whether the popularity of these philosophical views was the product of this or that transitory hold on power, but whether anybody now has any better ideas or any better utopias. We pragmatists are not arguing that modern Europe has any superior insight into eternal, ahistorical realities. We do not claim any superior rationality. We claim only an experimental success: we have come up with a way of bringing people into some degree of comity, and of increasing human happiness, which looks more promising than any other way which has been proposed so far.

In order to evaluate this response, consider some of the reasons why Europe no longer looks like the avant garde of the human race, reasons why it seems absurdly improbable that we shall ever have a global liberal utopia. Here are three:

1. It is not possible to have European democratic government without something like a European standard of living – without the middle class, and the well-established institutions of civil society, which such a standard has made possible. Without these, you cannot have an electorate sufficiently literate and leisured to take part in the democratic process. But there are too many people in the world, and too few natural resources, to make such a standard of living available to all human beings.

2. The greedy and selfish kleptocrats have become, in recent decades, considerably more sophisticated. The Chinese and Nigerian generals, and their counterparts around the world, have learned from the failures of twentieth-century totalitarianism to avoid ideology and to

274

be pragmatic. They lie, cheat and steal in much more suave and sophisticated ways than those used by, for example, the old Communist nomenklaturas. So the end of the Cold War gives no reason for optimism about the progress of democracy, whatever it may have done for the triumph of capitalism.

3. Achieving a liberal utopia on a global scale would require the establishment of a world federation, exercising a global monopoly of force – the sort of federation you can find described in any science fiction utopia set in the twenty-first century. (As Michael Lind has pointed out, the only science fiction stories which postulate a continuing plurality of sovereign nation states are apocalyptic dystopias.) But the likelihood of such a federation being set up is much smaller than it was when the United Nations Organization was founded in 1945. The continual splitting up of old nation states, ex-colonies and ex-federations makes a world government less likely with every passing year. So even if technology could somehow enable us to balance population and resources, and even if we could get the kleptocrats off the backs of the poor, we would still be out of luck. For sooner or later some uniformed idiots will start pressing nuclear buttons and our grandchildren will inhabit a dystopia like that shown in the film *Road Warrior*.

I think these are three plausible reasons for believing that neither democratic freedom nor philosophical pluralism will survive the next century. If I were a wagering Olympian, I might well bet my fellow divinities that pragmatism, utilitarianism and liberalism would, among mortals, be only faint memories in a hundred years' time. For very few unexpurgated libraries may then exist, and very few people may ever have heard of Mill, Nietzsche, James and Dewey, any more than of free trade unions, a free press and democratic elections.

None of these reasons why the dreams of nineteenth-century Europeans may be irrelevant to the twenty-first century, however, suggest any reason to be suspicious of the superiority of liberalism, pragmatism or utilitarianism to their various rivals, any more than the collapse of the recently converted Roman Empire gave Augustine and his contemporaries a reason to be dubious about the superiority of Christianity to paganism. Nor does contemplating such reasons help us do what Geertz asks us to do when he calls for the creation of 'a new kind of politics', one

> which does not regard ethnic, religious, racial, linguistic, or regional assertiveness as so much irrationality, archaic and ingenerate, to be suppressed or transcended, a madness decried or a darkness ignored, but, like any other social problem – inequality, say, or the abuse of power – sees it as a reality to be faced, somehow dealt with, modulated, brought to terms.[6]

When I first read this sentence in Geertz's book, I found myself agreeing. But on second thoughts I realized that I was agreeing with the spirit rather than the letter. I take the spirit to be that we should deal with people who exhibit such assertiveness as we should deal with all other potential fellow citizens of a world federation: we should take their problems seriously and talk them through. But if one takes Geertz's sentence literally, one can reasonably object that there is no contradiction between regarding something as an archaic and ingenerate irrationality and regarding it as a reality to be faced, somehow dealt with, modulated, brought to terms.

I think it important to insist on this absence of contradiction because it is often said that philosophical pluralists like myself must abjure the notion of 'irrationality'. But this is not so. We can perfectly well use the notion as long as we do so to signify a readiness to ignore the results of past experience, rather than to signify a departure from the commands of an ahistorical authority called Reason.

We have learned quite a lot, in the course of the past two centuries, about how races and religions can live in comity with one another. If we forget these lessons, we can reasonably be called irrational. It makes good pragmatic and pluralist sense to say that the nations of the world are being irrational in not creating a world government to which they should surrender their sovereignty and their nuclear warheads, that the Germans were being irrational in accepting Hitler's suggestion that they expropriate their Jewish neighbours, and that Serbian peasants were being irrational in accepting Milosevic's suggestion that they loot and rape neighbours with whom they had been living peacefully for 50 years.

Insofar as 'postmodern' philosophical thinking is identified with a mindless and stupid cultural relativism – with the idea that any fool thing that calls itself culture is worthy of respect – then I have no use for such thinking. But I do not see that what I have called 'philosophical pluralism' entails any such stupidity. The reason to try persuasion rather than force, to do our best to come to terms with people whose convictions are archaic and ingenerate, is simply that using force, or mockery, or insult, is likely to decrease human happiness.

We do not need to supplement this wise utilitarian counsel with the idea that every culture has some sort of intrinsic worth. We have learned the futility of trying to assign all cultures and persons places on a hierarchical scale, but this realization does not impugn the obvious fact that there are lots of cultures we would be better off without, just as there are lots of people we would be better off without. To say that there is no such scale, and that we are simply clever animals trying to increase our happiness by continually reinventing ourselves, has no relativistic consequences. The difference between pluralism and cultural relativism is the difference between pragmatically justified tolerance and mindless irresponsibility.

So much for my suggestion that the popularity of the meaningless term 'postmodernism' is the result of an inability to resist the claims of philosophical pluralism combined with a quite reasonable fear that history is about to turn against us. But I want to toss in a concluding word about the *un*popularity of the term – about the rhetoric of those who use this word as a term of abuse.

Many of my fellow philosophers use the term 'postmodernist relativism' as if it were a pleonasm, and as if utilitarians, pragmatists and philosophical pluralists generally had committed a sort of 'treason of the clerks', as Julien Benda puts it. They often suggest that if philosophers had united behind the good old theologicometaphysical verities – or if James and Nietzsche had been strangled in their cradles – the fate of mankind might have been different. Just as Christian fundamentalists tell us that tolerance of homosexuality leads to the collapse of civilization, so those who would have us return to Plato and Kant believe that utilitarianism and pragmatism may weaken our intellectual and moral fibre. The triumph of European democratic ideals, they suggest, would have been much more likely had we philosophical pluralists kept our mouths shut.

But the reasons, such as the three I listed earlier, for thinking that those ideals will not triumph have nothing to do with changes in philosophical outlook. Neither the ratio of population to resources, nor the power which modern technology has put in the hands of kleptocrats, nor the provincial intransigence of national governments, has anything to do with such changes. Only the archaic and ingenerate belief that an offended nonhuman power will punish those who do not worship it makes it possible to see a connection between the intellectual shift from unity to plurality and these various concrete reasons for historical pessimism. This shift leaves us nothing with which to boost our social hopes, but that does not mean there is anything wrong with those hopes. The utopian social hope which sprang up in nineteenth-century Europe is still the noblest imaginative creation of which we have record.

* * * *

NOTES

1 For a treatment of this topic with which I heartily agree, see Bernard Yack, *The Fetishism of Modernities* (Ithaca, N.Y.: Cornell University Press, 1997), especially the chapter entitled 'Postmodernism: the figment of a fetish'.
2 Clifford Geertz, *A World in Pieces* (forthcoming).
3 Alfred Lord Tennyson, *In Memoriam* (1850).
4 Geertz, ch. iii, p. 21.
5 Geertz, ch. iii, p. 23.
6 Geertz, ch. iii, p. 27.

Index to *Philosophy and Social Hope*

284